CRITICAL

The Life and Work of

Mother Teresa

Paul Williams, Ph.D.

ALPHA

A Pearson Education Company

International Standard Book Number: 0-02-864278-3
Library of Congress Catalog Card Number: Available upon request.

04   03   02   8   7   6   5   4   3   2   1

Interpretation of the printing code: The rightmost number of the first series of numbers is the year of the book's printing; the rightmost number of the second series of numbers is the number of the book's printing. For example, a printing code of 02-1 shows that the first printing occurred in 2002.

Printed in the United States of America

Publisher:
Marie Butler-Knight
Product Manager:
Phil Kitchel
Managing Editor:
Jennifer Chisholm
Acquisitions Editor:
Mike Sanders
Development Editor:
Suzanne LeVert
Senior Production Editor:
Christy Wagner

Copy Editor:
Krista Hansing
Cover Designer:
Ann Jones
Book Designer:
Sandra Schroeder
Production:
Svetlana Dominguez
Brad Lenser
Michelle Mitchell

CRITICAL LIVES

Mother Teresa

Appendixes

Introduction

I approached the subject of Mother Teresa with a considerable amount of trepidation. I had met her when she visited Marywood University, several years before she received the Nobel Peace Prize in 1979. By that time, Mother Teresa already was revered in Catholic circles as a "living saint." Everybody—faculty, students, clergy, guests, members of the press—treated her not simply with respect but outright obeisance. What she said to the audience about her work "among the poorest of the poor" was accepted without question. She seemed the epitome of a self-sacrificing Christian dedicated to the most intransigent interpretation of the New Testament. Her speech was long, rambling, and somewhat incoherent, but no one expressed the slightest sign of annoyance or impatience. The audience, myself included, was pleased and happy to be in the presence of such a sanctified figure—so far elevated above the banal mass of money grubbing, belly-stuffing, sex-seeking humanity.

Mother Teresa told us the same story she told audiences throughout the world about the formation of Nirmal Hriday, her home for the dying in Calcutta. One day, as the story goes, Mother Teresa came upon a bundle of rags in the midst of a bustee (slum) in Calcutta. Upon examination, the good nun discovered the bundle was really the body of a dying woman. Rats, dogs, and maggots had devoured much of the woman's face. Mother Teresa, although far from a robust figure, carried the body to a local hospital, only to be told that the hospital was overcrowded and would only admit patients who had a chance of recovery. Undaunted, our saint attempted to convey the woman to another medical facility. But her effort was in vain. She heard a rattle from the woman's throat and felt the body stiffen in her arms. With deep despair, she placed the body on the pavement, closed the poor creature's eyes, and prayed over the mortal remains in the pouring rain. "It was then that I decided to find a place for the dying and take care of them myself," Mother Teresa said.

She went on to say that members of her religious order—the Missionaries of Charity—had "picked up" more than thirty-six thousand dying and destitute street people in Calcutta so they could die "with dignity" at Nirmal Hriday.

The audience was moved—some to tears—by her words. As Mother Teresa left the podium, they sought to touch her, no doubt believing that holiness and healing radiated from her homespun sari in the same manner that such qualities flowed from the hem of the cloak of Christ.

Mother Teresa walked from the student center with her hands folded in prayer and her eyes to the ground. Already she displayed signs of a severe spinal disorder, making her seem to lean over, almost at a forty-five-degree angle, and giving her the uncanny semblance of a hunchback.

Some zealous souls, including Catholic nuns in the crowd, attempted to kiss her, but she never raised her cheek, so the kisses could only be planted on the top of her head. Later, we were told that Mother Teresa doesn't like displays of affection and that the only people permitted to kiss her were the lepers in her leprosaria.

At that time, Mother Teresa was sixty-seven years old and incredibly wrinkled. Her skin had a strange grayish hue that seemed to give her the appearance of being mummified. Her eyes seemed out of place with her other features. They appeared blue and lifeless—the eyes of statue in some pre-Tridentine sanctuary.

It was hard to account for her incredible charisma. Mother Teresa was neither attractive nor well-spoken. She displayed neither natural grace nor easy charm. She appeared approachable, always willing to sign an autograph or bless a rosary, and yet remote, always keeping admirers at an arm's distance.

While writing this book, I thought of Mother Teresa's words that day in Scranton nearly twenty-five years ago. Then, as now, it struck me as incredible that the small nun could carry a dying woman through the steaming, teeming streets of Calcutta. It also struck me as remarkable that sisters of her renowned religious order could collect so many dying people from the slums of a single city, thirty-six thousand in less than twenty-five years, or about five per day, every day. Having been told that over seventy percent of the patients at Nirmal Hriday survived, I envisioned Mother Teresa's home as a massive facility with thousands of beds. I believed that it must be staffed with physicians, nurses, and orderlies who would administer analgesics to those in the throes of agonizing death. I pictured nuns leaning over carefully scrubbed and smiling Dalits like cherubim and seraphim.

But then I encountered the reality. The Home of the Dying consists of an administrative office joined by two long and low barracks: one for men; the other for women. The facility contains ninety-five infirmary stretchers—not beds—in which the sick and dying lie uncovered and without medical attention. Even the cancer patients are denied means of pain management. For the purposes of sanitation, the patients are dragged from their beds and hosed down with cold water as they beg and scream for mercy. There are no physicians, no nurses, no orderlies, no analgesia. According to the sisters who operate the facility, Nirmal Hriday receives between four to five hundred new patients every year, not five or six per day.

Something didn't seem right. At first I thought that Mother Teresa misspoke and didn't really mean to say that the home cared for over thirty-six thousand patients. But two years later, she pronounced the same figure when she received the Nobel Peace Prize. What's more, she used the same figure when she delivered an address in Sydney, Australia, in 1974. To complicate matters, Mother Teresa told *Time* magazine in December 1989 that her sisters picked up over fifty-four thousand sick and dying slum residents and that "23,000 something have died."

I began to scratch my head. Maybe, I thought, Mother Teresa had no mind for figures. Surely this is a small matter to fault such a saintly figure who has done so much for so many in places most of us would not want to spend even a day.

But then I discovered that Mother Teresa also had no mind for facts, even important facts. Her sisters, as it turned out, "picked up" very few dying "destitutes." Her order has a fleet of ambulances that have been donated by charitable organizations throughout the world. But the ambulances are not used to transport patients to hospitals or leprosaria, let alone the Home for the Dying. They are used almost exclusively to transport the sisters from one section of the city to another. If you call the Missionaries of Charity for an ambulance to pick up an unwanted baby, a sick child, or a dying beggar, the sisters will instruct you to call the Calcutta Corporation at 102 and request a city ambulance. The emergency vehicles of Mother Teresa's order have sirens and flashing red beacons. They race through the crowded streets and are exempt from all traffic regulations. But the ambulances have been stripped of all provisions to transport a stretcher or to administer emergency medical attention. In truth, they represent nothing more than a religious taxi service.

Preparing this book I had to strip out pious fictions that surround almost every aspect of her life and work. For starters, Mother Teresa always spoke about her idyllic childhood in Skopje, Serbia. She neglected to say that her father was a victim of political assassination and that the family lived in abject terror under the Yugoslavian government.

She described her life as a nun in the Loreto convent as one of perfect peace and contentment. "To leave Loreto," she said, "was my greatest sacrifice, the most difficult thing I have ever done. It was more difficult than to leave my family and my country to enter religious life. Loreto, my spiritual training, my work there, meant everything to me." But the truth of the matter is that Mother Teresa came to detest the Order after she had been demoted as headmistress and sought ecclesiastical release from her solemn vows so that she could become a secular social worker.

Throughout her life, Mother Teresa insisted that her religious order exists solely by divine grace. "We don't accept government grants or church donations," she said. But her many ventures—

homes for unwanted children, facilities for lepers, centers for victims of AIDS and tuberculosis—were made possible by massive gifts of lands, buildings, supplies, and cash from both church and state.

And then there is the matter of the private contributions. In 1997, Reuters International News Agency calculated that Mother Teresa's religious order receives more than thirty million dollars annually from people throughout the world. Where does the money go? No one can provide an answer. The Missionaries of Charity keep no books or records for accounting purposes. This, too, is part of the "mysterium" of Mother Teresa.

The "mysterium" is intensified by the fact that she sought an exorcism on September 5, 1997, several weeks before her death.

Do the unanswered questions about this historical figure diminish her significant and truly awesome accomplishments? Will she be tried in the balance and found wanting? Or will Mother Teresa become, as she so stridently wished to become, an object of intercessory prayer and pious veneration?

Chapter 1

Shanti, Mother Teresa

It is one hundred five degrees in the shade. The city reeks of raw sewage and fetid decay. One million people were expected to line the streets for the funeral cortege, but less than half that amount is in attendance. The merchants in the bazaars are disappointed. The rich American and European tourists fail to arrive. Pickpockets roam among the crowd, but the pickings are scarce. Although it is still morning, prostitutes peddle their wares. Some are ten- and twelve-year-old girls in whorish attire. Others are young boys wearing lipstick. They offer oral sex for the U.S. equivalent of fifty cents.

On the sidewalks, thousands of homeless people cook meals of rice and rancid meat from restaurants in vented garbage cans. The stench of the food is overwhelming, and the insects are insufferable. The city is built on forty miles of swampland. Green flies, mosquitoes, wasps, bees, and maggots crawl over everything and everyone, but the people seem oblivious to this constant annoyance.

Many inhabitants of the *bustees*—the squalid huts that cram every square inch of the city—pay little attention to the funeral procession. They have no radios or televisions. They cannot read newspapers. They have no idea that this is one of the most significant events in the history of the modern Roman Catholicism.

Only two percent of the poor in the "city of joy" are Christian. The overwhelming majority—more than eighty percent—is

Hindu. At the city's holiest temple, bloody sacrifices are made every morning to the gold statue of Kali, the goddess of death and destruction. The people are fiercely devoted to this goddess, and small statues of Kali can be found everywhere, even in most wretched hovels.

Kali is "the Black One," the goddess of disease, death, and destruction. This goddess is usually depicted as a terrifying figure, wearing a wreath of skulls and holding a sword in one of her many arms. For centuries, Kali was the patroness of "thugs," who committed murders to her as sacrifices. The Hindus call Kali "Mother," just as they call the small nun from Albania "Mother."

Indeed, next to the temple of Mother Kali stands a life-size statue of Mother Teresa. The Hindus bow to one and pay obeisance to the other without any sense of irony or impiety. By the time of her death, Mother Teresa—who devoted her life to the innocent victims of violence, the dying in the streets, the refugees, the patients with AIDS or leprosy, the prisoners on death row, and the unborn—became associated with the most vengeful and destructive of India's goddesses. Many in the crowd call out Mother Teresa's name in Bengali as the funeral procession passes before them. While hailing the deceased nun, they hold up images of Kali. Such actions seem mocking until you realize that Mother Teresa set up her headquarters in a place that served for centuries as a temple to the blood-thirsty and demanding Hindu goddess. Both Mothers have come to represent death in the eyes of the poor and the homeless. That is part of the paradox.

In many ways, Mother Teresa does not belong to the western world and the Roman Church. She might have been born in Macedonia, but she was a true daughter of India. She lived here for seventy years. She learned to speak fluent Hindu and Bengali, she became a citizen of India, and the habit for her religious order was a simple Indian sari. What's more, Mother Teresa never tried to convert the Indian people from their beliefs. She said that Hindus should be good Hindus, Moslems should be good Moslems, and Christians should be good Christians. No less than Sir Richard Burton and T. E. Lawrence had, Mother Teresa had gone native and now belonged not to Eastern Europe, but to Asia. "We think of Mother not as a Christian, but simply as a Mother," says Samir Banerjee, a Brahmin priest from the Temple of Kali. "She was just the Mother of us all." Calcutta is one of the most densely populated places in the world. No one knows how many people live in this city. Some say twelve million; others say sixteen million. New York boasts a population of 11,480 per square mile, but Calcutta holds 85,500 in the same space. Each occupant of the slums occupies a living space of less than three square feet. They sleep on the pavement wrapped from head to toe in bits of *khadi* cloth. Calcutta at night seems to be strewn with millions of corpses.

But it is now daylight, and the streets are already congested with trucks, buses, taxis, handcarts, scooters, cycle rickshaws, horse carriages, and bicycles. The traffic moves at a snail's pace. The city is alive with the tooting of carrier tricycles, the honking of horns, the throbbing of engines, the ringing of carriage bells, and the shrieking of loudspeakers. The city reeks like a landfill with poisonous fumes, nauseating gases, and the all-pervasive stench of garbage. In the absence of adequate garbage collection, eighteen hundred tons of refuse are left to rot in the streets every day.

Thousands of men and women can be seen lifting up their cotton *longhi* and squatting over the gutter in answer to the "call of nature." An open cesspool runs through the crowded streets.

Mangy dogs wander among the crowd, along with meandering cows, goats, and buffalo. But the people fail to take notice as they go about their business. Some sell vegetables and fruit along with hot tea. The tea is served in leaves that are twisted into cones. Others offer such edible items as *muri*, rice roasted in hot sand; *barfi*, Bengali nougat wrapped in thin silver film; *mansours*, yellow sweetmeats made out of chick-pea flour and sweetened milk; and *pan*, quids made out of chopped betel nut, a pinch of tobacco, chutney, and cardamon, all wrapped in a betel leaf.

But most of the people in the three thousand slums of the city beg in order to survive. At the entrance to the big hotels on Chowringhee Road and Park Street where rich tourists are staying for Mother Teresa's funeral, a syndicate of racketeers controls the begging. The racketeers prefer to exploit deformed children, legless men on planks with wheels, or mothers in rags with emaciated babies. The beggars are paid three rupees a day. The racketeers take the rest. It is said that children are mutilated at birth so that they can merit the attention of the syndicate.

Those who do not beg peddle a wide array of goods—T-shirts, baseball hats, umbrellas (this day in September 1997 is the midst of monsoon season), cheap watches, silk scarves, gunny bags and purses made from jute, and, for this special occasion, rosary beads of all shapes, sizes, and colors, including a blend of shocking pink and bright turquoise. Venders sell Campa Cola, the Indian version of Coca Cola, and bottled water. Saddhus mingle among the tourists and the sellers. For twenty *paisas* coin (five U.S. cents), these holy men will lay their hands upon you and pour a few drops of holy water from the Ganges down your throat. Tourists are cautioned to drink only bottled water because the tap water comes from the Hooghly River. The river, an arm of the Ganges, remains ripe with sewage and garbage. On this hot and humid day, the Hooghly stinks to high heaven. But the people ignore the stench as they wash their clothes and bathe in its waters.

For the most part, the bottled water sold on the streets does not come from pure mountain streams but instead is filtered from the Hooghly into plastic bottles by enterprising street peddlers. Outbreaks of cholera occur on a regular basis in Calcutta.

On this day, members of the press express disappointment over the relatively modest crowd and the lack of public displays of emotion. Mother Teresa was the most beloved figure of her time. But there is no weeping or wailing at her passing. The event, which has attracted all the major news sources, seems scarcely newsworthy. Even in this place of unspeakable poverty and squalor, it lacks visual interest. When the cameras turn to the crowds, the poor people smile and wave as if they were being treated to a *michil* (a Hindu religious procession), a circus parade, or a chance at instant celebrity. If only there were some outpouring of grief—women falling into ecstatic swoons of sorrow, men hurling themselves before the funeral carriage, children weeping for the lost Mother— there would be copy for the newsmen, but such displays fail to materialize. "I've been shooting all morning," an ABC cameraman says, "and I don't have ten seconds of usable footage, let alone a lead." This, too, is part of the paradox.

As it is hauled through the streets, Mother Teresa's casket remains open for the benefit of onlookers. The white wooden box seems too large for the small nun and her body is almost shamelessly exposed to the merciless sun. The familiar, wizened face appears brown and discolored, as if putrefaction is already in progress. The effect is wrong. It conjures up images not of sainthood, but of the macabre. The bodies of great saints, as all hagiographers know, are not supposed to decompose.

The casket is hauled by a military gun carriage—the same carriage that transported the bodies of Mahatma Gandhi and India's first prime minister, Jawaharlal Nehru, to their funerals.

Everything seems strangely incongruous and surreal—the dead body seeming to melt in the sweltering heat; the flower petals falling from the rooftops into the gutters; the military gun carriage rambling through the narrow streets with the corpse of a frail and unimposing woman who is being hailed as a modern saint.

No one seems aware that the body of this woman might become a very valuable commodity. In years to come, her bones, her prayer books, and her clothing might be venerated as relics. They might be enshrined in great churches and cathedrals. They might become efficacious—capable of performing miracles and effecting cures. Yet she passes before the poorest of the poor and they neglect to reach out even for a strand of her hair.

The procession proceeds at increased speed. A few teenagers attempt to run along with the carriage for the sake of the cameramen, but they eventually fall back in exhaustion.

The coffin is conveyed from "Black Town," the native section of narrow lanes, slums, and bazaars, to "White Town," the Chowringhee section of spacious homes, broad avenues, and modern office buildings.

The funeral takes place not at a shrine or cathedral, but at the Netaji Indoor Stadium. It has been planned not as a religious service, but as an event. The stadium is filled to overflowing with invited guests. The best seats in the house are overstuffed, ornate armchairs and couches that appear to have been borrowed from imperial palaces. These seats are reserved for the presidents of Italy and Ghana; the queens of Spain, Jordan, and Belgium; assorted dignitaries; and Hillary Rodham Clinton.

> *Traveling from "Black Town" to "White Town" in the city of Calcutta is like journeying from hell to heaven. "White Town" was fashioned by the colonial British in the manner of a grand European capital. Some impressive structures include the Raj Bhavan (the state governor's residence), an imitation of Kedleston Hall in Derbyshire; the High Court, a copy of Cloth Hall in Ypres, Belgium; St. Paul's Cathedral, a marvel of Indo-European architecture; and the General Post Office, with its majestic dome and Corinthian columns.*

At a 1995 National Prayer Breakfast in Washington, Mother Teresa confronted President and Mrs. Clinton and other liberal Democrats. Her remarks that day were unexpected. When she was introduced, she first spoke of God, love, and families. She said that people must love and care for one another. Her words produced purrs of contentment.

But as the speech continued, her words became more pointed and disconcerting. She asked, "Do you do enough to make sure your parents, in the old people's homes, feel your love? Do you bring them each day your joy and caring?" At this point, several in attendance began to squirm in their seats. "I feel that the greatest destroyer of peace today is abortion," she said, and she told why in uncompromising terms. For several seconds, the audience became perfectly silent. Then applause began until it swept through the room. But not everyone was applauding. The president and the first lady, the vice president and Mrs. Gore, and members of the Clinton cabinet sat motionless and silent, like figures from a wax museum. Mother Teresa did not stop with these remarks. She went on to condemn artificial birth control and the Protestant distinction between faith and works. No one expected the old and ailing nun to utter such a fiery address. When she was finished, there was hardly a person in the room who had not been offended. A U.S. Senator turned to his wife and said, "Is my jaw up yet?"

But no jaws remain slack this day. Everything is proper and highly dignified. The eulogies are dry and without eloquence. The ceremony seems to be staged by an innocuous director for mass consumption. The choir of nuns sings in Hindi, Bengali, and English, accompanied by Indian instruments. An orphan girl places a small bunch of flowers on her coffin. A rehabilitated criminal, a leper, and a cripple present the "gifts of the altar" to the officiating Archbishop. Representatives of other religions—Hindu, Muslim, Sikh, Buddhist, and Parsee—offer blessings over the casket. It is ecumenical, contemporary, empty.

Following the ceremony, the dignitaries and mourners enter limousines to follow the gun carriage to Mother Teresa's final resting place.

Rain begins to fall as a reminder that September is monsoon season in Calcutta. Maybe this explains the absence of vast crowds to express a final good-bye to the most famous figure of India since Mohandas Gandhi.

Her final resting place is neither a site within Vatican City nor the Bojaxhiu family plot in Albania. It is instead the Motherhouse of the religious order she created almost fifty years ago. This is a good idea for the order. Her grave is sure to attract hosts of tourists in years to come, and with tourists come sizeable donations.

The Missionaries of Charity brothers and priests lower the coffin into the carefully prepared grave. Indian soldiers, stationed outside the house, raise their rifles and fire a final salute. The gunfire is jarring and unexpected. A group of sisters sing one of Mother Teresa's favorite hymns in Bengali, and the Archbishop bestows a final blessing. Those in attendance form a line to pour a fistful of dirt on the coffin before they are led to the long line of limousines.

Her gravestone bears no name, only this simple inscription from the Gospel of John: "Love one another as I have loved you."

Of course, she will be a saint. The pope has placed her canonization on a fast track. She will become a saint before such powerful and influential figures as Pope Pius XII, Dorothy Day, Archbishop Oscar Romero, and Pope John XXIII. The process that usually takes hundreds of years will take less than five in her case.

But she continues to attract critics and detractors. George Orwell once said that all saints must be presumed guilty until they are proved innocent. The attacks have already come—in the form of books such as *The Missionary Position: Mother Teresa in Theory and Practice*, by Christopher Hitchens; articles such as "Unmasking the Mother," by Germaine Greer; and programs such as a BBC production called *Hell's Angel*.

Such works claim that Mother Teresa ...

- Increased the misery in Calcutta by opposing birth control and abortion, even for women who had been raped by Pakistani soldiers in the genocidal war of 1972.

- Refused to provide pain-killing drugs to those who came under the care of her Home for the Dying.

- Requested leniency for Charles Keating, one of her benefactors, after he was found guilty in the savings and loan scandals of the 1980s.

- Accepted donations without reproach from such unsavory dictators as Jean-Claude Duvalier of Haiti.

- Permitted grossly unsanitary conditions to persist in her homes and shelters.

- Lorded her celebrity over the other sisters in her order, forbidding them to speak to any public official or member of the press without her permission.

Before Mother Teresa is beatified and sanctified, her life must come under complete scrutiny, and these charges must be addressed. Tribunals must be held in which witnesses for and against the "cause" of her canonization must give evidence. Miracles credited to her intercession must be authenticated. And a critical study of her life must be prepared.

The funeral Mass for Mother Teresa at the Netaji Indoor
Stadium in Calcutta.

(© David and Peter Turnley/CORBIS)

Chapter 2

Worldly Life and Death

Very few saints of the Roman Catholic Church, the twelve apostles being the exceptions, come from poor or ordinary families. Most are the sons and daughters of aristocrats or prosperous merchants who became sanctified by "slumming it." St. Francis of Assisi, for instance, spent his life in poverty—begging for daily bread, working at menial jobs, and preaching in the open marketplace. He wore a rough tunic with a cord and championed the virtue of apostolic poverty. But by birth, the good saint was not a poor peasant, but a lordly knight-at-arms, hailing from one of the wealthiest and most influential families in Assisi, Italy.

The same is true of St. Clare, the founder of the Poor Clares. She and her fellow nuns dressed in rags, lived on alms, and spent their time making clothing and providing shelter for the homeless. But St. Clare was not poor. She was the beautiful and rich daughter of the illustrious Offreducio family. She, like St. Francis, was born and raised in a palace.

St. Alexis, the patron saint of beggars, was a rich Roman noble who disguised himself as a beggar in order to avoid marriage. St. Serf, another saint of the poor, was not a serf at all, but rather the son of a sixth-century Scottish king. To be a saint, it seems as if one should start out with wealth and a good measure of social prominence.

Mother Teresa of Calcutta is no exception. She was the daughter of Nikola and Dranafile Bojaxhiu, who descended from prosperous and influential Albanian families. Nikola, who had been trained in France as a pharmacist, was a merchant and an entrepreneur who moved from his native town of Prizren in Albania to the city of Skopje in Serbia because of its location as a center of commercial activity in the Balkans.

> Albanians are divided into members of the Tosk and Gheg peoples, who are separated south and north by the Skkumbini river. The overwhelming majority (seventy percent) are Moslem, with an Orthodox Christian minority among the Tosks and an even smaller Roman Catholic minority among the Ghegs. The Ghegs, including the Bojaxhiu family, populated and continue to populate the much-disputed region of Kosovo. Although Kosovo has an Albanian majority, it was also the site of the Orthodox Serbs' holiest battlefield—the fourteenth-century rout by the Turks.

Skopje today bears little resemblance to the city of Mother Teresa's childhood. The Macedonian capital was left in rubble by an earthquake in 1963. Rebuilt by Japanese investors, Skopje was robbed of its historical character. The old city was transformed into a sprawling Socialist metropolis with sprawling vainglorious buildings that have since fallen into disrepair and decrepitude.

The wide avenues that surround the capital building and financial centers lead to incommodious alleys and narrow passageways filled with trash that never seems to get collected. The poverty and squalor is almost overwhelming. The surrounding slums lead to open marketplaces where hash and heroin can be obtained at every street corner. Skopje, the birthplace of the greatest Catholic saint of the twentieth century, is now the central trans-shipment point for illegal drugs from Southeast Asia.

The city seems as exotic and as dangerous as Calcutta. Prostitutes are everywhere, along with their pimps who stand before smoke-filled bars and dingy coffee shops. The crime rate is out of sight. If you remain in the old section when the sun goes down, there is a good chance that you will not survive until morning.

The unemployment rate is higher here than almost anywhere else in the world—save Calcutta, currently fluctuating between thirty and thirty-five percent. The main exports of this landlocked central European city are food, beverages, and tobacco. There are no major industries here. The Macedonian capital remains in the dregs of economic stagnation.

To compound its problems, the city remains a political tinderbox with pressure mounting between the Macedonian Greeks and the Albanian Moslems, who have poured into Skopje in recent years from Bosnia. Located in the midst of the Balkans, the birthplace of Mother Teresa has experienced many molesters. It has been traversed by every major European and Asian army. For this reason, the people are a mix of the occidental and the oriental. They are small in stature, with dark olive complexions, prominent noses, black hair, and dark, luminous eyes.

This is the starting point for any study of Mother Teresa. By her appearance and way of life, she appeared to represent both Eastern and Western cultures. Perhaps had she been born in Europe or Asia, her appeal would not have been so universal. Neither Arab nor Greek, and yet a mixture of both, her unique religious and cultural heritage granted her—in an age of political correctness—an aura of transcendence and universal appeal.

Throughout her life, Mother Teresa would say little about her family and her upbringing. When questioned about her childhood, she said, "Mine was a happy family. I had one brother and one sister, but I do not like to talk about it. It is not important now. The important thing is to follow God, the way he leads us to do something beautiful for him."

She rarely mentioned her family members by name, rarely spoke of her upbringing, and refused to associate herself with her homeland—not even when all hell broke loose between the ethnic Albanians and the Serbs in the years following the break-up of Yugoslavia.

Mother Teresa's early life is shrouded in mystery. She was born in 1910, but we know less about her upbringing than religious personages born in the Middle Ages—far less, for instance, than we know about St. Francis and St. Clare. For years, biographers listed her date of birth as August 27. But the date is incorrect. It represents the date she was christened Agnes Gonxha Bojaxhiu. The real date of her birth is August 26, 1910.

This little-known fact escaped the attention of both her admirers and her detractors. The incorrect birth date is recorded not only in a score of biographies, but also in the *Indian Loreto Entrance Book* (the official record of Loreto nuns who enter India). The fact that Mother Teresa never corrected this mistake displays her intent to keep her early years from public scrutiny. She often likened the obscurity of her early years to that fact that almost nothing is known of Jesus until he began his public ministry at the age of thirty. A hidden life displays humility, she said.

Dealing with Mother Teresa, most readers are apt to accept what she says about herself without question. They assume that a saint is incapable of uttering something untrue and contradictory to her beliefs. Mother Teresa, however, didn't always say what she meant, nor did she always mean what she said. She once told the press that nothing in the nature of a biography or a biographical study should ever appear about her. "Christ's life," she said, "was not written during His lifetime, yet He did the greatest work on earth—He redeemed the world and taught mankind to love His Father. The Work is His Work and to remain so, all of us are but His instruments, who do our little bit and pass by." Such a saintly statement is admirable. It displays her piety and sense of humility. Yet after making this statement, Mother Teresa authorized not one, but two, biographies of herself and carefully glossed over the more troublesome aspects of her life. To complicate matters, Mother Teresa was very often less than candid about herself. In 1970, she told author and broadcaster Malcolm Muggeridge that she came from peasant stock. "This," Muggeridge wrote, "is apparent in her appearance and bearing and way of looking at things." But Agnes Gonxha Bojaxhiu was not of peasant stock. She came from a prominent family. She also spoke to Muggeridge of her happy childhood in Yugoslavia. She neglected to tell the seasoned journalist that her youth was marred by violence, ethnic hatred, and political harassment. Most writers—even the harshest critics—accepted her as she appeared: a mother of mercy, a selfless servant of Jesus Christ, a modern saint. It was comforting to think that at least one human being was genuinely good.

But Mother Teresa was not one-dimensional. Little about her life and work is as simple and straightforward as it appears in her authorized biographies. Take the matter of her sister, Aga. Some biographers argue that Aga, also known as Agatha and Age, was born in 1913; others insist that Aga was an elder sister who was born in 1907. This confusion stems from the fact that Mother Teresa was careful to conceal all information regarding her past from public scrutiny. She spoke of her great love for her home in Serbia and her family. But throughout her life, she remained coldly indifferent to both. She rarely spoke of Aga or her older brother, Lazar, who was born in 1908, and she never visited them. She failed to attend the funerals of her mother and her sister in 1972, and she neglected to visit Lazar when he was dying of cancer in 1981. Perhaps in the spirit of cloistered nuns in the years before Vatican II, Mother Teresa became dead to her former life as Agnes Gonxha Bojaxhiu. Or perhaps she did not wish to conjure up the ghosts of the past.

In her few statements about her childhood, Mother Teresa spoke of her family in glowing terms, insisting that her father was an upright man who was a leading figure in Skopje's civil life. She mentioned that Nikola was a gifted linguist, fluent not only in Albanian and Servo-Croat, but also in Turkish, Italian, and French. By all accounts, he was a stern and strict disciplinarian who constantly reminded his three children that they must never forget their upper-class status and their Albanian heritage. "Never forget whose children you are and from what background you come," he told them. Despite Nikola's strictness, the children remembered the excitement with which they would greet him when he returned from a business trip and the many presents he brought back for them all.

Nikola had been well schooled in Venice and Paris, and was a licensed pharmacist, a profession he never practiced. Instead, Nikola was an entrepreneur. He traded in such commodities as sugar, oil, cloth, leather, and medicines and traveled extensively to different parts of Europe. His business boomed with the outbreak of World War I. He became one of the wealthiest men in Skopje, a leading landowner and a member of the city's council. In addition to his other business interests, Nikola was a building contractor who erected the first movie theaters in the Balkans.

The Bojaxhiu family lived in an expansive house (one of Nikola's many properties) that overlooked the city. Surrounded by fruit trees, the house contained a large garden and separate quarters for guests. Nothing is left of Mother Teresa's birthplace. It was completely destroyed by the devastating earthquake of 1963.

Mother Teresa's mother, Dranafile (known as Drone), was petted and pampered as a patrician wife. Her main task was to supervise the household servants and the education of the children. In one of her rare references to her family, Mother Teresa remembered how her mother often performed domestic chores to busy herself while her father was away. But as soon as Nikola returned, she transformed into a prim and proper wife in a neatly pressed dress without a hair out of place.

Drone, like her husband, came from Shikodra in northern Albania. Her ancestors were merchants and landowners with large estates in Novo Selo. She was a child of fourteen or fifteen at the time of her wedding, fifteen or sixteen when she gave birth to her first child, and less than twenty at the arrival of her last. Drone was at least fifteen years younger than her husband was. Of the two, she was by far the most religious. She took her children to Mass every morning and when she was not working in her house or helping others, she passed the hours away by reciting the rosary.

Although christened Agnes, Drone and Nikola called their youngest Gonxha, an Albanian word for "rosebud." By all accounts, Gonxha was a bright and happy child who showed an early aptitude for music and poetry. In an attempt to enhance the saintly image of his sister, Lazar later told the press that Gonxha never tattled when he and Aga filched sweets or committed other acts of innocuous misbehavior, adding that she never engaged in such behavior.

Although Mother Teresa rarely spoke about her father, she praised her father's hospitality to the poor in her authorized biographies, saying that an elderly woman regularly came to the Bojaxhiu house for meals. She reported her father as saying, "My child, never eat a single mouthful unless you are sharing it with others." However, her brother Lazar later admitted that such hospitality was offered not to poor Greeks or Moslems, but to poor relatives and fellow Albanians.

The Bojaxhiu family of Skopje was separated from the common Serbs not only by wealth and position, but also by culture and religion. In 1910, when Mother Teresa was born, Skopje was part of Serbia. Serbia and Albania were both ruled by the Ottoman Turks. When Nikola and Drone moved from Shikodra to Skopje, a distance of less than one hundred miles, they remained in the same empire, but in a different world. In Albania, the population was predominantly Moslem. In Serbia, the majority faith was Eastern (Greek) Orthodox. Nikola and Drone were members of a Roman Catholic minority that represented less than eight percent of the population.

> The Eastern Orthodox Christians and Roman Catholics of Central Europe disliked each other even more than they disliked the Moslems. Some date the hostility back to the fall of Constantinople during the Fourth Crusade; others say it stems to the "filioque" controversy of the fifth century. The Roman Catholics believe the Holy Spirit proceeds from the Father and the Son; the Orthodox believe the Holy Spirit proceeds from the Father alone. These two forms of Catholicism have different creeds, different liturgies, and different religious practices. Most notably, the Orthodox Christians refuse to acknowledge the primary of the See of Rome as the center of ecclesiastical authority. Theologians note that the division between the Greek Orthodox and Roman Catholic Church occurred during the Council of Ephesus in 421. The Roman Church, under Bishop Cyril of Alexandria, held that Mary is theotokos, the "mother of God." The Greek Church, under Bishop Nestorius of Constantinople, said that Mary is Christokos, the "mother of Christ."

When Agnes was two, the first Balkan war broke out as the various states attempted to carve up the remains of the collapsed Ottoman Empire. Serbia, without access to the sea, attempted to prevent the rise of an independent Albania by annexing Kosovo

and northern Albania. Austria attempted to prevent this annexa-
tion by a declaration of the Congress of Viore that proclaimed
Albania as an independent state.

But this declaration only served to intensify the resolve of the
Serbs who initiated a policy of mass murder of Albanians in Serbia
and northern Albania. In 1912, Serbian soldiers broke into the
home of an Albanian Catholic family, a stone's throw away
from the Bojaxhiu residence. They raped the wife and beat the
husband until he revealed the hiding place of his daughters. The
daughters—aged fourteen and sixteen—were dragged into an open
courtyard and gang-raped by the soldiers. Their screams echoed
throughout the neighborhood. In a nearby village, soldiers shot
into houses until the inhabitants came out with their hands on
their heads. The men and women were mowed down by firing
squads, while the children were bayoneted to save ammunition.
The reign of terror persisted until the outbreak of World War I in
1914.

The Bojaxhiu family would have heard reports of Serbian soldiers stealing money from peasants and merchants as they returned
from the marketplace, of men being hung in the forest by their
arms as bait for wild animals, of children going out for firewood
only to be seized and slaughtered. In one month—October 1912—
twenty-four Albanian villages were put to the torch by Serbian soldiers and more than five thousand Albanians were tied together
and mowed down by machine-gun fire in Pristina.

The Skopje of Mother Teresa's childhood was a violent and
brutal place where acts of barbarism were commonplace and where
no one was safe to travel the streets.

The situation worsened at the end of the Great War. Albania
retained its independence, while Serbia, Macedonia, Montenegro,
and a section of the old Austro-Hungarian Empire became combined to form the new nation of Yugoslavia.

Nicola and other Albanian nationals objected to the formation
of the new country and formed a political action society for Kosovo
to be incorporated into Albania. His stance was not popular with
the new Yugoslavian government. Mother Teresa's brother, Lazar,
said that government officials relentlessly harassed the Bojaxhiu

family. The situation for the children became unbearable when they were forced to attend public school—rather than the parochial school at the Albanian Roman Catholic parish—and to learn and speak Serbo-Croatian, the native tongue of the Serbs.

The harassment only served to strengthen Nikola's resolve. In 1919, he attended a political meeting of Albanian nationalists in Belgrade. He returned home terribly ill, suffering from severe stomach pains. He began to hemorrhage badly and was rushed to the local hospital. The next morning, he underwent emergency surgery but died the following day. Later reports showed that he had been poisoned by the Yugoslavian secret police.

The funeral of Nikola Bojaxhiu was a significant event in Skopje. Large crowds attended it, including members of council, business leaders and representatives of other religions. On the day of the funeral, every jewelry shop was closed. The children in all the schools received commemorative handkerchiefs. The number of handkerchiefs given away by local tradition was a testimony to the wealth of the deceased.

Nikola's political passion was passed on to Lazar. In 1928, when Albania became a monarchy under the Moslem ruler King Zog I, Lazar enlisted in the army of the newly crowned king as a second lieutenant. In 1939, Italy, under the fascist regime of Mussolini, invaded Albania. Lazar, then thirty-nine, welcomed the black shirts as liberators, joined the Italian army, and was stationed in Rome as a member of Mussolini's cabinet.

At the end of the war, Lazar, the Albanian nationalist, found that he could not go home again. The postwar communist government in Albania took action against all "traitors" who had allied themselves with the fascists. Lazar was tried in absentia, found guilty, and sentenced to death. The sentence was never carried out because Lazar remained in Italy, where he became wealthy by managing a pharmaceutical company that manufactured birth control pills, among other products.

Throughout her long life, Mother Teresa mentioned neither her brother's radical politics nor her father's political assassination. In one of her authorized biographies—*Mother Teresa* by Navin Chawla, she makes mention only of Nikola's "untimely" and "tragic" death in 1917. The silence of Mother Teresa over the political murder of her father defies explanation, especially because it had to be one of the most catastrophic and formative events of her early years. The strangeness is magnified by the fact that she gave an incorrect date for his death, stating that she was seven years old.

But she was not seven years old, she was nine, and the death of Nikola in 1919 must have had a devastating effect on the Bojaxhiu family. We know from later reports that Drone fell into deep depression and was unable to leave the house for many months. We also know that the tragedy bound the family even closer to the Albanian Roman Catholic parish of the Sacred Heart in Skopje.

The Sacred Heart parish performed not only a religious role, but also a sociological function by preserving the unique culture and identity of its parishioners. "We were very closer united," Mother Teresa told her official biographers, "especially after my father's death."

The Bojaxhiu family attended daily Mass and nightly devotions. Agnes learned to play the mandolin and played at ethnic celebrations. She and Aga joined the church choir, where they became known as the "nightingales" of the congregation. During the summer months, Drone and her children spent weeks at the chapel of the Madonna of Letnice on the slopes of Skopje's Black Mountain.

At least once a week, Drone would visit an old woman named Fife, who had been abandoned by her family, to take her food and to clean her house. She cared for Fife, an alcoholic with six children, as if she was a small child. Agnes would accompany her mother on such errands of mercy. "When you do good," Drone told her young daughter, "do it quietly, as if you were throwing a stone into the sea." In later life, Mother Teresa said that many of her distinctive sayings—such as her oft-repeated instruction, "Be only all for God"—were mere echoes of her mother's words. In 1922, when Agnes was twelve, she announced that she wished to become a nun. The announcement was the result neither of a conversion experience nor an apparition. "It was not a vision," she later said. "It was a personal matter. I never had a vision." The fact that

Mother Teresa's decision to enter religious life was not based on a supernatural event may disturb many members of her ever-growing cult who believe that all saints are expected to witness and perform miracles.

Her decision, in fact, appears to be based in the violent death of her father and her resulting position as a Roman Catholic Albanian in a Greek-Moslem world. Just as her family retreated into the ethnic enclave of the parish life under adverse conditions, Agnes Gonxha Bojaxhiu may have decided to retreat into the sequestered protection of convent life when faced with adulthood. She may have been compelled to canonization not by a higher calling or a blinding light, but rather by a terrible act of violence.

Chapter 3

Worldly Denial

As a teenage girl, Agnes came under the spiritual care of Father Jambrekovic, a Croatian Jesuit priest who became the pastor of Sacred Heart in 1925. He introduced her to the "Spiritual Lessons" of St. Ignatius Loyola that were to have a formative effect on her spiritual development. In later years, she said that each night before climbing into bed, Christians must ask themselves the three questions of St. Ignatius: "What have I done for Christ?" "What am I doing for Christ?" "What will I do for Christ?" Throughout her life, Mother Teresa would display a spiritual affinity toward Jesuits and Jesuit theology.

Father Jambrekovic also spoke to Agnes and other members of the Solidarity of Children of Mary about the Jesuit missions in Bengal, in the archdiocese of Calcutta. He read letters from the missionaries about their work in the "City of Joy." The letters captured Agnes's imagination and by the time she was seventeen, she had decided to become not only a nun, but also a missionary nun in India.

India offered escape from Yugoslavia, where her father had been assassinated, where her family was forced to renounce their ethnic heritage, and where the Bojaxhius had experienced harassment and oppression. It was a world away from the Balkans and the age-old conflict between the Albanians and the Serbs.

The thoughts of young Agnes about India were far different than those of most of us today. At that time, Calcutta represented not an urban nightmare but one of the most exotic cities in the world. Despite the heat, the tropical diseases, the snakes, the jackals, and even the tigers that prowled around wealthy estates in the middle of the night, Calcutta was known as "the Paris of the East." Western colonists began their day with a drive in a horse-drawn carriage or a Rolls Royce limousine under the shade of the banyan trees, magnolia bushes, and palm trees of the Maidan Park. On the wide avenues of the inner city, you could see as many high-society ladies in palanquins or barouches as the Champs Élysées of Paris or the London Mall. Every year, a glittering season of polo, horse racing, and social receptions drew the elite of the East to "the jewel of the British colony."

In books on India, Agnes would have seen photos of long gondolas propelled by men in frock coats and top hats and ladies in evening gowns along the Hooghly and of the riverside pathways of the Garden of Eden that led to a beautiful pagoda. She would have read of the luxurious ballrooms of the Chowringhee Houses and of the Old Empire Theater where Anna Pavlova presented her final dance recital.

Sure, poverty existed in Calcutta, as everywhere else in the British colonies. But the city was not synonymous with depravity and squalor. Strange as it may seem, it was a model of progress and prosperity. Thanks to its harbor, it attracted more industries than any other city in India: metal foundries, chemical and pharmaceutical plants, flourmills, and jute and cotton factories. Nicknamed the "Ruhr of India," its hinterlands produced twice as much coal as France and as much steel as the combines of the Ruhr region of Germany.

The city had been colonized and now it remained for the residents to be Christianized. The majority of the people were Hindu, worshipping such strange gods as Hanuman, the monkey god; Ganesh, the elephant-headed god of good fortune; and Surya, the Sun god. If they were not brought to the true faith, Agnes was taught by Fr. Jambrekovic, the Hindus, Moslems, Sikhs, Jains, and

Buddhists of India would be bound for eternal perdition. The greatest and most noble task of all, Agnes came to believe, was to save the pagan people by prayer and example. This was a parochial calling—not a humanitarian calling—and it was to this calling that the young Agnes Gonxha Bojaxhiu of Serbia so eagerly responded.

Agnes had grown into an attractive young woman with a triangular face, a noble nose, piercing black eyes, a dark olive complexion, and thick and curly black hair. She was distinctly Eastern European and many Irish nuns, who met her in her youth, fancied her a "gypsy," while religious sisters in India believed she was "Bengali."

As attractive as she was, Agnes was not a perfect specimen of youth, vitality, and good health. According to her medical records, she had a "weak chest" and was prone to chronic coughs. A family physician diagnosed her as "pre-tubercular," and her mother told the other children that Bonxha would not be with them for very long.

In addition to the "pre-tubercular condition," Agnes suffered from severe attacks of malaria that resulted in high fevers and states of delirium. Her health problems were so severe that the family spent holidays at the famous spa town of Vrnjacka Banja in the mountainous region of Montenegro.

Compounding these problems, Agnes was born with a clubfoot. Throughout her life, Mother Teresa tried to mask this condition, saying that ill-fitting sandals caused her halting gait. Even after her death, no mention was ever made of this deformity. This was understandable since a clubfoot was viewed by many people in the Balkans as a sign of the evil one.

The young Agnes was outgoing and popular with girls, but became shy and retiring whenever a boy appeared. In later years, an Australian journalist asked Mother Teresa if she missed having a husband and children, and she responded by saying: "Naturally, naturally, of course. That is the sacrifice we make. That is the gift we give to God." But even as a teenager, Mother Teresa displayed no interest in the opposite sex.

In the two years before she entered the convent, Agnes spent summers on retreat at the shrine of Cernagore where she sought the advice of her Confessor. He told her: "If the thought that God may be calling you to serve Him and your neighbor makes you happy, then that may be the very best proof of the genuineness of your vocation. Joy that comes from the depths of your being is like a compass by which you can tell what direction your life should follow. That is the case even when the road you must take is a difficult one."

Agnes applied to join the Loreto Sisters, the Irish branch of the Institute of the Blessed Virgin Mary. This order worked with the Jesuits in India and maintained the spiritual devotions of St. Ignatius. The constitution of this order was patterned exactly after the constitution of the Society of Jesus. Like the Jesuits, the Loreto Sisters were not subjugated to the authority of a local bishop; they remained directly under control of the Pope. Also like the Jesuit counterparts, the sisters represented an intellectual society within the Church. Their primary purpose was the formation and propagation of correct doctrine by academic instruction. They were known not for working among the poorest people in Calcutta, but for operating schools for the children of the wealthiest Catholic families. Her decision to enter the Loreto Order undermines the common assumption that Mother Teresa's original intent upon entering religious life was to serve the dying and the "poorest of the poor."

Acceptance into the Loreto Order mandated that Agnes speak English—a language she had hardly ever heard, let alone mastered. It surely would have been far easier and far more fitting for Agnes to enter an Albanian or French order of religious sisters that worked among the street people of Calcutta rather than an Irish order that catered to the elite if her purpose was to serve as a religious social worker.

Although Drone and Aga approved of Agnes's decision, Lazar expressed dismay. He had grown into a good-looking and worldly wise soldier who had "a way with the women." By this time, he held the rank of lieutenant in the grand army of King Zog I of

Albania. "How could you do such a thing?" Lazar chided Agnes in a letter. "You are throwing your life away." Agnes responded by writing: "You will serve a king of two million people. I shall serve the king of the whole world."

The Institute of the Blessed Virgin Mary was formed in 1822 by three Irish nuns—Frances Mary Teresa Ball, Ellen Arthur, and Anne Thierry. They took possession of the Rathfarhan Abbey that had been purchased by the Archbishop of Dublin to serve as their Motherhouse and novitiate. The purpose of the new order was to provide superior education to girls from Catholic families. The fame of this new order spread far and wide, and Mother Frances Ball and members of her convent became known as the Loreto nuns. In 1836, Pope Gregory XVI issued an official prescript concerning the Loreto nuns that ordained the following: "Those who associate themselves to this Institute cannot depart to another even though observing rules of a more rigid discipline without express permission of the Apostolic See." This mandate would impact the later career of Mother Teresa. In 1840, the Sacred Heart Church, one of the most beautiful chapels in Ireland, was built next to the Rathfarhan Abbey as part of the convent complex. At the urging of the Archbishop of Calcutta, the Loreto nuns established a school in Calcutta in 1841 for the daughters of wealthy Catholic families. They also opened convents at Darjeeling, Assansol, and Entally.

A few days before Agnes's departure for Zagreb, the first leg of her journey to the convent in Ireland, a farewell concert was held in her honor at the Church of the Sacred Heart.

On September 26, 1928, Agnes Bojaxhiu embraced her friends and family and boarded a train for a grueling trip across Europe to France, where she would board a boat for Ireland. She was young, frightened, and unsophisticated. No one in Skopje who waved good-bye at the train station would ever see her again.

If she stayed in Skopje, she would have faced a precarious and uncertain future. The Yugoslavian government had begun to colonize the area with Serbs and the native Albanian population in Serbia was forced to emigrate or undergo assimilated. As part of the assimilation process, they were forbidden to speak their native language and were compelled to change their surnames to include a

Serbian suffix such as "vic" or "vc." Under the new laws of colonization, Serbs were given gifts of 125 acres of land, free transportation to the new area of settlement, unrestricted use of state forests, and exemption from taxation for a period of three years. As the Serbs moved into Skopje and Northern Albania, a new and infinitely more terrible period of persecution was about to begin.

Agnes entered the Loreto Abbey at Rathfarhan, outside of Dublin, on October 12, 1928, where she received a cap of a postulant—that is, she became a candidate for admission in a convent. Her hair was cropped and covered by a black veil. She took a crash course in English for six weeks before being placed on a ship for India. Between language lessons, she was obliged to clean the floor of the convent on her hands and knees, work in the kitchen and laundry, and perform acts of penance, including self-mortification, a process of subduing the temptations of the flesh by the infliction of pain.

Agnes now organized her life around the "Divine Offices" or "canonical hours." At 2 A.M., the bell signaled the nuns, novitiates, and postulants to rise from their sleep for the recitation of prayers and the reading of the Psalms. At 5 A.M., the bell rang for the members of the convent to gather for morning prayers. At 6 A.M., after making their beds and performing acts of personal hygiene, the bell rang for morning Mass. At 9 A.M., following breakfast and morning duties, the bell rang for midmorning prayers and devotions. The members of the convent then went to their work or study stations. At noon, the bell rang for all to gather for a meditation on the suffering of the Lord. Following lunch, they performed their afternoon chores, which were interrupted at 3 P.M. when the bell rang for communal prayer and thanksgiving. The members of the community returned to their workstations or classrooms until the bell rang at 6 P.M. for vespers. Following vespers came the evening meal and quiet time for study and contemplation, until the bell rang for a gathering of thanksgiving for their calling.

This schedule would regulate the life of Mother Teresa for the next twenty years.

On December 1, 1928, Agnes Bojaxhiu, along with other postulates and three Franciscan missionary nuns, set sail for India. The long voyage through the Suez Canal, the Red Sea, and the Arabian Sea to the Indian Ocean could only have heightened the young girl's sense of complete separation from all that was familiar and her feelings of what she called "incredible loneliness."

Her first port of call, according to one of her authorized biographies, was Colombo in the island of Ceylon (Sri Lanka), where Agnes was astonished by the tall, fruit-laden palm trees; the half-naked men pulling carts through the congested streets; and the shrill voices of the women in the market places. This, she said, represented her first step into the Third World.

Her biography notes that Madras was the next port of call on the Coromandel Coast of India. Here she told her biographer that she was shocked profoundly by the "indescribable" poverty of the people. She said it was an experience for which she had not been prepared. She later wrote:

> *Many families live in the streets, along the city walls, even in places thronged with people. Day and night they live out in the open on mats they have made from large palm leaves—or frequently on the bare ground. They are all virtually naked, wearing at best a ragged loincloth. ... As we went along the streets we chanced upon one family gathered around a dead relation, wrapped in worn red rags, strewn with yellow flowers, his face painted in colored stripes. It was a horrifying scene. If our people could only see all this, they would stop grumbling about their misfortune and offer thanks to God for blessing them with such abundance.*

Here we encounter another problem with Mother Teresa's account of her early life. Later, she would contradict many of these earlier statements about her past—even of her first passage to India—by telling another authorized biographer that she deported at Bombay and took a train ride through the heart of India. Was she confused about this crucial event in her life? Or did she purposely distort the truth to enhance her own image? These questions, like countless others about the life and work of Mother Teresa, beg an answer.

We only know for certain that on January 6, 1929, Mother Teresa arrived in Calcutta. A group of Indian nuns awaited to greet the novices on the dock. "With a joy I cannot describe," Mother Teresa wrote, "we touched the soil of Bengal for the first time. In the convent church we first of all offered up our thanks to the Redeemer for allowing us to arrive safely at our destination. Pray for us a great deal that we may become good and courageous missionaries."

Mother Teresa would remain in the city for only a brief stay before setting off for Darjeeling, a hill station for the nuns of Loreto seven thousand feet above the teeming city in the foothills of the Himalayas. Darjeeling is one of the most beautiful places on earth. It calls to mind the Shangri-La of *Lost Horizon*. When Mark Twain visited the city, he wrote, "The one place that all men desire to see, and having seen it once—even a glimpse—would not give that glimpse for the shows of the rest of the world combined."

Most devotees of Mother Teresa assume that she lived and worked among the poor of Calcutta from the time she first set foot on Indian soil. In truth, she lived in an incredibly affluent area, surrounded by spacious tea plantations, English colonial homes, and luscious botanical gardens of Sikkum spruce, geraniums, arum lilies, azaleas, magnolias, and a variety of Himalayan conifers. She was high in the mountains, more than three hundred and fifty miles from the city with which she would come to be identified.

India was in a state of turbulence. The British Raj still prevailed, but its days were numbered. While Mother Teresa was serving as a postulant at the Loreto convent school in the privileged environs of Darjeeling, tens of millions of Indians were rallying for the cause of independence. They were divided into two factions: the nonviolent, largely Hindu movement led by Mohandas K. Gandhi and Jawaharlal Nehru and the militant Moslem League of Mohammed Ali Jinnah.

Two years earlier, the appointment of an all-British commission to study the question of India's independence had sparked bloody riots throughout the country, and Gandhi had landed in jail. But such events were far from the rarefied air of Darjeeling.

During her stay at the convent school, Mother Teresa did little to distinguish herself from the other postulants. One of the nuns who served at the convent at the time remembered her as "a simple, ordinary girl." Another said that she was "unremarkable, not particularly educated, not particularly intelligent." However, St. Marie Therese, who had arrived at Darjeeling the previous year, spoke of her as "a great girl, very jolly and bright, full of fun."

At the convent, English was the primary language and Mother Teresa was immersed in language classes, including courses in Bengali, while undergoing preparation for teaching at the Loreto School. She managed to complete her work and her studies, and, by May 23, 1929, she was ready to enter the novitiate, the period of probation and preparation that takes place before the taking of solemn vows.

As a novitiate, Mother Teresa received the holy habit. She, like the other nuns and novitiates, dressed like a widow in long black tunics, a cincture or belt to hold the dress in place, a wimple to surround the face, and a black veil.

For her new life, she selected the name Teresa of the Child Jesus. She chose this name not after the great Spanish mystic St. Teresa of Avila, one of the great doctors of Roman Catholicism, but rather St. Teresa of Lisieux, known as "the Little Flower." Her choice of names was limited. All novitiates had to choose the name of a canonized saint. Because most saints were men, the Loreto nuns quickly claimed the permissible female names. This forced novitiates and nuns to adopt such masculine names as Joseph, Cyprian, Anthony, John, and Augustine. The newly dubbed Teresa of the Child Jesus was one of the few religious women at the convent with a feminine name. Heaven already had smiled upon her. St. Teresa of Lisieux was a brand new saint, who had been officially canonized in 1925.

It is not surprising that Agnes Bonxha Bojaxhiu became devoted to St. Teresa of Lisieux. She, too, was associated with roses by her childhood name of Bonxha. She, too, had suffered the loss of a parent as a young child. She, too, suffered from weak lungs and had been diagnosed as tubercular. She, too, was expected to die at a young age. She, too, had experienced a call to her vocation as a young child. She, too, sought to please God by suffering indignities and humiliations without murmur or complaint. She, too, sought to sever all her worldly ties and affections in order to live only for God.

St. Teresa of Lisieux was born in 1873 to an affluent family in Normandy. Her mother died of breast cancer when St. Teresa was four. When her favorite sister entered the Carmelite Order, "the Little Flower" suffered what most of us would call a nervous breakdown. Her illness was cured when she had a vision of the child Jesus. When a second sister joined the Carmelite Order, the young Teresa became bound and determined to enter the convent. Despite objections from her father, Teresa, through prayers and pleas, managed to receive a special dispensation to become a Carmelite at the tender age of fifteen. Because of her physical frailty, Teresa was prohibited from performing acts of penance and mortification of the flesh, such as extreme fasting and self-flagellation. For this reason, she sought "little ways" to please God and gain admission to heaven. "Little ways" consisted of offering up minute annoyances and difficulties to the suffering souls in purgatory. Teresa believed that she must become child-like in her sanctity, accepting everything without complaint, and "trusting in Jesus, like a Father." At the age of twenty-three, she became seriously ill with tuberculosis. She suffered such extensive hemorrhages that she was barely able to complete her small book of meditations called The Story of a Soul, *before she died on September 30, 1897. Her last words were, "My God, I love you." The nuns noticed that her death room smelled of roses. She is celebrated as the patroness of flower venders.*

Despite her lack of higher education, Mother Teresa taught at the Loreto School at Darjeeling for the next two years. She taught almost every subject in the curriculum: English, history, arithmetic, geography, and religion. She was simply handed textbooks and given a classroom assignment. Like most nuns and religious sisters of the time, she learned the subjects along with the students. The students were well-to-do British girls and daughters of wealthy Indian families.

For a short stint, she helped the medical staff at a small medical center. It was here that she first came into contact with India's poor. She wrote:

> Many have come from a distance, walking for as much as three hours. What a state they are in! Their ears and feet are covered in sores. They have lumps and lesions on their backs, among the numerous ulcers. Many stay at home because they are too debilitated by tropical fever to come. One is in the terminal stage of tuberculosis. Some need medicine. It takes a long time to treat them all and give the advice that is needed. You have to explain to them at least three times how to take a particular medicine, and answer the same question three times.

In 1931, she was assigned to live at the Sisters of Mary convent in the Entally neighborhood of Calcutta and to teach geography at St. Mary's High School for Girls, one of the six schools in the city operated by the Loreto sisters that catered to daughters from well-heeled Catholic families.

The convent and the school were enclosed in a vast complex of more than one hundred acres surrounded by high gray walls. The convent itself was an impressive turn-of-the-century building with huge colonnades and bright green shutters. The convent parlor, with its wide plank oak floors, contained highly polished teakwood furniture and framed prints of Renaissance art. The grounds included playing fields, lush gardens, and meticulously cropped lawns. The school itself was a modern granite structure with yellow-washed corridors and airy classrooms. A guard stood at the tall iron gates to protect the complex from intruders.

It's wrong to assume that this assignment cast the young novitiate into the teeming streets of the "City of Joy." Throughout her career as a member of the Loreto Order, Mother Teresa lived a safe and sequestered life among her fellow nuns.

Nuns are under canonical order to live a cloistered existence. "Cloister" comes from the Latin *claustrum*, meaning something that is kept under lock and key. By their vocation, nuns are expected to renounce the world and not to engage in worldly activities, not even social work. They are to live their lives behind the thick walls of a convent and to have little association or contact with the outside world. They are called to a contemplative life, not to the active life of religious sisters.

During her stay at the Loreto School in Entally, Mother Teresa had no contact with the streets of Calcutta, with the people in bustees, the speeches of the "bampanthis" (the political activists), or the "michils" (processions) of the Hindus. She was not permitted to leave the convent for any reason without the permission of her Mother Superior.

As a novitiate and later as a nun, she was ordered to speak only when necessary, to refrain from jests and loud laughter, and to walk with her eyes constantly to the ground. She was prohibited from owning anything, "not a book, writing tablet, or pencil—not a single item."

A convent, according to Catholic doctrine, is a "glorious prison" that women may enter of their own volition. But once inside, they are forbidden to leave. Here they are to live, work, die, and be buried.

The Catholic distinction between nuns and religious sisters is often obscured in biographies and accounts of Mother Teresa. A nun lives in a convent and assumes solemn vows that cannot be broken. A nun is called to the "higher life," the life of prayer and contemplation. A religious sister, on the other hand, lives in communal houses and assumes simple vows that can be absolved, since they are not eternally binding. A religious sister is called to the "active life"—the work of performing acts of charity. While nuns remain in convents, religious sisters work in hospitals, orphanages, asylums, hospitals, and food kitchens.

Teresa's purpose as a young woman preparing for solemn vows was to live a life of prayer, regulated by the "canonical hours" and punctuated by chores such as teaching in the convent school. She was not called to social action, but to solitude.

Like most novitiates and nuns, she wore a hair shirt underneath her habit for the mortification of the flesh. The coarse garment, made from goats' hair and wrapped around the loins like a girdle, acted like sandpaper against her skin and caused constant discomfort. It was removed only for the purpose of bathing.

As someone immersed in Tridentine Catholicism—the Catholicism before Vatican II—Mother Teresa believed that holiness is related to sexual purity, to chastity, and to virginity. This belief forms the basis for her beliefs and teachings. Individuals, she said, should live wholly and utterly for God as though they do not possess bodies. God is spirit, she said, and we can turn to him only in spirit. There is a chasm in her ideology between the physical and the spiritual that cannot be breached.

A worldly saint, in Catholic theology, is a contradiction in terms, a theological oxymoron. There are no worldly saints, just as there are no saintly sinners. By definition, saints are individuals who have turned from the world, the flesh, and the devil. Very few Catholic saints were married, St. Thomas More and St. Elizabeth Ann Seton being notable exceptions. There is a cleft between the physical and the spiritual, the mortal and the immortal, the holy and the profane that remains embedded in the warp and woof of Catholic doctrine. When this distinction is denied, Catholic doctrine, in general, and Mother Teresa's teachings, specifically, seem irrational or senseless.

We know little of Mother Teresa's life behind the convent walls of the Loreto House, simply because her life—and the lives of her fellow novitiates—were almost completely uneventful. Every day brought the same routine, without let up. The bell rang for the seven Divine Offices, and the residents of the convent gathered for prayers and devotions. In between the canonical hours, they performed household functions, taught convent classes, and received religious instruction. At night, before climbing into her cot, Teresa often scourged herself with a small whip for the purpose of mortifying her flesh. Such penitential practices were encouraged.

The few contacts Mother Teresa had with the outside world were with the Bengali sisters, whose members were known as the Daughters of St. Anne. This order of religious sisters was affiliated with the Loreto Sisters. They operated a boarding school for Bengali girls within the convent compound. Many of the students came from broken homes; some were orphans. The Daughters of

St. Anne were Bengali women who dressed in saris and spoke in their own tongue. Students from this boarding school attended classes at St. Mary's high school, where Mother Teresa taught geography.

> Nuns and monks live their lives according to the Catholic practice of asceticism. Asceticism comes from the Greek askeses, meaning "training." As athletes engage in physical training, members of convents and monasteries engage in spiritual training. The motto for both remains the same: "No pain, no gain." The only way, according to ascetic theology, to gain spiritual perfection is through the subjugation of the flesh and all fleshly desire. The physical desire for food must be repressed by fasting; the desire for self-fulfillment must be repressed by self-denial; the longing for rest must be repressed by hard work. The scriptural basis for this teaching comes from St. Paul, who writes in his Epistle to the Romans: "If you live after the flesh, you will die, but if through the spirit you mortify the deeds of the flesh, you shall live." (8:13) Inherent in this theology is the belief that our attempts to make expiations for our sins and that worldly longings are pleasing to God.

The religious sisters were immediately attracted to the Albanian novitiate. By appearance, speech, and demeanor, she was radically different from her Irish co-religious. Many of the Daughters of St. Anne came to believe that she, too, was Bengali and came to refer to her as "the Bengali Teresa" in order to distinguish her from the Irish Marie Therese.

In 1937, Mother Teresa returned to the convent at Darjeeling to make preparation for her wedding. Her long engagement was over. At the age of twenty-seven, she was ready to become the bride of Jesus Christ.

Chapter 4

The Call and the Vision

On May 24, 1937, the young novitiate known as Teresa of the Child Jesus walked down the center aisle of the chapel within the Loreto convent at Darjeeling. She wore a white wedding gown and a garland of flowers around her head. The small chapel was filled with nuns and novitiates in black habits. The wedding Mass began with the recitation of the Introit and the singing of the Gloria.

Before consecration, Teresa was called to kneel before Archbishop Ferdinand Perier, who officiated at the marriage ceremony. The Archbishop asked, "Are you resolved to preserve to the end of your days in the holy state of virginity and in the service of God and His Church?" Teresa answered, "I am." The Archbishop continued by asking, "Are you resolved to accept solemn consecration as a bride of our Lord Jesus Christ, the Son of God?" Teresa replied, "I am." Archbishop Perier and all present then exclaimed, "Thanks be to God."

After offering a prayer of consecration, Archbishop Perier read the following words from the Song of Solomon: "Rise, my love, my fair one, and come away." In response, Teresa, holding a candle, knelt before the Monsignor to receive her veil and ring. The Archbishop said, "Dearest daughter, receive your veil and the ring that are the insignia of your fidelity to your Bridegroom, and never forget that you are bound to the service of Christ and of his body, the Church." The newly consecrated Teresa replied by saying, "Amen."

At the close of the ceremony, Teresa retired to her cell for a three-day retreat in solitude that was known as her honeymoon. Following this period of prayer and fasting, she sat down with her fellow nuns for the wedding feast.

At the age of twenty-seven, Teresa had assumed the most solemn vows that a Catholic can make. Only the cloistered religious—monks and nuns—make solemn vows of poverty, chastity, and obedience. The other orders, including Jesuits and parish priests, simply make promises that are not nearly so binding and unbreakable.

> *Nun comes from the Coptic (Egyptian) word for "good" or "beautiful." It was applied to the first convent for women established by St. Pachomius in 330 on the opposite side of a river near Tabennisi, where the same saint established a monastic society for men. The four hundred women who became the first nuns divided their time between prayer (private and common) and manual labor. They raised their own food, cleaned and decorated the chapel, and spun flax and made clothes for the monks and themselves. They also engaged in spiritual exercises under a "Mother Superior" and were expected to memorize the Holy Scriptures, especially the Psalms. Whenever a virgin died, her spiritual sisters prepared her for burial in a wedding gown and placed her body on a riverbank. The monks, upon receiving a signal, crossed the river on a ferry to convey her body to the opposite side for burial in a common cemetery. Except for such occasions, the monks—except for a priest and a deacon for Sunday Mass—were not permitted to cross over to the convent.*

The new Bride of Christ returned to the convent in Calcutta and continued her teaching at Loreto Entally. On select occasions, such as trips to the marketplace with the Mother Superior or periodic visitations to the local Catholic Hospital, Teresa became more aware of the conditions of human life on the streets of Calcutta. The sights started to haunt her. "I felt it very deeply that while I should be snug in my bed behind the convent walls, down the road there were those who had no shelter."

In 1937, Sister Teresa was appointed principal of St. Mary's and superior of the Loreto nuns at Entally convent. With the appointment came a new title. Henceforth she would be addressed as "Mother Superior" or "Mother Teresa."

The nuns remember her for the great emphasis she placed on personal hygiene. Sr. Francesca, who continues to serve as a secretary at the convent, says: "In the morning Mother Teresa used to take us for our baths. She would stand there, ring the bell for us to pour water on ourselves, ring for us to soap ourselves, ring the bell for us to pour water again, and ring for us to come out. She would stand by the door with a bottle of permanganate of potassium. As we emerged, she would put this in our mouths and make sure we gargled!"

At this time, she wrote one of her few letters to her mother, Drone, who was now living in Tirana, the capital of Albania. She shared this news: "This is a new life. Our center here is very fine. I am a teacher and I love the work. I am also Head of the whole school, and everybody wishes me well."

But Mother Teresa's calm and happy life as the headmistress of a parochial school for privileged girls within a convent would soon be shattered by a series of cataclysmic events. In 1937, an earthquake shook the Bihar region of India between Varanasi and Dhanbad, causing hundreds of thousands of deaths and catapulting entire villages in the direction of Calcutta. Hundreds of thousands swarmed into the narrowest of alleyways. The streets became lined with salesmen and beggars, with homeless families camping on the sidewalks, with piles of building materials and refuse, with makeshift altars and small temples.

The situation was worsened by the outbreak of World War II. Although there was minimal fighting in Calcutta, the war had terrible consequences for the people there. When the Japanese overran the neighboring country of Burma, millions of refugees poured into the city. As the center of the entire British operations in the East, Calcutta became subject to the constant threat of air raids and naval attacks from the Japanese war ships and aircraft carriers that lined the Bay of Bengal. The upper regions of the Indian Ocean suddenly became closed to trade and supply ships. In Calcutta, food shortages suddenly became commonplace. Medical supplies were practically nonexistent. By 1942, famine struck—the

Great Famine, as it came to be called—and it lasted until 1944. More than two million people starved in the teeming streets of Calcutta. Their bodies were eaten by rats, scavenger birds, and hungry dogs.

The British high command took control of the Sister of Loreto's complex for use as administrative headquarters and a military hospital for soldiers sounded in Burma. The convent and school were moved to a location on Convent Road. Here the nuns and religious sisters under Mother Teresa continued their daily routine of prayer and teaching as regulated by the Rule of St. Benedict. Babies were placed daily on the doorsteps of the new location; beggars constantly banged on the doors for alms; the sick and dying begged for food and shelter. The nuns were under siege not only by the Japanese, but also by the poor of Calcutta.

With the war came a shortage of priests, and Mother Teresa came to turn to a young Jesuit priest from Belgium named Father Celeste Van Exem to perform daily Mass at the convent and to serve as a confessor to the nuns and religious sisters. Father Celeste, who would come to play a principal part in the creation of the Missionaries of Charity, said that his impression of Mother Teresa at that time was one of a very simple nun, very devout but not particularly remarkable.

Despite the increasing nightmare of life in the streets, Mother Teresa remained removed from the want and poverty outside the convent walls, from the increasing tension between Moslem and Hindu forces, and from the effects of the collapse of the colonial government. Father Celeste affirmed this when he later said, "Some accounts have tried to make a connection between Mother Teresa's life behind convent walls and the poverty and communal killing in Calcutta in those days, but these accounts are completely wrong, only a hypothesis."

The situation within Calcutta worsened after the war. The Indian National Congress pressed for independence from British rule, and the prospects of self-rule only heightened the tensions between Hindus and Moslems. Under Gandhi, the Hindus envisioned a united India. The Moslems, under Mohammed Ali Jinnah, agitated for the partition of India and the creation of a new homeland for Moslems that would be called Pakistan. On August 16, 1946, the Moslem League conducted a mass meeting in the Great Park of Calcutta. Passions were raised to a fever pitch, sparking bloody riots between Moslems and Hindus.

For four days and four nights, a communal frenzy swept over the crowded city. The scarce food supplies went underground, and Mother Teresa was faced with the prospect of three hundred starving children within her convent. She had to take immediate action. The small Albanian nun went out into the streets alone. Violence was erupting all about her. Thousands lay dead and dying in the streets. Finally, she was stopped by some British troops who drove her back to the school with a lorry-load of rice. The experience was jarring. She had come face to face with the world outside the convent walls.

Some biographies of Mother Teresa report that she watched out of her window every night and witnessed the burgeoning nightmare that was taking place in the Motijhil slum. One author argues that such sights compelled Mother Teresa to leave the comfortable convent and work with the impoverished people in the streets. But such accounts are erroneous. Mother Teresa's room was situated on the opposite end of the complex, overlooking lush gardens and not the squalid slums.

Neither war nor political upheaval would shatter Mother Teresa's sequestered life. The bombshell would come in the form of a simple note from the Abbess of the Loreto Order. The note would inform her that Mother Cenacle, her predecessor, would return to replace her as principal of St. Mary's High School and as Mother Superior of the Loreto Convent at Entally. Mother Teresa had been discharged because of questions regarding her competence. She was ordered to return to her former functions as an ordinary nun and to submit to the authority of her new superior.

Why was Mother Teresa removed from her position? One reason is that she lacked the educational training to serve as a high school principal. She had never stepped foot in a college. She showed little or no interest in academics. She could not take part in intellectual discussions with her fellow nuns. She knew little of art and literature, let alone the intricacies of scholastic theology.

The British Parliament in 1947 passed the Indian Independence Act as proposed by Viceroy Lord Mountbatten. Some provisions of the act were as follows:

- On August 15, 1947, two sovereign states, India and Pakistan, will be formed and the King of England no longer will be called the Emperor of India.

- The assemblies of India and Pakistan will prepare their respective constitutions.

- The British will have no authority over India or Pakistan after August 15, 1947. By that time, all British troops will be withdrawn.

- After August 15, 1947, the British Parliament will not have the right to make any law that affects the self-rule of the Indian peoples.

At midnight, August 15, 1947, the Indian "Tricolor" replaced the "Union Jack." Jawaharlal Nehru was named the first Prime Minister of India, and the process of political partition between the Moslems and the Hindus was set in motion.

Another reason was that she was Albanian, not Irish, and thus, in the eyes of those with power, projected the wrong image of a headmistress of an elitist parochial school. The wealthy parents of the children in the convent school often assumed that she was a Bengali rather than an Albanian nun, who should not occupy a position of prominence over Irish nuns, let alone children from wealthy British families.

Mother Teresa was devastated by the dismissal and frustrated that she had no means of redress, let alone recourse to action. She could not leave the Loreto Order to join another religious community. Such a transfer would have to meet with papal approval. This approval would be highly unlikely because she had no friends with ecclesiastical weight and importance. She could not renounce her solemn vows. She was married for all time to Jesus Christ and unsanctioned divorce meant eternal damnation. Annulment of her vows would also require papal approval, and she lacked the means and influence to win the favor of the Vatican bureaucracy.

She fell into a state of depression that gave way to periods of uncontrollable weeping. Father Celeste told a reporter that this was the only time that he saw Mother Teresa emotionally distraught. "I have seen her upset at the death of a Sister, things like that, but I never saw her cry. But then there were tears in her eyes." Depression gave way to physical illness. She suffered severe stomach spasms and chronic fits of uncontrollable coughing. Traces of blood appeared in her handkerchiefs. It was feared she was consumptive. The physicians advised a return to Darjeeling.

The rattling train ride on September 10, 1946, was to transform her life. As the train ascended into the Himalayas, Mother Teresa experienced what she described as "a call within a call." A voice seemed to come to her from the adjacent seat in the empty compartment, commanding her to leave the contemplative life in the convent for an active apostate in the streets. "It was an order," she said. "To fail to obey would have been to break the faith."

Many interviewers have attempted to obtain more information about this life-transforming experience, but Mother Teresa also refused to provide more information. She later confessed, however, that the call was not a vision, but "a communication that came as a form of inspiration."

At Darjeeling, Mother Teresa took part in a religious retreat that was directed by Father Pierre Fallon. Father Fallon noticed that Mother Teresa seemed to be completely engrossed in prayer and meditation and remained in isolation from her religious sisters. He further observed that at intervals she furiously scribbled notes on small slips of paper.

When she returned to Calcutta, Mother Teresa conveyed these notes to Father Celeste. He found in them the essence of her plan: "She was to leave Loreto but she was to keep her vows. She was to start a new congregation. That congregation would work for the poorest of the poor. There would be no institutions, hospitals, or big dispensaries. The work was to be among the abandoned, those with nobody, the very poorest." He also became convinced that she had experienced a genuine calling. He later told a reporter,

"From the beginning I had a feeling that it was a real vocation, a real call, and subsequently all that has happened is difficult to explain in a natural way. Mother was not an exceptional person, she was an ordinary Loreto nun, a very ordinary person, but with a great love for her Lord. So she was happy to offer a second sacrifice. She made her first sacrifice when she left her mother. Then she made another sacrifice, perhaps as big as the first, when she left Loreto."

Father Celeste met with Mother Teresa and offered his support and consultation. The first step, he told her, was to obtain the approval of Archbishop Ferdinand Perier. He instructed her to write a simple letter of explanation that he would convey to the Archbishop in person.

If Father Celeste thought Archbishop Perier would readily agree to release Mother Teresa from the convent, he was sorely mistaken. The Archbishop informed Father Celeste that Mother Teresa would have to wait at least a year while he pondered the matter and consulted with Father John Baptist Jansen, the Father General of the Society of Jesus, and Father Joseph Creusen, a specialist in the canon law of nuns. When Father Celeste said that he knew both men well, the Archbishop became alarmed and said, "I forbid you to write to them."

Father Celeste responded by saying that Mother Teresa's request was the result of a divine calling. "Your Grace," Father Celeste said, "it is the will of God. You cannot change the will of God." Archbishop Perier turned to the priest with a sneer and said, "I am the Archbishop, and I do not know the will of God, and you, a young priest in Calcutta, you know the will of God the whole time."

At the end of 1947, Archbishop Perier finally permitted Mother Teresa to write to her own Superior, the Mother General of Loreto at Rathfarman in Ireland, to request permission to leave the order. The Archbishop, however, demanded that the letter be shown to him before it was placed in the mail.

Mother Teresa wrote the letter in a simple and straightforward manner, saying that she felt called by God from the cloister to the streets. Father Celeste typed it and it was placed before Archbishop Perier for his approval.

Approval was not immediate. The Archbishop objected to Mother Teresa's request for an "indult of exclaustration." *Indult* means the special privilege to perform or execute an act that is not permitted by canon law. *Exclaustration* refers to the right of a nun to leave the contemplative life of the cloister and to retain her solemn vows and special religious status. The Archbishop insisted that a request be made for an "indult of secularization." This meant that Mother Teresa should seek to relinquish her vows and revert back to the status of a laywoman.

Mother Teresa was so intent on leaving the Loreto Order that she agreed to comply with the Archbishop's directive. She sent a letter to the Mother General at Rathfarhan requesting separation under an "indult of secularization." By submitting this request, she expressed her willingness to strip off her habit and her wedding ring in order to obtain freedom from her stay in the convent.

The response from the Mother General was immediate and totally unexpected. She wrote:

> My dear Mother Teresa,
> Since this is manifested as the will of God, I hereby give you permission to write to Rome. Do not speak to your own Superior, do not speak to your own Provincial. I do not speak to my own counselors. My consent is sufficient. However, when you write to Rome, do not ask for an indent of secularization but of exclaustration.

The Mother General obviously wanted to settle the matter as simply as possible. She did not wish to create a situation among the Loreto nuns in Calcutta by denying Mother Teresa's request and having a malcontent in their midst. She diplomatically agreed to allow Mother Teresa to leave the convent, perhaps believing that exposure to the grim realities of the streets of Calcutta would send the unsettled nun screaming back to the convent in a matter of weeks. Implied in the letter is the Mother General's willingness to make the right connections for papal approval. She obviously wanted to assume complete control of the delicate matter.

In an act of rather willful rebellion, Mother Teresa ignored the explicit instructions of the Mother General and immediately presented the letter to Archbishop Perier for his reaction. The Archbishop reiterated his initial position: Mother Teresa should send a petition to Rome seeking an induct of secularization rather than exclaustration. This would make clear her desire to separate herself—once and for all—from the Irish nuns of Loreto. Mother Teresa agreed without a word of protest. She sent a letter to Rome asking that she be absolved of her solemn vows so that she could serve as a secular social worker. Her willingness to leave the Church undermines her steadfastness and fidelity and represents one of the major criticisms to claims of her saintliness. "No saint," one critic said, "would ever seek separation from Mother Church."

These dealings between Mother Teresa and her superiors remained clandestine. No one in the Loreto School or convent knew of her secret plans to leave the convent. She went about the daily rituals of work and prayer as though nothing was amiss, let alone that she had applied for an indent of secularization. St. Marie Therese Breen admitted, "It came as a shock to us when we heard, because it had never been discussed between us as these things are private, so we never knew until she left."

At the end of July 1948, Archbishop Perier received the Vatican decree regarding the fate of Mother Teresa. She was granted the right to establish a new order of missionary nuns and had been given the right to leave the convent with the indent of exclaustration for one year. The decree was stunning because Mother Teresa had not sought or requested this indent. The good Mother General at Rathfarman had demonstrated the Irish gift for ecclesiastical politics. She had obtained what was best for the reputation and integrity of her order.

The decree was monumental. It represented the first time in history that a nun was permitted to work outside a cloistered environment. Indeed, it served to nullify the very notion of a nun as one who lives in a life of prayer and contemplation in a convent. It broke down the long-standing distinction between a nun and a religious sister and had profound ramifications on the future direction of Catholic vocations. Because of this decision regarding

Mother Teresa, nuns would act like sisters, and sisters would become sanctified social workers. Thousands would leave the convents and solemn vows would represent promises that could be broken. This, too, for better or worse, remains a part of Mother Teresa's legacy.

> Mother Teresa was the first woman in the history of the Roman Catholic Church to receive an indent of exclaustration to perform missionary work outside the confines of a convent. Mary Ward, who is credited with being the inspirational source of the Loreto Order, served as Mother Teresa's prototype in her appeal to Rome. Mary Ward entered a convent of Poor Clares at St. Omer in England as a lay sister. Not suited for a life of prayer and contemplation in a convent cell, she sought to perform charitable work in the community. At the age of twenty-four, Mary, with a group of devoted companions, opened schools for the poor and rich with the convent at St. Omer as her base. Her idea was for women to perform the same tasks for the Church as men in the Society of Jesus. She sought freedom from enclosure, from observance of the canonical hours, from the wearing of a habit, and from the jurisdiction of the diocesan. She sought in 1624 what Mother Teresa sought in 1947. St. Paul V declared that solemn vows and strict papal enclosure were essential to all communities of religious women. The "Jesuitesses," as the followers of Mary Ward were called by their detractors, were officially suppressed by the Church in 1630. The ruling of Pope Pius V remained in effect until Pope Pius XII issued his ruling in favor of Mother Teresa's indent of exclaustration.

On April 20, 1948, Father Celeste met with Mother Teresa at the large convent building at Entally. He presented her with the Vatican document and said, "Mother, you have the decree of exclaustration. I have three copies for you to sign: one copy for you, one copy for Rome, one for the bishop. You have the decree of exclaustration for one year. You can do the work. Your Superior is now the Archbishop of Calcutta. You are no longer a Loreto nun."

"Father," came the response from Mother Teresa, "can I go to the slums now?"

Father Celeste told her that it would take several months before the paperwork was finalized and that she should not mention the decree to anyone. On August 16, Mother Teresa went to her cell and removed her habit. She dressed in a simple sari and slipped through the convent gates under the cover of night.

The next day letters went out to every Loreto institution in India with the news of Mother Teresa's departure from the order. They were neither to criticize nor praise her action, but only to keep her in their prayers.

Chapter 5

Calcutta and the Missionaries of Charity

Mother Teresa began her new life as a missionary to the poor just as India began its turbulent new life as a country. With the partition of India in 1947 came chaotic disorder. War broke out between India and Pakistan, and more than one million died in the conflict. More than four million Moslems and Hindus fleeing from the war-ravaged areas of Bihar and East Pakistan poured into the crowded streets of Calcutta. Three thousand slums appeared overnight. The population soared more than ten million, making Calcutta the second largest city in the world next to New York. The people were now condemned to live on less than ten square feet per person. In the absence of public toilets, the residents of the slums were forced to perform bodily functions at every curb. The streets became open sewers. Mounts of garbage collected at the curbs, attracting millions of flies, mosquitoes, cockroaches, and rats.

The problem of filth brought with it the rise of epidemics. People died in droves of cholera, hepatitis, encephalitis, typhoid, and rabies. International health agencies, such as the Red Cross, began to speak of Calcutta as an open cesspool, a city poisoned by fumes, nauseating gases, and toxic discharges—a devastated landscape of crumbling façades, collapsed roofs and walls, broken roads, leaking sewers, and burst water pipes. It had become Kipling's "City of Dreadful Night."

By 1950, when the India-Pakistan conflict subsided, seven out of ten families in Calcutta survived on less than one rupee a day— a sum insufficient to buy a half-pound of rice. Along with the poverty and disease, Calcutta became a powder keg of violence and anarchy, where masses turned to the promise of communism. The inflammatory speeches by political agitators caused riots and looting throughout the city. No one was safe—not the wealthiest merchant, not the most powerful politician.

The unbearable climate intensifies the urban problems. Calcutta remains torrid for eight months without reprieve. The heat melts the asphalt on the roads and expands the metal structure of the great Howrath Bridge to such an extent that it measures four feet more by day than by night. At the end of the long summer comes the monsoon season during which the alleyways, shacks, and streets are transformed into lakes of mud and excrement. It is small wonder that the inhabitants of this "inhuman city" turn to worship Kali, the terrible goddess who wears a necklace of snakes and skulls. And it's an even smaller wonder that the most common slogan on the walls of the rotting building says, "Here there is no hope."

> *The most popular goddess among the Hindu population of Calcutta is Kali, the Mother Goddess. She represents dissolution and destruction, the polar opposites of Mother Teresa and her Missionaries of Charity. Ironically, she is the Indian deity most closely associated with the Catholic nun among the inhabitants of the streets. Kali's appearance is fearsome: baleful eyes, a protruding tongue, and four arms. In her upper-left hand, she wields a bloody sword, and in her lower-left hand she holds the severed head of a demon. With her upper-right hand, she makes a gesture of defiance, with her lower-right hand she bestows benefits. Draped around her is a chain of severed human hands and she wears a belt of dismembered limbs. As the divine mother, she is often depicted as dancing in sexual union with Shiva, the third member of the Hindu trinity.*

By the time Mother Teresa set out on her mission of mercy, Calcutta had the lowest life expectancy rate in the world. More than ninety percent of the people suffered from dysentery or some form of malnutrition. Tuberculosis remained rampant. Among the teeming millions of poor roamed thousands of lepers. Mother Teresa did not go immediately to the streets to work with the people. Archbishop Perier sent her to work with the Medical Mission Sisters in Patna. The sisters taught her how to identify the telltale signs of cholera; how to treat sores and common childhood diseases such as measles, mumps, and chicken pox; how to treat a wound and administer an injection; and how to serve as a midwife for women in labor. At Patna, she also learned how to maintain a makeshift ward for emergency services.

The Patna sisters gave her practical suggestions about working with inhabitants of the *bustees*. She and her co-workers should never eat what the poor ate, especially not the sweetmeats inflamed with chili and other incendiary spices often applied to mask the stench of rancidity. Indeed, she was cautioned not even to eat the rice sprinkled with salt. Even the most innocuous food cooked by cakes of cow dung in *chulas* could cause dysentery.

The sisters related to her the importance of realistic work habits. Mother Teresa and those who worked with her should never work more than seven or eight hours a day. Above all, they must never labor in the midst of the noonday sun, and each and every worker must have a weekly day off for rest and recuperation.

The sisters also instructed her about dressing for street work. She and her co-workers must never wear anything dark or heavy because such clothing could quickly produce heat exhaustion. Each worker would need three white and light saris: one for wear, one to wash, and one for emergencies. They must keep their heads covered at all times for protection against the sun and lice.

Father Celeste visited Parna in November 1948 to check on Mother Teresa's progress. "At the hospital," he told Mother Teresa's biographer Navin Chawla, "I saw a group of sisters and nurses chatting. I said to the group, 'I have come to see Mother Teresa, where is she?' 'But, father, I am here,' said a voice from the back. Mother Teresa was there all along, but I failed to recognize her because she was wearing a sari." The white sari with blue borders bore the insignia of the cross and the rosary. It was to become the uniform of her religious order.

Upon the completion of Mother Teresa's medical training, Archbishop Perier assigned her to stay with the Little Sisters of the Poor, who operated a home for the elderly at 2 Lower Circular Road. She began her street work not in the most wretched of slums, but at Motijhil, one of the better sections of the city. For Calcutta, Motijhil is lower middle class. It is lined with small houses that have television antennas. This section of Calcutta offers electricity, drinking water, and adequately maintained sewer lines.

Because Mother Teresa had spent most of her life as a teacher, she immediately sought to establish a makeshift school for small children. She visited the parents of students who had attended the St. Teresa School where she had served as headmistress. Several parents were more than willing to place their children under Mother Teresa's care for a few hours in the morning. Why not? The Mother was making them an offer that no Bengali woman of sound mind could refuse: free childcare.

The school, Mother Teresa later told her friend and biographer Franca Zambonini, was free because the children received nothing but simple instructions in reading, writing, and arithmetic without pencils, paper, chalk, slate, blackboards, books, charts, maps, or anything else. The students didn't even have a roof over their heads, let alone desks and chairs. They sat on the ground under a tree while the good Mother spoke to them for hours. Her only visual aid was a stick with which she drew figures in the dirt.

The story reads like an account from Alban's *Lives of the Saints*, with Mother Teresa writing letters from the Bengali alphabet in the dirt before adoring children. But there are some problems with this account. The inhabitants of Motijhil are mostly Biharti Moslems who do not speak Bengali. Their primary language is Urdu or Hindi. Another problem arises with the question of Mother Teresa's actual command of the Bengali language. Several Bengali reporters who interviewed her said that she possessed no understanding of the language and was only capable of uttering a few catch phrases, such as "I will pray for you," and "Jesus lives in the leper." This claim is supported by the fact that Mother Teresa never wrote anything in Bengali, not even notes to the Bengali workers in her employ. All of her notes, messages, and letters were written in English. For this reason, it is very possible that Mother Teresa relied on interpreters at the start of her career as a religious social worker.

Mother Teresa was granted a small allowance from the Loreto Sisters that she used primarily for transportation, food, personal hygiene items, and cleaning supplies. By midweek, her meager funds were spent, forcing her to forego the tram fare and walk back and forth to the simple site of her mission in her rough leather sandals, a parting gift from the Patna sisters. It didn't take Mother Teresa long to learn the most basic lesson of life outside the convent: You can't do anything without money.

In search of funding, she turned to one of the wealthiest financial institutions in Calcutta: the Church. She visited two parishes in search of contributions for her street school. The priest at the first parish in Sealdah said that he was pleased to hear of her work but refused to open his purse. Mother Teresa trekked to a second parish, this one at Park Circus, where the priest, upon hearing her pitch, opened his wallet and shelled out one hundred rupees.

This gift represented a small fortune to Mother Teresa. She immediately returned to Motijhil where she rented two rooms for five rupees a month. One room was to be used as a classroom, the second as a dispensary. This was a significant accomplishment because her mission was less than two weeks old.

Upon learning the great spiritual lesson: "Ask and it shall be given unto you," Mother Teresa went about asking members of the Sodality of the Blessed Virgin Mary and various Altar and Rosary Societies for donations. Within a matter of days, her classroom was equipped with tables, chairs, blackboards, books, slate tablets, and boxes of chalk.

By January 1, 1949, she had thirty children, mostly ragamuffins, in her classroom that was situated across the street from a large water tank. "The little children," she wrote in her journal, "were dirty and untidy, but very happy." Before beginning instruction, she marched them to the water tank where she gave them a complete cleaning and delousing. To her dying day, Mother Teresa remained a stickler for cleanliness.

By reaching out to Catholic social and charitable groups, she also managed to recruit three volunteer teachers, and, within one week, the classroom was packed with sixty youngsters. The money and gifts came pouring into the new mission. Mother Teresa had come to represent a new phenomenon in Calcutta. Here was a beggar who was begging not for her own needs, but for poor children. Her appeals were answered with open pocketbooks.

On January 14, 1949, after being in the missionary business for less than a month, Mother Teresa received her "first rude shock." She knocked on the door of a rectory and asked the priest at Park Street for a contribution of fifty rupees. "What surprise!" she wrote in her journal. "He treated me as if I was doing something very wrong. He advised me to ask my parish priest to finance me. Great was his surprise when I said I shall finance myself by begging. He went off, saying he did not understand and did not say good-bye. It was the first good blow and a hard one. Coming up Camac Street, tears often filled my eyes."

But such refusals were rare. Mother Teresa now engaged in a major campaign for contributions. She sent out thousands of "begging letters" from her room in the nursing home of the Little Sisters of the Poor and amassed a small army of volunteers to engage in "begging expeditions." She called her new enterprise Nirmal Hriday, a Bengali term meaning "Pure Heart."

In her quest for cash, Mother Teresa even met with government officials in an effort to secure government funding for her school. In her journal, she wrote: "I went with Sabriti (one of her volunteers) to meet with Miss Roy, the Inspectress of Schools. She was ready to give a grant for the school. I told her I wanted to teach the children the things they need most and I wanted to be free." This was a bold move. She was attempting to obtain public money for a parochial venture. What's more, she was seeking such funding without ecclesiastical approval. Her efforts came to no avail. Miss Roy informed Mother Teresa that her school would have to be in operation for more than a year before the government could consider support. The school had been in existence for less than three weeks when Mother Teresa made the request. She was moving fast.

No sooner did the little school get underway than Mother Teresa opened a dispensary, not at Motijhil, but at a room provided to her at St. Teresa's parish school, where an Irish nun from the Loreto Convent was serving as principal. The dispensary was well stocked with medicines that she had managed to obtain from local chemists' shops, along with a screening apparatus for tuberculosis. Before long, lengthy lines of people formed down the block at opening time. Many were rickshaw pullers and "coolies" who carried heavy weights on their heads in the marketplaces.

Her fund-raising efforts are best exemplified by the story of her visit to a pharmacy with a long list of medicines that she wanted to obtain for her dispensary. The pharmacist said that he couldn't possibly help. Mother Teresa responded by sitting on the floor and reciting countless rosaries. At the end of the day, the pharmacist took a fresh look at the list and said, "Here are the medicines you need. Take them with the firm's compliments."

Upon establishing one school, she decided to open another, this one in Tiljara. In her journal entry of January 4, 1949, she wrote, "I begged the parents in Tiljara to get the children to school. I shall do everything in my power to help these poor creatures. Their misery is much more terrible than at Motijhil." Within three weeks, the school and its fully stocked dispensary were opened. On February 2, she wrote, "This is our Lady's day. Last year, on this day, Mother General's letter arrived. At Tiljara, I had twenty-three children. The children are very nice and so very respectful. They love their games—God be praised for it all."

At this time, Mother Teresa made an entry in her journal that confounds both her critics and her admirers. She wrote, "When Our Lady thinks it fit to give me a few children of my own, then only, Nirmal Hriday will spread its love everywhere in Calcutta. I keep on telling Her, 'I have no children,' just as many years ago She told Jesus, 'They have no vine.' I put all trust in her Heart. She is sure to give to me in Her own way."

This entry clearly shows that Mother Teresa, at the age of thirty-eight, actually held hopes to free herself from her solemn vows and the confines of religious life. This hope comprised the essence of her petition to her Mother Superior as well as the

Vatican. She sought an "indent of secularization." Such a separation from the Church, in turn, could grant her the opportunity to marry and to have a family of her own. It also implies that she did not want to remain under an "indent of exclaustration." She was still a young and attractive woman. At this stage in her life, she sought self-fulfillment, not sainthood.

During these years, Mother Teresa was ordered by Archbishop Perier to keep not only a journal, but also a diary. Her admirers often quote fragments of the diary, including this entry: "Oh God! If I cannot help these people in their poverty and their suffering, let me at least die with them, close to them so that in that way I can show them your love." Were these words really inscribed in the secret record of Mother Teresa's trials and tribulations? No one knows. The diary has not been preserved. It was allegedly in Father Celeste's hands for many years until she persuaded him to return it because she wanted to destroy it. "There may have been revelations of her own reactions and emotions that she preferred not to share," explained Eileen Egan, one of her authorized biographers.

Mother Teresa's new work consumed all her time and energy. Although she soon amassed a small army of volunteers, most of the volunteers had other jobs and responsibilities. They worked at the mission for several hours and left, sometimes before they completed their work. Even worse, some days the volunteers were not able to come. In her journal, Mother Teresa noted, "I went to see the sick but there was too little time and the teacher was anxious to get to her own children."

The woman Mother Teresa most admired in 1949 was Jacqueline De Decker, a lay Belgian missionary. De Decker earned a degree in sociology before coming to India in 1947. For her work among the poor in the bustees, she dressed Indian style in saris and sandals. She became known as the "saint of the streets." Mother Teresa sought her out, and the two became fast friends. In 1949, De Decker was stricken with the first symptoms of a serious spinal disorder that would eventually disable her. She returned to Europe for the first of many back operations, and she continued her friendship with Mother Teresa by correspondence. Throughout her life, Mother Teresa always referred to De Decker as her "second self."

But not everyone in the Roman Catholic Church was pleased with the growth of her mission. Several priests complained that it was unsightly to see a nun walking the streets without a habit and performing the tasks of a secular social worker. Moreover, they said that any success she achieved as a solitary nun would not last. The complaints reached the ears of the Mother Provincial of the Loreto Order in Entally. The Mother Provincial met with Mother Teresa and pleaded with her to return to the convent for the good of the order. Mother Teresa responded to the request by strengthening her resolve to succeed. She wrote to the Mother Provincial, "I believe some are saying what is the use of working among the lowest of the low that since the great, the learned, and the rich are ready to come, it is better to give full force to them. Yes, let them do it. If the rich people can have the full service and devotion of so many nuns and priests, surely the poorest of the poor and the lowest of the low can have the love and devotion of us few—'the Slum Sister' they call me, and I am glad to be just that for His love and glory."

But although she met criticism, she also encountered widespread admiration and acclaim. Within a matter of months, she became a celebrity in the City of Joy. At the end of February 1949, an official from the Ministry of Education visited the Motijhil School and issued these words of praise: "Sister, I admire you and envy you. Your love for these destitute classes is great and here we are of this country doing nothing for our own. I shall go to the Prime Minister and tell him what you are doing." The Prime Minister was informed of her work and expressed his appreciation to Archbishop Perier.

Heaven continued to smile on Mother Teresa's efforts. On February 28, 1949, she was offered her own rent-free living quarters in the second floor of the residence of Michael Gomes and his family. Gomes was a devout Roman Catholic and a close friend of Father Celeste. Located at 14 Creek Lane in one of the most affluent sections of the city, the house was surrounded by a high wall and beautiful gardens of cascading bougainvillea.

Upon leaving her room with the Little Sisters of the Poor, Mother Teresa became the first nun in the history of the Roman

Catholic Church not to reside within the confines of a religious community. She was now almost totally independent. She had no routines to observe, no hours to keep, and no Mother Superior to obey. To add to her blessings, she also obtained the services of Charu Ma, a widow who formerly worked at the St. Mary High School, as her personal cook and housekeeper. Charu Ma was to stay with Mother Teresa until she died.

With her newfound freedom, Mother Teresa began to entertain thoughts of forming her own religious order. Such thoughts were no longer idle daydreams. Within two short months, she had managed to open two schools and two dispensaries, collect an incredible amount of donations, and even establish her own headquarters.

She attempted to recruit a group of disciples. On March 1, 1949, Mother Teresa sent a note to Subashini Das, a wealthy Bengali student she had known at St. Mary's High School, and asked the young girl to visit her at her living quarters. Once the girl arrived, Mother Teresa asked her to become a member of a "little society" that she was forming of religious social workers. She offered to share her quarters with Subashini, to provide meals, and to give the girl a small allowance. Because such job opportunities were rare in Calcutta, the young Bengali girl immediately accepted.

On March 19, Mother Teresa took her new church to the Baithak Khan Church, where Father Celeste was stationed and, without church approval, consecrated Subashini as a member of her society. Subashini now became known as Sister Agnes. Within a week, Mother Teresa's recruiting efforts resulted in an additional new disciple: Magdalena Patin, another student from St. Mary's, who became known as Sister Gertrude. Several weeks later, a sixteen-year-old girl, Sister Margaret Mary, became the third member of the "little society."

By the end of May, the second floor of the Gomes household became crowded with eight additional postulants. "They were regulated by a bell system," Michael Gomes told Navin Chawla. "According to the ringing of a bell, they had to eat, go to work, pray, or rest. During the recreational time, they played games such as tug of war. You could hear their laughter down the street. They had to study a great deal as well. They were not allowed to give up their studies, and, in fact, Mother Teresa would tutor them in the evenings." Sister Agnes, the first disciple, remembers, "We lived as nuns, but we had not yet been recognized as a separate congregation. The Archbishop had yet to approve our way, and there was no constitution yet. But we were convinced that approval would come."

Several recruits to Mother Teresa's new society left high school in their last year without taking their final examinations. This caused considerable anguish for parents, who were distraught to see their daughters leaving school without a secondary school diploma. Sister Florence recalls, "After Mother had been to Patna, she came fishing to our homes talking to our parents and to us. We were sitting for our school final exams then, so our parents thought study was more important than anything. But Mother said, 'No, no. The sooner you come, the better.' She was young looking and very dynamic; she inspired us. So we joined her." At least one set of parents severed contact completely with their daughters because they had become so angry with them for quitting school and joining the mission.

The young women, dressed like their spiritual leader in white saris with blue bands, were soon a familiar sight not only in the residential neighborhood of Creek Lane but also in various slum areas of the city. The new recruits ran the schools in the morning and operated the dispensary in the afternoons every day except Sunday. They visited sick families and helped to place the seriously ill and the dying in hospitals.

Another primary function of the women was to go from parish to rectory, Catholic home to Catholic societies, banks to businesses, to solicit alms and donations. Without a continuous flow of cash and goods, the new society could not continue to exist, let alone expand its activities.

To aid in the fund-raising, Father Celeste placed advertisements about Mother Teresa in *The Statesman*. He later said that he could not list the Mother's address as 14 Creek Lane because this comfortable location would inspire neither confidence nor contributions. He opted instead to list the address of his church so that the little society would receive ample support from the start. It also became important for Mother Teresa to be depicted as a national rather than a parochial figure. For this reason, she applied for and was granted Indian citizenship.

In July, Archbishop Perier came to a decision regarding Mother Teresa and her work. Her leave from the convent had been granted for only one year, and the time had come to decide what to do about her religious status and her missionary work. The decision for the Archbishop was not easy. Mother Teresa had become the target of harsh criticism. The parish priest at St. Thomas's Church spoke of her work as "the wiles of the devil." It was not right, the priest argued, for a nun to act as a layperson. Indeed, he said, her mission undermined the concept of religious vocation and religious community. It was disgraceful that she—as a nun who had taken vows of poverty—was living in a comfortable apartment with a cook and attendants. It was outrageous that she was recruiting young women to join her society without canonical approval. Send her back to her cell, the priest insisted, and lock the door.

Upon hearing such objections, Archbishop Perier said that he would not approve Mother Teresa's work as a street nun unless the St. Thomas priest retracted his objections. Fortunately for Mother Teresa, Father Celeste, who was friendly with the priest, came to her rescue. He met with the critical prelate and persuaded him to withdraw his comments as a personal favor. Reluctantly, Archbishop Perier gave his approval for Mother Teresa to persist in her missionary work.

But the Archbishop was not pleased with Mother Teresa's "little society." He insisted that the society submit a petition and a constitution for official sanction by the Sacred Congregation of Religious in Rome. Father Celeste relayed this information to Mother Teresa and asked her to prepare a preliminary constitution for the creation of the religious society that she wanted to call "the Missionary Sisters of Charity." For weeks, Mother Teresa worked on her proposal. She finally submitted her efforts to Father Sanders, a Jesuit priest, who judged that the document was not fit for ecclesiastical inspection. The English was poor and several articles in the bylaws ran counter to canon law.

The task of a constitution was handed over to Father Celeste, who modeled the proposal on the Loreto Rule, which, in turn, had been based on the Jesuit model. "I took into account the existing canon law and the constitutions of some other congregations," Father Celeste later explained, "but most important of all, the Inspiration that Mother had received on the train journey to Darjeeling and which recurred throughout her retreat. I had read the inspiration sheets only once, but I knew what she wanted in them. She had to leave her convent and live like the poor, she should not have a big house or big institutions, her work would be in the slums and on the pavements of Calcutta. If they acquired large houses and institutions, it would only be for the helpless, such as abandoned infants and children, or lepers and dying destitutes. Theirs was to be a religious society, not social work. It was charity for Christ in the poor."

As completed by Father Celeste, the constitution had two hundred seventy-five rules. To show that the order represented not a laxity in discipline for religious women, the document upheld not only the three solemn vows of poverty, chastity, and obedience, but also a fourth vow of wholehearted and free service to the poorest of the poor. This vow, Mother Teresa said, would bind the Missionaries of Charity to feed, clothe, shelter, and nurse the sick, the dying, and the outcasts.

Father Celeste and his fellow Jesuits refined the document. He then gave it to a member of his congregation, who was employed at the High Court in Calcutta, to prepare it for official submission. The prepared document was delivered to Archbishop Perier, who took it with him to Rome in 1950.

The Jesuits had performed their work well. The only question raised about the proposal concerned proper dress for the sisters. The Sacred Congregation said that postulants and novices should assume different habits so they could be distinguished from fully professed sisters. It was decided that postulants should wear plain white saris with short sleeves as a habit, novices should wear white saris with full sleeves, and sisters should assume the distinctive dress of Mother Teresa.

On October 7, 1950, the constitution the Missionary Sisters of Charity—but not the congregation itself—received papal approval. A Mass was celebrated in a tiny chapel that had been created out of one of the rooms in the second floor of the Gomes' residence. Father Celeste read the Decree of Erection that began as follows:

> For more than two years now, a small group of religious women under the guidance of Sister Teresa, a lawfully uncloistered religious of the Institute of the Blessed Virgin Mary, have devoted themselves to helping the poor, the children, the adults, the aged, and the sick, in this, our Metropolitan City.

The very first words of the decree were false. The small group of religious women had not been laboring for two years, but less than nine months. The constitution, which had been prepared by Jesuit priests, not the members of the order, maintained that the society would live in perfect poverty without possessions or property. Mother Teresa, however, was preparing to violate the guiding principle. She had her mind set on purchasing a large building at 54A Lower Circular Road to serve as the Motherhouse of her new order.

Chapter 6

The Motherhouse and Nirmal Hriday

The Motherhouse of the Missionaries of Charity is a three-story structure that is enclosed in a three-building complex within the heart of Calcutta at 54 Lower Circular Road (now called Acharya J. C. Bose Road).

The entrance of the Motherhouse is a small door in the alley. The parlor is a waiting room in which a sister sits behind a simple wooden desk. It is furnished with a long table, benches, and several mismatched chairs. The walls are lined with photographs of Mother Teresa with Pope John Paul II and various world leaders. The parlor opens into a spacious courtyard with a flower garden. In the midst of the courtyard is a well where the sisters perform their morning ablutions. The chapel is a large rectangular room without any ornamentation except a large statue of the Virgin Mary. The altar is a plain table. Entering the chapel is like entering a mosque because you are obliged to remove your shoes. The third structure serves as a refectory—that is, a dining room for the religious sisters.

Numerous accounts have been written about the miraculous way that Mother Teresa obtained possession of this complex. According to the stories, the sisters prayed and prayed for a perfect location for their Motherhouse. Suddenly, an angelic man appeared at 14 Creek Lane to tell Mother Teresa and the sisters that the ideal spot would be a property at 54A Lower Circular Road. The man led Mother Teresa to the place and disappeared into the putrid air. Mother Teresa then met the owner of the complex, a Moslem physician by the name of Dr. Islam. According to the pious accounts such as the authorized biographies by Navin Chawla and Kathryn Spink, Dr. Islam was astonished that the saintly nun knew of his intention to sell because he had discussed the matter only with his wife. When he heard of Mother Teresa's charitable work among the poorest of the poor, Dr. Islam said, "Money isn't everything." He then retired to the nearby Mosque of Maula Ali to pray. When he returned, the good doctor had tears in his eyes and said, "God gave me this house. I give it back to him."

This story reproduced in all official accounts of Mother Teresa's life intimates that the Moslem doctor was so moved by the Christian nun's unselfish devotion that he handed over the keys to his property without seeking a penny in payment. But that is not really the case. Dr. Islam sold the complex for an undisclosed amount of money. Part of the payment came from cash that Mother Teresa and her workers, including Father Celeste, had obtained from their fund-raising efforts. Another part came from a sizeable loan of one hundred twenty-five thousand rupees that Mother Teresa obtained from the vicar-general of the diocese.

From the start, Mother Teresa imposed strict discipline on the members of her society who resided in the complex. The sisters rose at 4:40 A.M. to the call of "Benedicamus Domino" ("Let us bless the Lord") and the response, "Deo gratias" ("Thanks be to God"). They dressed in their saris at bedside with a sheet over their heads so that no sister could behold another's nakedness.

They gathered in the courtyard to wash at the well before entering the chapel for morning prayers, meditation, and Mass. At 5:45, they left the chapel and entered the refectory for a breakfast of cereal, milk, bread, and tea. Following this meal, they were all obliged to swallow a multitude of vitamin pills. By 6:30, they lined up for their morning showers, were carefully supervised by Mother Teresa, who remained a stickler for cleanliness to the end of her days. They had to scrub their carefully cropped heads with lice-killing compounds. After the shower, they had to wash the saris that they wore the previous day in buckets of hot water. Following this, they scoured the Motherhouse from top to bottom.

At 7:45, the sisters went off in pairs to work at the schools, dispensaries, and various slum areas. They were ordered to remain silent and to spend the time in travel by foot or tram by reciting rosaries. By noon, all the sisters were obliged to gather in the chapel for a recitation of prayers and devotions. Next came lunch and naptime. Every sister in the society was sent to bed for a half-hour so that no one became cranky.

At 2 P.M., the sisters gathered for prayer and afternoon tea, followed by spiritual readings and instructions by Mother Teresa. By 3, the sisters reported back to their work sites, where they labored until 6, the time for the adoration of the Blessed Sacrament, Benediction, and the recitation of litanies in the chapel.

The evening meal was served at 7. The sisters ate in silence while a member of the society read the Spiritual Exercises of St. Ignatius or an account from Alban's *The Lives of the Saints*. Between 8 and 9, the sisters were allotted time for recreation. This was the only occasion in which they were permitted to speak to one another about matters not relating to work. At 9 came evening devotions, followed by bedtime and the rule of absolute silence.

As the daily schedule was structured, so was the schedule of training for the sisterhood. The basic requirements for admission to the order were healthiness of mind and body, the ability to learn, and a submissive disposition. No academic or intellectual standards were set.

Father Celeste wrote the "vestition" ceremony, whereby novices were received in the new order. For the service, he used the ceremony of the Loreto nuns—the same ceremony by which Mother Teresa became a Bride of Christ—as his model. In the revised service, the novices came to the cathedral dressed as Bengali brides. There was another change. In the midst of the service, Mother Teresa removed her shears and cut off the hair of the Bengali girls as a sign of their sacrifice of life in the flesh. The ceremony, replete with the hair cuts, usually lasted three to four hours.

In her journal, Mother Teresa wrote of how strictly the rule of silence was observed in the Motherhouse, so much so that it seemed empty even though thirty to forty sisters resided there. She mentioned how the novices were obliged to wash themselves and their clothes in common buckets and how they were forced to clean their teeth with ashes. She also wrote of the "garment" things (underwear) that were contained in a small *potla* or bundle. The *potla* was used to raise the pillow of anyone who coughed at night so that perfect peace could be maintained.

Along with the Motherhouse, Mother Teresa came to acquire other property, most important, a section of the temple of Kali in a section of South Calcutta called Kalighat. The temple of Kali is the place where the Hindus bring their dead to be cremated on the banks of the River Hooghly. One of the most congested places in the overcrowded city, the temple area is surrounded by hundreds of small shops and stalls where items essential for worship are sold: marigolds, incense, vessels, powders, imitation jewels, images and statues of the Hindu deities, fruits, and caged birds. The narrow lanes are crowded with thousands of people—mendicants in vermilion *tilaks*, beggars holding tin cups, fakirs performing bizarre acts, penitents leading goats to slaughter, troubadours singing canticles, rich families carrying offerings of fruit and food in gold paper, and pall bearers chanting ancient Vedic hymns as they carry bodies to the burning *ghats*.

Around the corner from the temple stands a long, low structure with windows obstructed by plaster latticework. The structure contains two great halls that were built as hostels for Kali worshippers who wanted to pass the night at the temple. But these halls no longer house pilgrims. They are filled with sick and dying poor people from the sidewalks and *bustees* of the "inhuman city." There is no door in the imposing sculpted porch. Anyone can enter at any time. A wooden board bears this inscription in Bengali and English: "Municipality of Calcutta, Nirmal Hriday—The Place of the Pure Heart—Home of Dying Destitutes."

What inspired the creation of Nirmal Hriday? In one of her authorized biographies, Mother Teresa provides this account: "One day as I was leaving our house, I came across a man lying upon the sidewalk who was at the brink of death. I went to get help at a nearby hospital, but when I returned after a few minutes, he was already dead. It was a shame. I felt guilty. Then the idea occurred to me of creating a home where these dying people could finish out their lives, where someone would help them."

> According to Hindu mythology, Kali's father made a sacrifice to guaran- tee the birth of a son, but he neglected to include Kali's husband, Shiva, in the ceremony. Kali, insulted by the omission, committed suicide. The grief-stricken Shiva roamed the earth with the dead body of his wife in his arms, threatening havoc and destruction wherever he went. Vishnu saved the world from ruin by hurling a discus at Kali's corpse, causing it to break apart into many pieces. Every spot where a fragment of Kali's body fell became hallowed. The most sacred spot of all was the spot where the toes of her right foot came to rest. This spot was called the Kalighat. This temple of Kali is a vital center of worship and devotion for Hindus, and it is the wish of every devout Hindu to be cremated in the burning ghats of the mother goddess.

In another account, she says she received the idea when she came upon a bundle of rags on the pavement. Upon closer inspec- tion, Mother Teresa discovered that the bundle was really a middle-age woman who was barely conscious. In one version of this account, rats and wild dogs had devoured half the woman's face; in another version, rodents had gnawed her toes to the bone. With Herculean strength, the good nun managed to transport her to Campbell Hospital. The hospital officials refused to admit the dying woman because they had no empty beds. When asked where she might take the poor woman, Mother Teresa was told to take her back where she found her. She took the dying woman in her arms and set off at a trot for a second hospital. Suddenly, she heard a rattle. The body stiffened in her arms and she knew that it was too late. Putting down her burden, she closed the poor creature's eyes and made the sign of the cross as she prayed before her in the rain. "It was then," she maintains in this pious account, "that I decided to find a place for the dying and take care of them myself."

What really gave rise to the place where the most ragged person could die in dignity? Perhaps the answer lies in the newspaper reports in the daily newspapers that spoke of poor people dying like dogs in the gutters of Calcutta. One report, published in *The Statesman* in 1952, told of a naked beggar boy of thirteen who lay down to die by a roadside in a residential neighborhood of Calcutta. A Good Samaritan found the boy and called an ambulance. The boy was transported to a hospital, but, being emaciated and naked, he obviously did not have money to pay for a stay. The hospital refused to administer treatment and the matchstick boy was deposited back where he had been found to die in the gutter. The story was a sensation. It was picked up by the Associated Press and published in newspapers throughout the world. International attention became drawn to the plight of thousands in India who are denied even the right to die with a modicum of dignity.

Mother Teresa, accompanied by Father Celeste, went to the municipality to meet with the chief medical officer, Dr. Ahmad, in an effort to address the problem. Dr. Ahmad had a brainstorm. He proposed that Mother Teresa and her sisters set up a shelter for the dying at the city's most famous temple at Kalighat. A Christian mission at a Hindu temple! This would show that the shelter was a cooperative effort between public and parochial sectors. He showed her the two great halls at right angles to each other, linked by an adjoining passage, and offered them to Mother Teresa and her new religious order. "This is God's doing," the nun reportedly said. "The place is ideally situated. It is to the precincts of this sacred spot that the destitute come to die, in the hope of being cremated in the temple pyres."

She would later claim that working among the dead and the dying in the spirit of true charity was one of her most rewarding experiences. "A beautiful death," she said, "is for people who lived like animals to die like angels—loved and wanted."

Few came to realize that Mother Teresa not only obtained the building free and clear, but also received a salary on a regular basis for her work with the municipality. But the payments were not the cause of uproar. What really enraged devout Hindus was the fact that municipal officers had handed over a section of the sacred temple free of charge to Roman Catholic sisters. Even worse were stories that the sick and dying were being offered food and shelter as payment for their conversion to Catholicism. Violent protests erupted when the sisters attempted to drag the bodies of dying beggars into the shelter. Rocks were hurled at the building. Windows were smashed. Hindu priests led huge crowds to recite sacred chants to Kali at the entrance of Nirmal Hriday. Threats were made on the life of Mother Teresa and her co-workers. At one point, Mother Teresa later told reporters that she dropped to her knees before the demonstrators and cried out in Bengali, "Kill me! And I'll be in heaven all the sooner!"

The protests continued until the shelter came under police protection. The Brahmin priests then petitioned the municipal authorities to end the sacrilegious arrangement. The Christian corpses within the Hindu temple represented a cause of ritual impurity that demanded immediate attention. A city councilor introduced a motion demanding the removal of the shelter from the Kali temple to another location. Upon considering the matter, the city fathers resolved that as soon as a suitable place was found, the Nirmal Hriday Hospital be removed from its actual premises.

Mother Teresa responded to this situation by informing the press and public officials that the shelter actually served the Hindu and Moslem population. She maintained that one of her patients had been a young Hindu priest in an advanced state of tuberculosis. The priest had been denied a bed in the hospitals and had been left to die in the streets. Mother Teresa said she nursed him and gave him a special corner to himself where he died in peace and tranquility. The name of the Hindu priest was never revealed, and temple officials dismissed the account as fabrication.

In another gesture to suppress criticism and outrage, Mother Teresa ordered the sisters to carry the bodies of all Hindu patients to the temple for cremation. What's more, she agreed to assume that the dying, who were unable to speak or state their religious affiliation, were Hindu and should be prepared for the burning *ghats*. She further agreed that the bodies of all males of unknown religious affiliation be examined for circumcision. If circumcised, they should be assumed to be Moslem and the local *Anjuman* should be contacted to collect the remains.

This agreement gave rise to the strange spectacle of Catholic sisters carrying the bodies of dead Hindus to the temple of Kali for purification and cremation. It also gave rise to stranger developments. The sisters, assuming that most of the unidentified patients were Hindu, began administering water from the Ganges for ritual purification. Other sisters, assuming that unconscious circumcised males were Moslem, read the *Koran* over their deathbeds. "Every person has an origin in God," Mother Teresa said, "and, in every human being, God dwells. For me, my God is Jesus. For a Hindu, he may be Shiva or Vishnu or Brahmin. For a Moslem, Allah." The important thing, she continued, is for a person to die according to what is written in the book. "Be it written according to the Hindu or Moslem or Buddhist or Catholic or Protestant or any other faith."

Despite such public pronouncements, the furor over Nirmal Hriday persisted even when the ninety-five cots became filled with the sick and dying from all sections of the city. Mother Teresa was determined to have the shelter operate at full capacity. At times, when ambulances failed to appear at the scene, the sisters conveyed the bodies to the home of the dying in wheelbarrows.

She invited Doctor Ahmad and other officials to visit the shelter. When they entered, they saw Mother Teresa leaning over a beggar whose face was a large, gaping wound. As they pressed closer, they saw that she was using tweezers to pull maggots from the raw flesh. The stench of the wound was so foul that the officials recoiled in disgust. They heard her say to the patient, "You say a prayer in your religion, and I will say a prayer as I know it. Together we will say this prayer and it will be something beautiful for God."

Coming out of Nirmal Hriday, Dr. Ahmad said, "Yes I will send this woman away, but only after you have persuaded your mothers and sisters to come here and do the work that she is doing. This woman is a saint." This was the first public proclamation of the saintliness of Mother Teresa. It came from a Moslem.

But the uproar continued for months to come, and the religious sisters continued to be pelted with stones. Additional stories about the holiness of the foreign nun were circulated among the Hindu populace. According to one story that appeared in the daily press, Mother Teresa noticed a group of people outside the Kali temple.

As she drew near, she saw a man stretched out on the ground with turned-up eyes and a face drained of blood. A triple braid denoted that he was a Brahmin priest from the temple. No one dared touch him. They knew that he was suffering from cholera. Mother Teresa bent over him, took the body of the Brahmin in her arms, and carried him to Nirmal Hriday. Day and night, she nursed him until he eventually recovered. Weeks later, we are told, he appeared before his people with Mother Teresa by his side and said, "For thirty years I have worshipped a Kali of stone. But here is the real Kali, a Kali of flesh and blood." Following the appearance of this story, Mother Teresa later admitted, stones were never again hurled at the shelter, nor at the little sisters in white saris. In 1953, at the age of forty-three, Mother Teresa already had been hailed as a saint and she had discovered the power of the press.

Mother Teresa attempted to find a physician to oversee Nirmal Hriday. After making inquiries in the Catholic community, she came upon Dr. Marcus Fernandes, whose sister had been a student at Loreto. From the time he entered the home of the dying, he found the haphazard nature of the treatment contrary to good clinical procedure and made several recommendations to Mother Teresa. He pointed out that many patients whom the sisters believed to be dying of cancer were actually suffering from malnutrition. He said that they would recover if fed a balanced diet with vitamin supplements. But, according to the widow of Dr. Fernandes, he could not persuade her to accept his advice. "She did not want them treated," the widow told Anne Sebba. "She expected people to die and would simply say, 'Well, she's gone to God.' She was not particularly interested in medicine."

Others who worked or visited the home for the dying related similar accounts. Once, when the sisters tried to save a sixteen-year-old on the verge of death, Mother Teresa blessed the youth and said to the sisters, "Never mind, it's a lovely day to go to Heaven."

As stories spread about the work of Mother Teresa among the dying in the streets in Calcutta, contributions and medical supplies came into Nirmal Hriday from all corners of the globe. According to sources, a good deal of the money was wasted and the facilities showed no signs of improvement. Dr. Fernandes found state-of-the-art x-ray machines that had been donated new in 1953 covered with rust and dust eighteen months later in a remote corner of the shelter. When he asked Mother Teresa why she had permitted such a waste of expensive and much needed equipment, she said that the sisters did not know how to use it.

Patricia Fernandes, the English wife of the Bengali doctor, worked with Mother Teresa on numerous other projects during this time, including the maintenance of a huge warehouse to store the donations. "I met with Mother Teresa on many occasions, and, quite unusually apparently, she came to our flat." The reason for the visits was for Dr. Fernandes to treat a minor skin ailment for Mother Teresa. When the treatments were complete, Dr. Fernandes sent her a bill that she refused to pay. At that point, the doctor and his wife severed all association with the street nun. "My assessment," Patricia Fernandes told a reporter, "was that she was an extremely ruthless and hard woman. My husband had quite severe differences of opinion with her and she would never listen or take any advice on anything."

Many others who worked with Mother Teresa, including Major E. John Somerset of the Calcutta Medical College and Hospital, are of the same opinion. Few, however, could dispute her achievement or the importance of her home for the dying, even though Mother Teresa persistently inflated the extent of her work. "Over the years," Mother Teresa told Navin Chawla, one of her authorized biographers, "we have rescued over fifty-four thousand people from the streets, about half of whom have died a beautiful death. Those who die with us die in peace and in dignity." Surely, they may have died in dignity, albeit in pain and agony, but, just as surely, there is no way the small facility at Nirmal Hriday could have provided care to fifty-four thousand in thirty years. According to the sisters who operate this facility, the Home for the Dying only contains ninety-five cots and admits fewer than five hundred new patients a year.

Chapter 7

Shishu Bhawan:
The Children's Crusade

Mother Teresa's career was off and running. By 1955, at the age of forty-five, Mother Teresa was a celebrity in Calcutta. She became a favorite subject for stories by Desmond Doig, a roving reporter for *The Calcutta Statesman*. Doig, an Indian-Christian of Anglo-Irish origin, had been following the career of Mother Teresa since she first created a new religious order to work with the poor. "I was tipped off by a Catholic functionary and fellow newspaper-man," Doig later recalled, "to 'watch this woman: she's quite extraordinary. She's going to be a saint.'" Doig not only watched but also reported every move that Mother Teresa made and nearly every act of charity she performed.

Mother Teresa attracted not only fame but also millions of dollars in donations. By this time, she supervised her own religious order of fifty sisters plus a small army of volunteers, operated a Motherhouse and a religious complex in the heart of Calcutta, ran Nirmal Hriday—the home for the dying—at the temple of Kali, and oversaw several schools and medical dispensaries. Through her friendships with government officials, Mother Teresa and her sisters were protected by the police and transported from place to place in official vehicles. She even amassed a fleet of vans that served as mobile medical dispensaries. The white vans with the insignia of the Missionaries of Charity became a common site in the busy streets.

She also befriended members of the high and mighty of the local social set, including Aruna Paul, wife of the British-based businessman Lord Swaraj Paul; Lady Sue Ryder, wife of Major Dudley Gardiner; and Ann Blaikie, wife of a chief executive of the British Tobacco Company. These social luminaries lived in the huge colonial mansions of the elite suburbs of Alipore. They frequented the same clubs and socialized with one another at tea and garden parties. Mother Teresa granted them the opportunity to demonstrate their altruism by visiting her missions and making cash contributions.

But of all her prominent friends, the most powerful and influential was the rich and beautiful Amrita Roy, whose uncle was Dr. Bidhran Chandra Roy, the Chief Minister of Bengal. She no longer had to deal with petty bureaucrats to solve problems with provisions of water and electricity. The doors of the government house were opened to her and she received immediate attention. When Mother Teresa spoke to Dr. Roy about the need for an orphanage, he came up with the funds for her to purchase a two-story building with a large courtyard located several hundred yards from the Motherhouse on Lower Circular Road. Upon seeing the house that became known as Shishu Bhawan, "the Children's House," Dr. Roy said: "Bigger, Mother, we need a much bigger home here. Enlarge this one. Try to buy the adjoining property. I shall help you."

Dr. Roy provided Mother Teresa not only with a property but also with a government grant. The Missionaries of Charity were to receive thirty-three rupees per month for every child in their care. Five years later, after Shishu Brawan attracted millions in private support, Mother Teresa decided to stop accepting these payments because they required excessive record keeping.

On February 15, 1953, Shishu Bhawan welcomed its first guest, a premature baby wrapped in a piece of newspaper, picked up from the street. He weighed less than three pounds and lacked the strength to suck at the bottle Mother Teresa placed between his lips. He had to be fed with a nasal tube. The baby miraculously survived. Soon the facility contained a dozen babies bundled together in cots and playpens.

While some sisters carted dying bodies to Nirmal Hriday, others carried infants to Shishu Bhawan. Many of the children were crippled and deformed. They were found in alleyways, under railway platforms, and even in public drains. As word spread about the home for children, Hindu parents brought their unwanted daughters to the home, often leaving them in baskets at the front door. The police picked up young thieves and pickpockets and placed them in care of the sisters. Hospitals discharged sick and abandoned patients to the facility. No child, according to Mother Teresa, was refused. In a matter of weeks, she claimed, Shishu Bhawan became packed with babies and unwanted waifs.

Many of the babies—products of premature birth and botched abortions—died shortly after arrival in the home. "I don't care what people say about the death rate," Mother Teresa said, "even if they die an hour later. These babies must not die uncared for and unloved, because even a tiny baby can feel." She called her new home a place of last resort. "I cannot give the love a real mother can give," she said, "but I have never refused a child. Never. Not one. Each child is precious. Each is created by God."

Mother Teresa would later boast that her orphanage in Calcutta contained cooking facilities to feed more than a thousand children a day. Yet reporters who visited Shishi Bhawan discovered that the facility in fact feeds fewer than seventy a day, just fifty for lunch and twenty for dinner. Moreover, such charity is not administered free and clear. To obtain a bowl of porridge, a child or adult is compelled to produce a food card from the Motherhouse.

Mother Teresa also often spoke of divine miracles that accompanied her work with the children at Shishu Bhawan. Usually, these stories bore a resemblance to the miracle of the loaves and the fishes. In 1979, she told a crowd in Dublin: "We have witnessed God's under care for us in a thousand different ways. In Calcutta alone, we cook for 7,000 daily [a figure that has been disrupted by numerous critics]. If one day we do not cook, they do not eat. One Friday morning, the Sister in charge of the kitchen came to me and said, 'Mother, there is no food for Friday and Saturday. We should tell the people that we have nothing to give them either today or tomorrow.' I was shocked. I didn't know what to tell her. But about nine o'clock in the morning, the Indian government for some unknown reason closed the public schools. Then all the bread for the schoolchildren was sent to us. Our children, as well as the seven thousand needy ones, ate bread and even more bread for two days. They had never eaten so much bread in their lives. No one in Calcutta could find out why the schools had been closed. But I knew. It was God's tender care."

Three sisters were assigned to three typewriters, where they spent the day typing appeals for donations that were sent throughout the world. The appeals offered "parents" in rich countries the opportunity to "adopt" a child for pennies a day. This effort evolved into the General Child Welfare Fund. It soon became the leading producer of revenue for Mother Teresa's missionary society.

By 1958, Shishu Bhawan had facilities for ninety children and a rapid turnover of occupants. Many of the children were put up for adoption in the spirit of political correctness that warded off any charges of parochialism: Hindu children could be adopted only by Hindu parents, Moslem children by Moslem parents, and Christian children by Christian parents. The new facility not only served to place unwanted children in caring homes, but it also became an incredible cash cow. "Every day," Mother Teresa said, "we have one of two families, even high-caste Hindu families, who come to adopt a child. According to Hindu law, an adopted child becomes a legal heir and can inherit property." To obtain such heirs, many prosperous Indian families have shelled out enormous sums and given elaborate gifts (including expensive real estate) to the Missionaries of Charity.

Girls who showed little aptitude for academics or training were prepared for marriage in accordance with the Indian custom. This custom involved a broker to arrange a union between a prepubescent girl of eleven or twelve and a teenage boy of fourteen or fifteen. Mother Teresa provided each of the young girls with a dowry of saris, utensils, furniture, and money. In exchange, she received a fee as a matchmaker. Strange to say, the fact that a Christian nun came to serve as a marriage broker for Hindu children never created much of a controversy. Indian custom requires that a girl should be pledged to her future husband well before puberty. The marriage takes place only after the girl experiences her first menstruation. Then the father of the "bride"—the role Mother Teresa often assumed—goes to the father of the groom and informs him that the girl is now capable of bearing a child. A festive ceremony is held and the young girl leaves the home of her parents to live with the boy to whom she may have been pledged for several years. Most Hindus give birth to their first child before attaining the age of fifteen.

> *For an Indian father, there is no more powerful obsession than that of marrying off a daughter. The role of a girl in Indian society is a thankless one. No domestic task, no drudgery, is considered too much for her. Up before everyone else and the last to go to bed, she leads the life of a slave. On the streets of Calcutta, the girls have the task of foraging through garbage for food, sewing together the rags that serve as clothes, and delousing the heads of other members of their families. From an early age, girls are taught to renounce all personal inclinations and to relinquish all play to serve their parents and brothers with a smile. Hindu fathers believe that their daughters do not belong to them. They are only lent to them for service until the time they marry.*

The new enterprise flourished. By 1960, the Missionaries of Charity opened houses in six cities throughout India that housed several hundred thousand children on any given day. Mother Teresa sent her sisters to scour the streets in search of destitute pregnant women, offering them a shelter and free medical care. Unmarried mothers were persuaded to hand over their babies to Shishu Bhawan.

The good Mother also administered classes on sex education for the poor people of India. These classes were held at Natural Family Planning Centers, where the sisters imparted the intricacies of natural birth control by the rhythm method. The participants were taught to keep a record of their cycles of ovulation by strings of brightly colored beads. The results of such efforts were questionable. One highly distressed Hindu girl showed up at a planning center confused as to why she was expecting a child. "I hung the beads round the neck of Kali," the girl protested, "and still I am pregnant."

To verify the effectiveness of "natural birth control," Mother Teresa commissioned a study (the only medical venture ever to receive her financial support) called "Symptothermia Vis-a-Vis Fertility Control." This study conducted by gynecologist Ajay Ghost attempted to show by a sample of seventeen hundred slum women of Calcutta that the rhythm method, with the help of a thermometer, a temperature chart, and the ability to check the character of cervical mucus, could help prevent pregnancy.

The heavily flawed report was published in *The Journal of Obstetrics and Gynecology of India* in 1982. As outlined in the report, the "beautiful method" required beggar women who lived in make-shift shacks with walls of cardboard and paper to rise at the crack of dawn to check and see if their cervical mucus had turned "slippery mucoid." After this examination, they were supposed to check their BBT (basal body temperature) with a fertility thermometer and to record the reading on their "daily charts." This task-taxing procedure appeared to be of limited use to the female slum dwellers of Calcutta since less than two percent possessed any reading skills.

Nevertheless, in her 1979 Nobel Prize speech, Mother Teresa would claim that in Calcutta alone, 61,273 fewer children had been born because of the use of the rhythm method. This figure, like most figures rattled off by Mother Teresa, seems to have little basis in fact. Mark Tully, the BBC's former correspondent in India and an admirer of Mother Teresa, said, "It is not known how this figure is arrived at." Eighteen months later, while speaking in Washington, D.C., Mother Teresa doubled the amount by claiming that her "beautiful method" had resulted in 134,000 fewer babies in Calcutta.

In 1968, when Pope Paul IV issued *Humane Vitae,* his encyclical on birth control, Mother Teresa pronounced that married couples who employed means of artificial contraception would not be eligible to adopt children from her orphanages. Such couples, she insisted, cannot love freely and unconditionally.

As she opposed artificial birth control, Mother Teresa also vehemently opposed sterilization and abortion. During Indira Gandhi's first term as prime minister, the Indian government sponsored a policy of sterilization for both men and women. The policy offered inducements in the form of financial rewards. Mother Teresa became the leading opponent of the political measure. She informed the prime minister that she would not be blessed for what she was doing. Shortly afterward, Mrs. Gandhi was defeated at the polls and later was assassinated.

To curb abortion, the Missionaries of Charity sisters plastered posters throughout the city with the face of Mother Teresa uttering this message: "Please do not destroy your child. We will take your child." When confronted with statements that India was suffering from a state of severe overpopulation, she said that there never could be too many children in India because God always provides. "He provides for the flowers and the birds," she said, "and for everything in the world that He has created. And those little children are his life. There can never be enough."

Her antiabortion campaign kicked into high gear when India became one of the first countries in the world to legalize abortion. "Many people are very concerned with the children of India," she said, "where quite a number die, maybe of malnutrition, of hunger, and so on, but millions are dying deliberately by the will of the mother. If a mother can kill her own child, what is left?" In time, she would become the leading proponent of the pro-life movement. Speaking at the Presidential Prayer Breakfast in 1995, she said: "As I am the pencil of God, I know what God likes and does not like. He does not like abortion and contraception."

The Medical Termination of Pregnancy act that was ratified in 1971 met with little success. Even though safe abortions are available at hospitals and clinics, the Indian women rather opt for illegal abortions. The World Health Organization says that more than twenty thousand Indian women die in unsafe abortions every year. Of the fifteen million illegal abortions that take place worldwide every year, seven million occur in India. To perform this procedure, street practitioners employ barbaric methods of induction, including wooden sticks wrapped with cotton wool; twigs with rags soaked in arsenious oxide, arsenic sulphide, and red lead; boiling water combined with acidic solutions; abdominal rubs that force the fetus from the womb; and turpentine, cantharide oil, and potassium permanganate tablets.

Mother Teresa presented Shishu Bhawan, like Nirmal Hriday, as a public rather than a parochial undertaking. Her concerns, she maintained, were humanitarian rather than sectarian. She refused to engage in the counting of saved souls for Jesus Christ or attempts to convert those around her—the poor, the sick, the dying, even the children—to the "true" faith. "I do convert," she told her biographer Navin Chawla. "I convert you to be a better Hindu, a better Catholic, a better Moslem, or Jain or Buddhist. I would like to help you to find God. When you find Him, it's up to you to do what you want with Him."

To show her advocacy of multiculturalism and the legitimacy of all religious beliefs, she refused to allow babies to be baptized in Shishu Brawan, unless she knew for certain that the parents were Christian.

In the constitution of the Missionaries of Charity, Mother Teresa wrote, "Our object is to quench the thirst of Jesus Christ on the cross by dedicating ourselves freely to serve the poorest of the poor, according to the work and teaching of our Lord, thus announcing the Kingdom of God in a special way. Our special task will be to proclaim Jesus Christ to all people, above all to those who are in our care." But in her life and work, Mother Teresa refused to proclaim Jesus Christ as the sole means of salvation. She upheld religious plurality rather than religious exclusivity— refusing to baptize a child or anoint the dying. Indeed, the Catholic saint—who delighted in being called "Ma Kali"— undermined the most basic premise of Roman Catholicism: that it alone retains sole possession of the truth.

Chapter 8

Titagarh: The Leper Colony

A dreaded disease of biblical times inexplicably vanished from Europe in the sixteenth century, but it persists in India and third-world countries amid conditions of poor sanitation, extreme poverty, crammed living conditions, malnutrition, and inadequate medical attention.

In India, there are more than four million cases of leprosy. The disease strikes without warning, attacking the nerves and removing the protective symptom of pain. Lepers can suffer serious injuries—burns, lacerations, fractures—without suffering the slightest discomfort. Such injuries eventually give rise to ulceration and sepsis. The skin of the afflicted turns clown-white and flaky. Failure to obtain treatment leads to deformities, including the rotting away of fingers and toes, the depression of noses, and the loss of eyebrows.

In the past twenty-five years, important breakthroughs have been made in the treatment of leprosy. Particularly significant was the discovery of the sulphone drug dapsone, or DDS, that arrests the disease and, in some cases, cures it. But such treatments are effective only if leprosy is detected in its early stages—that is, before the deformities appear.

Because the disease is often contagious, lepers in all third-world countries are ostracized from all sections of "safe" society, even the society of bustees in the "inhuman city" of Calcutta. In biblical times, lepers were required to ring a bell and cry out "Unclean" wherever they went.

From the 1930s to the 1950s, when the great migrations to Calcutta occurred, lepers suddenly appeared in the crowded slums. They were driven to the very edge of the city and ended up living in a swamp by the railway tracks in an area called Titagarh. No one dared set foot in this settlement for fear of contagion—not social workers, not missionaries, not even the police. The bustee of Titagarh became a center for smuggling and the distillation of illegal liquor.

Within this leper colony, there was no drainage for sewage, no drinking water, no electricity, and no adequate housing. The lepers lived in makeshift huts without roofs to protect them from the torrential monsoon rains and the cold of late December. Goondas, or gang leaders, ruled Titagarh and exacted a tribute from every inhabitant. Because the lepers lacked any means of earning an income, they were forced to raid and loot the nearby communities to pay off the goondas. The ravaging bands of lepers regularly combed the crowded slums for anything that might fetch a few rupees.

Once the Missionaries of Charities opened dispensaries throughout Calcutta, it was inevitable that the religious sisters would come into contact with the unclean inhabitants of Titagarh. At one dispensary outside the walls of the Loreto Convent at Entally, more than one hundred lepers began to show up every week for medicines, vitamins, food, and supplies. Although many of them were missing limbs, they made their way fifteen miles to the facility because they were not permitted to board trains or buses.

Mother Teresa responded by establishing a Leprosy Day on which she called upon the well-minded citizens to make a contribution to the plight of the poor lepers of Titagarh. Mother Teresa proclaimed Leprosy Day to be January 30, the day on which Mohandas Gandhi, the father of modern India, was assassinated by a Hindu extremist in 1948. The pleas for donations were made in the name of "the father of modern India." Pictures of Gandhi were plastered on collection boxes with these words: "Touch a leper with your compassion." It was the first time in history that a Hindu was used to champion a Christian cause. Giving to Mother Teresa became synonymous with giving to Gandhi.

The fund-raising campaign was a masterpiece in planning and execution. Ann Blaikie, an Englishwoman and the wife of the most prominent British solicitor in Bengali, set about to obtain contributions from business, industry, and the affluent inhabitants of "white Calcutta." Desmond Doig ran a series of articles replete with photographs in The Statesman. Dr. Sen, a Hindu specialist in leprosy treatment at the Carmichael Hospital for Tropical Diseases, retired from his position to offer his services free of charge to the lepers of Titagarh.

The money once again came pouring in. Mother Teresa received not only gifts of land and property but also several ambulances. With the ambulances, she instituted mobile leprosy clinics that permitted the sisters to provide services at eight sites throughout the city.

When the ambulances arrived, the religious sisters traveled to several areas around Titagarh and found themselves surrounded by a virtual sea of lepers. Some came clinging to crutches; others dragged themselves along the mud and muck on planks or crates with wheels. Three folding tables were set up. One was for the distribution of food and medicines, another was for injections of DDS and other drugs, and a third was for the dressing of wounds and amputations. The stench, according to Sister Gabrielle, an Indian sister from Mauritius, was overwhelming, and the scene seemed to come straight out of Dante's Inferno. As soon as a leper placed his stump on the table, a host of maggots would come crawling out of it. Bits of flesh fell away from legs and arms that were completely rotted to the bone. Bones crumbled upon the slightest pressure like worm-infested pieces of wood. The doctors performed amputations amid a sticky swirl of flies and mosquitoes and sudden squalls of dust. The attendants had nothing to relive the pain of the patients, no morphine, no curare, not even bhang, which is opium-treated hashish. To quiet the screaming, the sisters sang lullabies.

Clearly, there was a need for a permanent facility. In the interim, Mother Teresa took over the Gobra Hospital as a center for leprosy, but residents and developers complained to officials because they didn't want such a facility in the midst of the city. She next tried to open a treatment facility in another area, but when she and her sisters arrived to occupy the site, the local residents greeted them with a hail of stones and rocks, screams of rage, and threats of murder. Mother Teresa's reaction to this situation was perfectly practical: "I don't think God wants us to open a clinic here," she said.

It became obvious that the facility would have to be constructed far from the madding crowd at Titagarh, which represented a massive undertaking. Workers had to build two large tanks in the swamp, using the excavated earth to fill in the remainder of the marsh. Next came the construction of an administration building and housing barracks. Then came the erection of the rehabilitation and production centers. A hospital followed, with separate wings for men and women and a large cafeteria. Finally, hundreds of small cottages were built to house the lepers and their families.

When the facility opened in March 1959, Ann Blaikie, the chairperson of the fund-raising committee, thanked the Volkart Foundation Trust for providing funds for the construction and the Titagarh Municipal Council for the gift of the land. She thanked the Philips Electric Light Company for providing utilities and permanent support for the operation. So many donors had contributed to the new clinic that the speech went on for hours. The social elite, seated on garden chairs and holding umbrellas to protect themselves from the midday sun, rose to take bows when their names were announced. Also in attendance were two hundred forty Titagarh lepers who had gathered for a promised lunch and the handout of free gifts. After the ceremony finally concluded, wealthy women in white dresses distributed buns, biscuits, oranges, and blankets to the lepers in rags. It was an incongruous sight, as Desmond Doig reported: "A crippled woman peeled an orange to feed her child; a man fumbled with fingerless hands to offer cake to a pariah puppy cradled in his arms."

Mother Teresa christened the colony Gandhi Prem Niwas (the "Gandhi Abode of Love"). She placed flowers before a portrait of the Father of India, folded her hands, and bowed before him. She was no longer the Mother Superior of an order of one hundred nineteen sisters and the "Ma Kali" of Kalighat, but (as everyone would soon discover) the "Mother of India" and a model of political correctness. Throughout her career, Mother Teresa would connect the image of Mohandas Gandhi with her work among the lepers. In addition to the opening celebration, a ceremony of official dedication for the clinic at Titagarh was held on October 2, Gandhi's birthday. This clever choice of a date ensured the attendance of the governor of Bengal, A. L. Dias, and his wife. It also permitted Indian officials to see Christian sisters laboring not under images of the crucified Jesus, but rather under the martyred Gandhi.

At the settlements, the religious sisters discovered ways to make the lepers productive. Hundreds of looms were installed in the main building and the lepers were taught to make saris, shirts, and dresses, not only for members of the order, but also to sell in marketplaces throughout the world. Some ended up in such stores as Macy's, Lord and Taylor, and Bloomingdale's. As the lepers worked at their charkhas (the Hindu word for "spinning wheel"), they were told that they were providing a great service for Mother India. Gandhi had said that the charkha represented the greatest weapon against American and British economic influence. As the means of spinning the simplest of cotton into clothing for the masses, it became the symbol of India's freedom movement. Each day, as the lepers of Titagarh made clothing from dawn to dusk, they were surrounded by pictures of Gandhi on one wall and Mother Teresa on the other. Visiting the colony, Dr. Don Huber asked, "Is this for the glory of God or the glory of Gandhi?"

Other means of productive labor were discovered. The lepers were put to work making sandals and shoes from rubber cuttings and cast-off tires. They made baskets and bricks. The children kneaded circles of cow and pig dung for use as fuel in the small cooking stoves, known as *chulas*, that lined the streets of Calcutta.

> Although India was grief-stricken by the assassination of Mohandas Gandhi on January 30, 1948, his example never brought permanent peace to the nation. Sectarian violence took thousands of lives in the ensuing decades. In 1983, Prime Minister Indira Gandhi (not related to Mohandas, but the daughter of India's first prime minister, Jawaharlal Nehru) ordered Indian troops into the holiest of the Indian Sikhs, the Golden Temple in the Punjab; four hundred Sikhs were put to death. A year later, Sikh guards responded by assassinating Indira Gandhi. Moreover, the partition of the Indian Empire into India and Pakistan did not result in the comfortable meshing of one nation and subsequent divisions between the people. After years of civil strife, East Pakistan declared its independence as Bangladesh in 1973.

Fearing that lepers from far and wide would swarm to Prem Niwas, the Indian government provided the Missionaries of Charity with thirty-four acres in the neighboring state of Bihar, one hundred and fifty miles from Calcutta, to create another leper colony. With international aid and money from the Propagation of the Faith (a Catholic missionary society devoted to the conversion of the world to Roman Catholicism), the new leprosarium, called "Shanti Nagar" ("The Place of Peace"), was transformed from a jungle into a well-planned community with ponds stocked with fish, mango trees, vegetable gardens, flowering shrubs, and livestock pens.

Mother Teresa had discovered another rule of social economics: One good leprosarium will eventually give rise to another. By 1975, the Missionaries of Charity operated more than one hundred leper colonies throughout the world.

Some practices performed at these facilities caused considerable controversy. To better identify with their patients, the sisters were not permitted to wear surgical gloves, not even when pulling maggots from festering sores. They were instructed by Mother Teresa to stick their fingers right into the wounds as signs of their identification with the "poorest of the poor." This resulted in the exposure not only of sisters to contagion but also of patients to infection.

Another source of contention came from Mother Teresa's insistence that the lepers not employ any means of artificial contraception or participate in the national sterilization program. She refused to take into consideration the fact that lepers almost always infect their children with the terrible disease. "A child," Mother Teresa countered, "is their only joy in life. The rich have so many other things. If you remove a child from the home of the poor or from those with leprosy, who is going to smile at them and help them to get better?"

> *The Roman Catholic Church insists that Catholics must always keep their acts of lovemaking open to God's intervention of new life. For this reason, the Church condemns all artificial means of birth control (including condoms, pills, withdrawal, and post-coital dousing procedures) as immoral and unnatural. Pope Paul's encyclical on birth control,* Humanae Vitae, *states: "Every act that intends to impede procreation must be repudiated whether the act is intended as an end to be attained or a means to be used, and whether it is done in anticipation of marital intercourse or during it, or while having its natural consequence."*

Encouraging lepers to have children, according to Mother Teresa, often resulted in experiences of the "beautiful." She told her biographer Navin Chawla, "Very often we see a leper woman who is scarcely able to walk, walking for miles, just to come to the Sister to make sure the child is all right. She has spotted the sign of leprosy in the child so she comes walking … all the way walking. We had the wonderful case of a woman who scarcely had any feet to walk on and she had walked more than six miles. She came with this baby in her arms and said, 'Sister, see, my child has leprosy.' She had seen a spot. The Sister examined the child and took the smear but it was not leprosy, and the woman was so happy that her child did not have leprosy that she took the child and walked all the way back again. She didn't even stop for a rest. That's a very beautiful thing."

Chapter 9

High Flying, Adored

Mother Teresa was frustrated. According to canon law, the work of her new order was confined to the diocese of Calcutta for ten years, and Archbishop Perier was adamant in enforcing this rule. It was intolerable. The entire world seemed to be crying out for the services of the Missionaries of Charity and she was unable to respond because of an ecclesiastical technicality. But time was of the essence. Mother Teresa was already fifty, and she wasn't willing to wait.

In 1959, she established branches in Ranchi, Jhansi, and Delhi. Jawaharlal Nehru, the Prime Minister of India, attended the opening of a Missionaries of Charity children's home in Delhi. "He was sick," Mother Teresa recalled, "but got up from bed and came. I asked him if I could tell him about the work. He said, 'No, Mother, you need not tell me about your work, I know about it. That is why I have come.'" The most powerful person in India was now paying homage to her. Prime Minister Nehru commended her to the president of India for the prestigious Padma Shri award. She became the first person who was not born an Indian to receive the award.

Despite such success, Mother Teresa began to experience periods of doubt and rejection. These feelings are recorded in a journal that she was told to keep by Father T. Picachy, the future Archbishop of Calcutta, who served as her spiritual confessor from 1959 to 1960. At one point, she wrote, "Now, Jesus, I go the wrong way. They say people in hell suffer eternal pain because of loss of God. In my soul, I feel just the terrible pain of loss, of God not wanting me, of God not being God, of God not really existing." At another point during this same one-year period, she wrote, "Jesus, please forgive the blasphemy—I have been told to write everything—that darkness surrounds me on all sides. I can't lift my soul to God: No light, no inspiration enters my soul." But she expressed such doubts to no one, not even her closest companions. They remained locked in her writing desk far from public scrutiny.

In autumn 1960, she accepted an invitation to address the National Council for Catholic Women at its national convention in Las Vegas. By this time, she was known in America, having appeared in 1958 on the front page of a national Catholic monthly called *Jubilee, a Magazine for the Church and Her People* as a saintly figure who worked among the poor, the dying, and the lepers.

Mother Teresa had never made a public appearance. Her speech was poorly constructed and her delivery was halting. But she was a natural. Her lack of professionalism made her seem more devout and saintly than the other speakers. More than three thousand women were in attendance and were riveted by the harrowing street stories of the small and unassuming nun in Calcutta. Mother Teresa told the crowd what she would tell crowds for the next thirty years. She was not present to beg and plead for donations. She was present to allow the audience to do something beautiful for God. Sitting in a booth at the convention, thousands dropped checks into her bag that had to be emptied several times. She had hit the proverbial jackpot.

She went from Las Vegas to Peoria, Illinois, where Catholic women familiar with the work of the Missionaries of Charity had been sponsoring her Mother and Child clinics for several years. She addressed another large group in Chicago, received another standing ovation, and left with more sacks of cash. Then she went on to Washington, D.C., for a scheduled meeting with Sen. John F. Kennedy, the Democratic presidential hopeful. The meeting with the future president never occurred because his advisors warned Kennedy to stay away from officials and dignitaries of the Roman Catholic Church for the sake of Protestant votes.

Her last stop in the United States was New York City, where she visited major funding services for her operations, including Catholic Relief Services, which was the headquarters of Bishop Fulton J. Sheen, a highly influential religious broadcaster and the chairman of the Propagation of the Faith. She also went to the World Health Organization (WHO), where she met with the director, Marcolino Candau, hoping for help for the leprosy patients and their children at Titagarh. Candau advised her to apply through the Indian government so that the appeal would not seem to be coming from a Catholic agency. It was sound advice. Mother Teresa applied for medical supplies and equipment through her friend Dr. Bidran Chandra Roy, Chief Minister of West Bengal, and all of her needs were immediately met. By the time she departed from the Kennedy Airport to London, she had amassed a small fortune in cash and had opened pipelines for continuous contributions.

Although it rained all week in London, the sun continued to shine on Mother Teresa's whirlwind tour. She was invited one evening to the palatial home of the Indian High Commissioner, Vijaya Lashmi Pandit, the sister of Prime Minister Nehru. She encouraged Mother Teresa to expand her efforts in a nonsectarian manner as a citizen of India and expressed hope that "such work in the Gandhi spirit would keep growing." The highlight of her stay in London was her television debut, an interview on BBC with journalist Derek Hart that had been arranged by Oxfam, a volunteer aid agency. Mother Teresa's lack of polish and sophistication seemed arresting and charming. She was on her way to stardom.

The next leg of her trip brought her to Germany to meet the officials of Misereor ("Let Us Have Mercy"), a Catholic overseas funding agency. Misereor published a major story on Mother Teresa and her Missionaries of Charity in its widely read magazine *Welteland* ("World Misery"). The article featured startling photos of starving children and dying people on the streets of Calcutta. The article captured the interests of the editors of another photomagazine, *Erdkreis*, which featured a story about Kalighat.

When Mother Teresa arrived in Frankfurt on a bitterly cold day, she was dressed in her simple white sari with a rough woolen blanket over her shoulders. The small Albanian nun was greeted by a host of press photographers from the leading newspapers. It was a perfect photo opportunity for Mother Teresa, who walked to the waiting limousine with her head lowered in prayer and rosary beads wrapped around her hands.

The officials at Misereor said that they were anxious to help Mother Teresa with her work, even offering to come up with cash for a new home for the dying in Delhi. There was only one stipulation. The allocation of grants from the agency required the preparation of financial forms for the purpose of possible audit. Mother Teresa responded by telling the Misereor officials that the members of the Missionaries of Charity were much too busy to spend their time on bookkeeping. Such an expenditure of time on paperwork would cause the poor to suffer. "Every donation," she said, "was scrupulously recorded and acknowledged and put into the stream of resources to support centers already in operation or to start new ones." But the Missionaries of Charity would prepare no separate financial reports for Misereor or any other sponsoring agency.

From Germany she went to Rome, where her fame preceded her. She made arrangements to meet with Pope John XXIII to receive his permission to expand her operations in other countries. She assumed that approval would be automatic. But the pope, who would inaugurate sweeping changes within the Catholic Church, had reservations about Mother Teresa and her work. He was less than pleased at the notion of a nun leaving a convent and working in the streets as a social worker. He was suspicious that she had applied for the nullification of her solemn vows to separate herself from the Loreto Order. He was distressed that she expanded the operations of her mission without ecclesiastical approval.

Nevertheless, the pope could not dismiss her efforts or her request. She had organized a new and revolutionary order with 119 sisters that had amassed millions in contributions. She had established a home for the dying, a settlement for lepers, and a shelter for the children. She was held in high esteem by leading officials, including the president and prime minister of India. Stories about her had been circulated in newspapers and magazines throughout the world.

Instead of granting the Missionaries of Charity approval to become a Society of Pontifical Right, the pope merely gave her a blessing and turned the matter over to Gregory Cardinal Agagianian and Archbishop Pietro Sigismondi of the Sacred Congregation of the Propagation of the Faith, Propaganda Fide. They would take five years to sanction Mother Teresa's petition.

When she returned to Calcutta, Mother Teresa realized that she had awakened a massive response throughout the Western world. She had made tremendous connections that would allow her to expand her mission throughout the known world. She had garnered enough financial support to make her new order the most successful religious enterprise within Catholicism. She had received acclaim and recognition. And she was beginning to win international rewards for her work with large cash prizes attached. Following the Padma Shri Award came the Magsaysay Award for International Understanding in honor of the president of the Philippines. This prize came with a check amounting to fifty thousand rupees, or about seven hundred and fifty dollars. The doubts that she may have once harbored were vanished. She was now completely confident that God's grace was upon her. Sure, she had to sit and wait for the approval of Propaganda Fide. But that would come. As St. Paul said, "All things work for the good to those who serve the Lord."

On June 3, 1963, Pope John XXIII died of stomach cancer. His successor was Giovanni Battista Montini, who became Pope Paul VI. Paul VI is widely recognized as the most ineffectual pope in recent history. When the process of *aggiornamento* ("updating") led to the wholesale abandonment of traditional beliefs and practices, he refused to address the issue by taking rebellious priests and bishops to task. Instead, he carried out extensive liturgical reforms in the name of aggiornamento ("updating") that resulted in vernacular rites (the translation of the Mass into the spoken language of the people) that offended the sense and sensibility of traditionalists. He allowed the Vatican Bank, under the director of Mafia chieftain Michele Sindona, to become the subject of a series of international scandals. And he produced an encyclical on birth control, *Humanae Vitae*, that resulted in divisiveness and the undermining of ecclesiastical authority.

Still, Paul VI's ascendancy to the throne of St. Peter was a true blessing for Mother Teresa, who had failed to obtain the favor of his predecessor. He would become an ardent believer in her saintliness and would grant his blessings to all of her undertakings. In November 1976, shortly before his death, Paul VI declared that Mother Teresa "was his greatest consolation in the Church."

As soon as he put on the shoes of the fisherman, Paul VI decided that he wanted to become a "pilgrim pope" by visiting countries throughout the world. For six years, he traveled incessantly, appearing in Israel, Portugal, Turkey, Colombia, Switzerland, America, Uganda, Asia, the Pacific Islands, and Australia. His pilgrimages would come to an end in Manila, the Philippines, when a deranged Bolivian artist pulled out a knife and attempted to kill him in 1970.

However, his first pilgrimage was to India, where he accepted an invitation to attend a Eucharist Congress in Bombay. The trip was arranged by Archbishop James Robert Knox, the Papal Internuncio to New Delphi. Archbishop Knox spent ten years in India, where he became one of the most vocal supporters of Mother Teresa and her Missionaries of Charity.

To illustrate the new pope's humanitarianism and concern with the poor in the midst of the era of social consciousness, Archbishop Knox persuaded the Pope to visit Mother Teresa's home for the dying at Kalighat. Hearing the news about the pope's visit, Mother Teresa made elaborate plans for his arrival. She called upon her one hundred twenty sisters to perform "many acts in silence in preparation of the pope's visit." The facility was scrubbed and whitewashed. The cots were covered with fresh, white linen. The patients were dressed in hospital gowns. A photograph of the new pontiff replaced the one of Mohandas Gandhi in the entry. Statues of saints were hauled into the former Hindu temple for the occasion, and the long, narrow dormitories were lined with stations of the cross.

The arrival of the pope became a media celebration. Photographs of the new pope blessing the dying bodies of the poor of Calcutta appeared in publications throughout the world. Before he left the facility, the pope blessed Mother Teresa and gave her a gift: the keys to his new Lincoln Continental. Wisely knowing that a servant of the poor could not drive through the slums in a spanking new luxury car, Mother Teresa decided to auction it off to the highest bidder. At that time, it was possible to purchase a Lincoln for less than seven thousand dollars. With her newly acquired business sense, she managed by coaxing the audience of affluent businesspeople to get one hundred thousand dollars for her Missionaries of Charity. Among the poorest of the poor, there were no flies on Mother Teresa.

The car was just the first of many gifts from Paul VI. At Christmas, he sent her a donation from his own purse to give five thousand poor children and lepers a good meal and a present. Shortly afterward, he sent her another gift for the purchase of four thousand beds and mattresses for the poor. By the end of the year came yet another gift: a specially made British motor truck called a "lorry" that proved to be too wide for the narrow streets of Calcutta.

The pope obviously did not know that Mother Teresa had replaced his photograph with that of the toothless Gandhi and that the white linen had been removed from the cots of Kalignat. He also did not know that most of the bodies of those who died there were not prepared for Christian burial but rather were hauled off for burning at the Temple of Kali.

In February 1965, Paul VI issued a decree in which he proclaimed Mother Teresa's Missionaries of Charity to be a Society of Pontifical Right. She now could establish operations throughout the world. She was free from ecclesiastical bureaucracy. She wasn't answerable to a Mother Superior or Archbishop. She was as free as any Jesuit of Episcopal authority. Receiving the news of the decree, Mother Teresa said, "This is the biggest miracle of all because, as a rule, Congregations are not raised to the Pontifical Order so fast; it takes most of them many years, thirty, forty years sometimes. This shows the great love and appreciation the Holy father has for our work and for our Congregation."

Immediately after Mother Teresa received this approval, Archbishop Knox, who had arranged the papal visit, asked Mother Teresa to set up a community in Venezuela. The Bishop of Barquisimeto had expressed his need for a group of sisters to live among the poor in his community who had medical care and schooling.

In July 1965, the first Missionaries of Charity home outside India opened in Cocorote, Venezuela. The Bishop gave her an empty rectory to serve as a convent house and the Catholic Women of Brooklyn pledged funds to provide ongoing support for the venture. Four Bengali sisters were chosen as the first pioneers and three more joined them within three months. It was an immediate success.

> *Catholic nuns and sisters have suffered an enormous decrease in number since the close of the Second Vatican Council in 1965. Before then, there were one hundred eighty thousand women in religious orders throughout the United States. By 2000, that number had dropped to less than eighty thousand. Catholic hospitals and grammar schools that once were staffed by nuns and other religious personnel had to turn to more expensive lay professionals. Every Catholic religious order, including the Loreto Order and The Society of Jesus, have suffered massive personnel hemorrhages. The average age of a Loreto nun is now sixty-seven; that of a Jesuit priest is sixty-two. The only exception has been Mother Teresa's Missionaries of Charity, which continues to attract hundreds of new recruits every year.*

Within the next few years, new homes of the Missionaries of Charity popped up everywhere. In December 1967, a home opened in Columbo, the capital of Ceylon (now Sri Lanka). In August 1968, one was opened in the slums of Rome, much to the delight of the pope. In September 1968, the Missionaries of Charity took over a compound in Tabora, Tanzania, that the White Sisters had operated for many years but now could not attract enough new recruits to maintain their missions. In September 1969, Mother Teresa's order opened a center for aborigines in Bourke, Australia.

The growth of her movement was incredible. While the Catholic Church suffered severe losses in religious vocations, the Missionaries of Charity, against all odds and contrary to all reason, continued to grow and flourish. From 1970 to present, a new center has opened somewhere in the world every six months.

Pope Paul VI blesses Albanian-born nun Mother Teresa Bojaxhiu, who was awarded by Pope John XXIII in 1971 for her work among lepers in India.

(© Bettmann/CORBIS)

Chapter 10

Brotherly Love and Betrayal

As the Missionaries of Charity expanded throughout the world, Mother Teresa decided to establish a branch of her religious order for men. This decision was unique in the history of the Roman Catholic Church. No order for men ever evolved from an order for women. It was always the other way around. The Franciscans gave rise to the Poor Clares and the Jesuits spawned the Loreto Order. But Mother Teresa had changed things. What's good for the goose would be good for the gander! The male branch of the Missionaries of Charity would permit individuals of every race and gender to join in Mother Teresa's campaign to serve the lepers, the dying, and the poorest of the poor. It would grant everybody the opportunity to gain God's favor by working for Mother Teresa. Father Celeste loved the idea, but there was one hitch. In the Roman Catholic Church, it is not permissible for a woman to be the head of a male congregation. But there was nothing in canon law that said a male and female religious order could not be yoked under a joint leadership. The male order, it was decided, would be modeled after the Missionaries of Charity's constitution. The brothers would take the same vows as the sisters and undergo the same novitiate. The superior in charge would be appointed by the pope with the approval of Mother Teresa. This only made sense because the Missionaries of Charity would pay the cost of instituting and of maintaining the brotherhood.

But the director of this "pious order," who would be called the "General Servant," would have to come, as did Father Celeste himself, from the Society of Jesus. Jesuits were not subjected to the authority of any bishop or archbishop. They were directly under control of the pope. And Paul VI was very fond of Mother Teresa and most supportive of her work.

Father Celeste and Mother Teresa came upon the perfect candidate—Father Ian Travers-Ball, a Jesuit from Australia. Father Ball was young, personable, and engaging. Regarding his first encounter with the Missionaries of Charity, Father Ball told a reporter, "I came to India in 1954, as a young Jesuit. I became interested in the poor when working in the Hazaribagh coal mining area of Bihar. She had a group of men whom she was directing, but she was looking for someone to head the Order. I walked in quite by chance."

On February 19, 1966, Father Celeste conducted a simple ceremony in which Father Ball and a small group of Bengali men became Missionary Brothers of Charity. The brothers wore no distinctive dress, neither cowls nor collars. They were dressed in white shirts and cotton trousers like common street people. At the close of the ceremony, Mother Teresa presented them with a small crucifix that they were to wear over their hearts, their sole mark of identification as members of a religious order.

> Originally, religious brothers within the Roman Catholic Church were pious men who did not have the requisite education for priesthood. The brothers performed manual tasks, such as cooking, gardening, illuminating manuscripts, and repairing the church or monastery. Many were artisans who built many of the great cathedrals throughout Europe. In the Middle Ages, lay brothers were often attached to convents so that they could perform arduous or physically strenuous work for the nuns (such as clearing forests or draining a swamp). Similarly, religious sisters were often attached to monasteries so that they could cook and clean for the monks. This gave rise to scandal (nuns giving birth to the babies of monks) and was outlawed by the Lateran Council.

Along with their new dress, they assumed new names. When Father Ball rose from his knees at the close of the Mass as Brother Andrew, Mother Teresa turned to the religious sisters and said, "This is a holy man—really very holy."

In the beginning, all went well. The brothers worked with the sisters by providing much of the mule work, lifting heavy crates of medical equipment and food supplies for storage in warehouses and lifting the sick and dying on stretchers for transportation to hospitals or the home of the dying. At Kalighat, the brothers were expected to care for the male patients while the sisters tended to the female patients. They resided on the first floor of Shishu Bhawan, where they operated a shelter for homeless boys. The brothers and sisters gathered each morning for Mass in the Motherhouse and each evening for devotions.

In July 1966, Mother Teresa provided the brothers with a property at 7 Mansatala Row, Kidderpur, Calcutta, that became their very own Motherhouse. "There were about fifteen of us when we first moved in," Brother Andrew said. "The lifestyle of a group of men will necessarily be different from that of women. We could not, for instance, live on top of each other the way the women have managed to do. Men need to go out for a walk, or have a game of football on a Sunday afternoon, or watch some wrestling. The Sisters don't go out for anything except their work. Household arrangements, too, could not be the same for us. I do not feel bound to follow the small details."

The next year, she secured from the government a large property in the slum area of Dum Dum, Calcutta's major airport, to serve as a shelter for homeless boys. In less than a year, more than forty boys occupied the facility called Nabo Jeevan ("New Life"). Twenty were sent to private boarding schools. Fifteen were sent to local schools as day scholars. The brothers tutored the handicapped, the crippled, and the tubercular at home. On another section of the property, the brothers built a shelter for thirty men who were sick, disabled, or destitute. Through Mother Teresa's efforts, the brothers also acquired a farm about twenty miles away from Calcutta, where they engaged in simple agricultural work.

In June 1968, the first group of novices completed its novitiate and made their profession as full Brothers. At this time, Brother Andrew officially left the Society of Jesus and became the director of the new order. The Brothers continued their work with lepers. At first they continued to assist the Sisters with the mobile dispensaries. Later, they went regularly to Dhapa, the largest leper colony in Calcutta, where they tended to the sick.

In due course, they began to work with the Sisters in Titagarh. The problems in this leprosarium on the other side of the railway tracks became too much for the women to handle. The *goondas* or mob bosses continued to exact tribute from every inhabitant of Titagarh. Robbery and rape became commonplace. Those who failed to come up with the tribute money were murdered. Bodies kept appearing in a nearby swamp. The Brothers helped to restore order by ousting the ruffians (with the help of the Indian government) and instituting a mandatory work program in the gardens, at the piggery, or on the looms. Even those with stumps for arms were obliged to labor on the charkhas. Order was restored.

The problems began when the members of Mother Teresa's new male order became political activists. While the Vietnam War was raging, the Brothers set up a house in Saigon. The first and second floors of the house provided shelter for fifty or so homeless people. The third floor was the place where the Brothers lived. In no time at all, many of the Brothers began to protest American involvement and joined the crowds chanting, "Yankee, Go Home!" To make matters worse, several Brothers spent a good part of their time not in prayer and meditation or performing acts of mercy, but rather drinking at the local watering holes, smoking local marijuana, and consorting with bar girls and prostitutes.

In 1975, after the Communists took over the houses of the Brothers in North Vietnam and Cambodia, Brother Andrew wrote this letter to Mother Teresa: "This year has been heartbreaking. We lost five houses ... The buildings don't matter. But to be separated so finally from all the people one came to know and love is unbelievably painful. I shall never be the same again after this, and I know that I shall have an ache in my heart for them until the day I die. The full story of the fall of Saigon and the change-over will never be told. The journalists who stayed on lived mostly in the overcrowded parts of the city. They did not really have the chance to share the feelings of the people I knew in Saigon in the reports of the media or in the general idea that people outside Vietnam have of what has been happening there."

After their departure from Saigon, five Brothers—one Dutchman and four Americans—left Vietnam to work in the Skid Row section of Los Angeles, where they championed the cause of the poor and homeless and worked for the extension of state and federal welfare programs. They wore street clothes, smoked on street corners, drank in the local bars, and peppered their speech with profanities.

Los Angeles was merely the starting point for other operations. The Brothers quickly established Motherhouses in Latin America, Japan, France, Sweden, and England. Brother Andrew justified expansion into ostensibly prosperous societies by stating that such societies have their own special brand of poverty. He wrote in a letter:

> Sometimes people wonder why we go to more prosperous places like Los Angeles, Tokyo, Hong Kong, when there is such desperate poverty in India and on such a large scale. I believe there is much more terrible poverty than that found in India. Hong Kong illustrates this for me. When I was in Calcutta recently during the floods which devastated so much, it struck me one day that the people of Calcutta are more humanly rich than people in Hong Kong. It is a strange paradox that may be saying something to us. It is true of much of the more affluent world. In Hong Kong we have a small home for severely mentally disabled men. We get public funds—and much interference. The men in the home are severely retarded. They have been in various institutions where they did not respond to training or treatment. They lived with their families in the impossibly small rooms of Hong Kong housing conditions. Since joining us, all have responded well—and the big thing, it seems to me, is that they are happy. But that is not enough, we are told. They must be doing something, they must be programmed. There can be few places as rushed in the world as production-centered Hong Kong. The stress and pressures here are great. It seems we are not allowed to be satisfied that these disabled men are happy. They have to be got into the rush, into the rat race that is driving everybody

*else mad. There are basic questions involved in this about
where the dignity and values of a man lies, whether it is in
his being or in his performance. And so, India, with its
greater material poverty, has a quality of life that is often
lost when the goals are materialistic and must be got down
in a report. I feel, in places like Hong Kong, we are meant
to be a little witness to this as* Animal Farm *bears down on
all sides.*

This passage tells us much about the Brotherhood. Even in
places like Hong Kong, they received public funding and worked
not as Christian missionaries but as secular social workers. Their
primary purpose was to address the problem of alienation as a result
of modern production and to promote social acceptance rather
than spiritual salvation. In his writings and statements, Brother
Andrew makes scant reference to the scriptures, let alone God or
Jesus. He often sounds like a Hyde Park socialist addressing capitalists from an orange crate.

The Brothers were getting out of control. In Los Angeles,
Brother Andrew ruled that the members of his order need not
travel to Calcutta to receive instruction or approval from Mother
Teresa. Those who wanted to become a member only needed
appear at a nearby Motherhouse and sign up for service.

Brother Andrew drafted the constitution of the Missionary of
Brothers in the spirit of Vatican II. The opening words were
indicative of his orientation toward love and peace rather than
piety and prayer:

*The general aim of this society comes from the lips of
Christ our Lord himself: "I give you a new commandment: Love one another. As I have loved you, so you
are to love one another. If there is love among you then
all will know you are my disciples."*

He set forth the special aim of the Brothers as follows:

*To live this life by dedicating oneself to the service of the
poorest of the poor in slums, on the streets and wherever
they are found. Leprosy patients, destitute beggars, the
abandoned, homeless boys, young men in the slums, the*

unemployed and those uprooted by war and disaster will
always be the special object of the Brothers' concern.

This appeared to be congruous with Mother Teresa's constitution for the Missionaries of Charity. But there was a major difference that wasn't immediately apparent. The model for Brother Andrew's order was not Mother Teresa's religious order, but rather Dorothy Day's Houses of Hospitality in America. As Brother Andrew saw it, the major purpose of the Brothers was not to set out specifically to serve various target groups in the slums (orphans, lepers, the dying), but to offer shelter and hospitality to all who came to their door. Unlike the Sisters, the Brothers slept in the houses with the poor, not in a separate monastery or Motherhouse. They ate with the poor and accepted whatever food the poor were offered, unlike the Sisters, who ate only carefully prepared food in the Motherhouse. When the Brothers were invited as guests, they were obliged to accept whatever hospitality they were offered, unlike the Sisters, who were obliged to remain under the Divine Office.

Mother Teresa, upon reading the revised constitution, became—in Brother Andrew's words—"annoyed and piqued," and showed it. She summoned him to the Motherhouse in Calcutta, but he failed to appear. He rather reminded her that she was neither his superior nor the superior of the Missionary Brothers of Charity. "From the beginning Brother Andrew went his own way," one observer said. "To a small extent, it showed the spirit of Mother, but it was not the Constitution of Mother."

When Brother Andrew and Mother Teresa met in 1976, tempers flared. Mother Teresa complained about the absence of prayer life within the order, the slackness of discipline, and the general untidiness of the brothers. Brother Andrew responded by saying that such matters were not her concern.

Realizing that she had lost control of her creation, Mother Teresa went to Rome and formed a new male order, The Brothers of the Word, that were to adhere to the rules of the Missionaries of Charity. She diverted funding from the Missionary Brothers to her new order of "contemplative" brothers and established a Motherhouse in Rome.

Brother Andrew said that he was "peeved" at the furtiveness with which Mother Teresa had acted without saying a word to him. Later, after Mother Teresa became a religious icon beyond reproach, Brother Andrew attempted to put a different spin on the matter by saying: "The failings of great souls call for a tolerant eye in view of their magnificent accomplishments, especially from much lesser mortals."

By 1986, Mother Teresa managed to have Brother Andrew relieved of his position as General Servant of the Missionary Charity of Brothers after "quite a saga of fears, uncertainty, and sadness." The following year, he was summoned by Church officials to a meeting, the purpose of which he did not know. "On arrival," he said, "I was presented with a list of occasions over the past twelve years when I had drunk too much, behaved foolishly, and gave a bad example. Arrangements had been made for my own good to go immediately for treatment at a clinic for alcoholics." While Brother Andrew confessed to becoming intoxicated on numerous occasions, he insisted that he was not an alcoholic and was not in need of treatment. His superiors then told him to go for psychiatric treatment. Brother Andrew professed that he was not crazy. He was then granted dispensation of his vows and permission to leave the order.

Several years later, Brother Andrew wrote: "Perhaps this humiliating story of Brother Andrew who was admired, praised, and loved by many wonderful people may in a strange way offer a little comfort to other humiliated, hard-pressed, embarrassed people, struggling with a disgrace, a failure, a fall in their own lives or in their dear ones—a painful break-up of a relationship, abandonment, a lonely pregnancy, a police case, being written off."

While the story may have conveyed "little comfort," it also served to impart a very important lesson: "Don't mess with Mother Teresa."

Chapter 11

The Mystery of the Co-Workers

Mother Teresa expanded her activities not only with the formation of an order for brothers but also with the creation of an organization for secular volunteers. Everyone—Catholic and Protestant, Hindu and Moslem—was to be recruited for service to the "poorest of the poor." She envisioned her mission to become the largest and most influential charity in the world, a mission united by Co-Workers in ecumenical humanitarianism.

Mohandas Gandhi gave the title "Co-Workers" to all those who joined with him to put an end to British rule in India. It was a title of identification and distinction, and it served to identify members of Gandhi's Indian National Congress Party, just as, say, the title "comrade" served to identify Bolsheviks during the Russian Revolution. Co-Workers were those who boycotted all things British and who joined in the march to the sea. According to British law, Indians could not produce salt, but could only buy it from British owned salt factories. In 1954, Gandhi organized a 24-day march to the sea. For this march, he gathered the support of hundreds of thousands of Hindu and Moslem Indians, all of whom became Co-Workers. As Co-Workers, the followers of Gandhi sat at the *charkhas* spinning cotton, as a sign that they were self reliant as a people, as a unified group. The Co-Workers supported Gandhi's social programs of combating leprosy, promoting literacy, and eliminating the caste system.

In 1953, a group of pampered and prominent wives of British dignitaries in Calcutta read of the nun who left her cloister to work in the streets with the poorest of the poor. The thought appealed to them. Here was a woman who broke from tradition to serve all of humanity. In her own way, the Albanian nun was more progressive, more liberal, and more liberated than the most forthright woman in their sewing circles. Small wonder that they wanted to join her. One such woman was Ann Blaikie, the wife of a wealthy lawyer and businessman. She and several of her friends, including a woman named Margaret Mackenzie, decided to collect unwanted toys and clothes from the rich, white boys and girls in the British community of Bengali for donation to the poor "colored" kids as Christmas presents.

When they presented the packages to the Missionaries of Charity, Mother Teresa thanked them and said that she now needed presents to give to the Moslem children during Ramadan and for the Hindu children during Riwali, the festival of lights. Blaikie and her friends were delighted with this response. Of course, they would provide packages. After all, they, too, were open-minded.

Eventually, as they grew closer with Mother Teresa, these women decided to form a society. But they didn't want the society to be another Altar and Rosary Society of the Roman Catholic Church. Most of the women, after all, were members of the Church of England. No, they wanted the society to be open to all races and religions. At first, they thought of calling themselves "Ambassadors of God" because they would be working with religious Sisters. But even this name was much too parochial and exclusive. They wanted to gain the support not only of Anglos but also of affluent Hindus, Sikhs, and Moslems. At last, they came upon the perfect name. In the spirit of the "Great Soul" (the "Mahatma"), they would call themselves "Co-Workers."

Later, Mother Teresa would say that the International Association of Co-Workers was a "most disorganized organization" from the start. But by 1955, Blaikie and her friends were producing an *International Newsletter* on a regular basis. They sent the

Newsletter to hundreds of foundations, philanthropic societies, and private charities throughout the world.

> *Dorothy Day was the leading Catholic female figure in the first half of the twentieth century. Born in Brooklyn in 1897, Day began her professional career as a correspondent for such communist newspapers as* The Call *and* The New Masses. *She got involved in the most controversial issues of the time: women's rights, free love, and birth control. Day had a series of lovers, became pregnant, and had an illegal abortion. In 1924, she got married, but the marriage lasted less than a year. In 1926, she found herself pregnant again, but this time she refused to have an abortion.*
>
> *When the baby was born, Dorothy became a Catholic and began publishing a journal called* The Catholic Worker *that represented an uneasy blend of liberalism and Catholic theology. She also opened a "House of Hospitality" in the slums of New York that provided food and shelter to the destitute. "What we would like to do," she said, "is change the world—make it a little simpler for the people to feed, clothe, and shelter themselves as God intended." She expressed regret for her participation in the sexual revolution of the 1920s and was opposed to the sexual revolution of the 1960s. She died in 1980. After a lifetime of voluntary poverty, she left no money for her funeral. It was paid by the Archdiocese of New York.*

Nothing about the Co-Workers would be distinctly Catholic or Christian. Rather, it was an undertaking of secular humanitarianism open and accepting of every race and religion. The unifying principle was to serve not the glory of God, but the memory of Gandhi. Mother Teresa later said that the name was chosen as a tribute to the one who called his helpers "Co-Workers" because they worked with him "for the brotherhood of man."

By 1960, Blaikie returned to England, where she formed "the Mother Teresa Committee" to promote the work of the Missionaries of Charity throughout the United Kingdom. From England, she continued to publish the *International Newsletter* that became transformed from a couple of roughly typed and mimeographed sheets of paper into a sleek, two-color glossy magazine.

As the Co-Workers increased in number, they issued pleas to help the starving children of India throughout Europe and America. One particularly successful notion was the "bread campaign." Schoolchildren in England emptied their pockets of pennies each day to purchase slices of bread for Indian orphans. In Germany, schoolchildren gave their pennies for daily vitamin pills; in Denmark, schoolchildren donated for glasses of condensed milk. In no time at all, the Co-Workers were raking in megabucks. Eileen Egan, a spokesperson for the Missionaries of Charity, said, "The generosity of the American people increased each year until for several years the donations exceeded $1,000,000." In Germany, the contributions exceeded $1.5 million. The organization also collected large sums from the people of Holland, Belgium, France, Sweden, Italy, Australia, and other countries where branches of the Co-Workers set up shop.

While visiting various groups of Co-Workers throughout Europe in 1974, Mother Teresa called upon those who were rich in material things to become aware of their spiritual poverty, to make themselves weak with the weak and poor with the poor. "Do not give from your abundance," she said, "but rather give until it hurts." She added, "Our sisters are working around the world and I have seen all the trouble, all the misery, all the suffering. From where did it come? It has come from lack of love and lack of prayer."

By 1978, more than eighty thousand Co-Workers were scattered over five continents—all engaged in fund-raising for Mother Teresa and the Missionaries of Charity. In that year, twenty-two hundred bails of supplies, along with one million tablets of dapsone for the treatment of leprosy, were shipped from Great Britain alone. The British Co-Workers also sent huge cash donations for Christmas meals and for flour to make bread, along with massive containers of clothes and blankets.

The International Association of Co-Workers was growing at a much faster rate than any charitable fund in the world. By 1990, it had amassed more than ten million dollars in assets and property. Navin Chawla, one of Mother Teresa's official biographers, wrote this about a "link" for relief supplies in Antwerp: "To give some idea of the size of these shipments, in 1990 alone, seventeen million Belgian francs' worth of milk powder and two hundred thousand Dutch guilders' worth of protein biscuits were purchased and supplied to Africa, South and Central America, and Asia. In addition, three million Belgian francs' worth of clothes were purchased at one-tenth their retail value and sent out to nine countries of West Africa."

At the time of the mysterious death of Pope John Paul I in 1978, the Vatican was enmeshed in a series of international financial scandals. One of the most notorious involved Mafia Chieftain Roberto Calvi, who served as the head of Banco Ambrosiano in Milan. Using the Vatican Bank as a conduit, Calvi set up eight dummy corporations in Panama. The Vatican Bank, through Archbishop Paul Marcinkus, produced "letters of patronage," informing Ambrosiano lenders that the Panamanian firms were secure and responsible firms whose purposes were known and approved by Holy Mother Church. More than $1.3 billion was loaned to the shell corporations. These corporations, in turn, purchased shares of Ambrosiano stock. When asked for collateral, the corporations simply posted the Ambrosiano stock that they had purchased. The loan money was transferred to the dummy corporations through the Vatican Bank, thus enabling the Vatican Bank to earn huge fees for currency conversions. The Vatican Bank also profited by selling its shares of Ambrosiano stock at artificially high prices engineered by Calvi and his optimistic announcement about the future of the corporations. When the scheme went bust, Calvi's body was found hanging from Blackfriars Bridge in London.

Problems arose. The United Kingdom granted Co-Workers charity status in the United Kingdom. This status mandated keeping financial records for auditing purposes. But the organization had become massive and unwieldy, with millions of dollars flowing from one country to another at such a monthly rate that accurate accounting was impossible. The Co-Workers, in short, had become an administrative nightmare. In the wake of the Ambrosiano affair and other scandals involving the Vatican Bank, Pope John Paul II expressed concern. This prompted Mother Teresa to issue this statement to her Co-Workers:

I want to make it very clear I do not want our Co-Workers to be involved in fund-raising. It was necessary before for us to have Flag Days, Leper Days, Children's Days, and all this. We had to do this because nobody knew we existed, but now the work has involved so many people that we just get—even in India where we never used to get anything before—we used to get about 20,000 rupees after working hours and hours—those who were in Calcutta they know how hard they had to work—now without even asking, without any difficulties we get quite a lot of money and help for the lepers .... Let us avoid publicity under that fund-raising name because it has become a target with other organizations and people are beginning to doubt, so let us not give them a chance.

In 1993, when Ann Blaikie became seriously ill, Mother Teresa suddenly and without warning shut down the entire organization of Co-Workers throughout the world. The news media besieged the Catholic Media Office in London with questions from the news media about the unexpected move, but no answers were forthcoming. The bank accounts of the Co-Workers were closed and the assets were liquidated. Anyone who now wanted to make a contribution to Mother Teresa's work would have to make a donation to the Missionaries of Charity. The Co-Workers who worked long and hard to do "something beautiful for God" were left out in the cold without any expression of gratitude or appreciation.

On July 22, 1994, when questioned about the Co-Workers, Mother Teresa said: "Co-Workers can continue to be friends with each other within a country or around the world. Friendship is a gift from God. But these long-distance friendships can be kept on a private level as you do with other friends, so there is no need to have national or international associations of Co-Workers to foster such friendships." Two years later, Mother Teresa asked her friends and supporters "to pray for the few who still find it difficult to accept my decision because they do not as yet see it as the will of God for the Co-Workers."

The Co-Workers had flourished for twenty-five years, becoming one of the most successful fund-raising agencies in the world. But it disappeared with all its books and records—its vast bank accounts and enormous investments—with the wave of Mother Teresa's wand. "It was all for the good," said one Co-Worker from Bath. "Mother Teresa was always one step ahead of the media. She knew how to avert a scandal."

Chapter 12

Enter Malcolm Muggeridge

Mother Teresa's rise to international stardom might not have happened without Malcolm Muggeridge. One of the great journalists of the twentieth century, Muggeridge considered himself an agnostic, even though he flirted with the idea of becoming a priest at his family's estate in South Croyton. He later said that his upbringing was as a "socialist."

Upon his graduation from Cambridge University in 1924, Muggeridge went to India as a teacher and later came to serve as the assistant editor of *The Calcutta Statesman*, where he wrote about the Indian struggle of independence and helped to make Mohandas Gandhi a household word in western Europe.

During the 1930s, Muggeridge became the chief correspondent for *The Manchester Guardian* and covered Stalin's "Terror Famine" in the Ukraine. During this time, he lost his communistic sympathy.

Returning briefly to India, he accepted a post as assistant editor for the *Calcutta Statesman*. While there, he completed his biography of Samuel Butler and gained recognition as a scholar. During World War II, he joined the Army Intelligence Corps and served in Mozambique, Italy and France.

After the war, Muggeridge became a critic and correspondent for *The London Daily News*, the editor of the British humor magazine *Punch*, and a popular curmudgeon on BBC. By 1960, he had become a prominent feature of London's literary life not simply because of his biting wit as a writer but also because of his affairs with prominent women. Bernard Levin, who worked with Muggeridge at *The Evening Standard*, said, "Muggeridge in some ways epitomized the riven nature of the decade, for as much as he was a sinner when he started he was a saint at the end, and although his formal canonization was expected to be somewhat delayed, many lived in the immediate expectation of his assumption into heaven as the Blessed Malcolm, while some claimed that the process had already started, and swore they could see light under his boots."

During the 1960s, Muggeridge—the renowned socialist and vocal agnostic became to modify his stance on religion while writing a book called *Jesus Rediscovered*. It was at this stage in his career that he met Mother Teresa and became the perfect person to launch her to international super-stardom.

In 1968, the BBC commissioned the esteemed journalist to conduct an interview with Mother Teresa for a Sunday-night series called *Meeting Point*. Ann Blaikie, on behalf of the "Mother Teresa Committee," made the arrangements.

Before the interview, Muggeridge had never heard of Mother Teresa or the Missionaries of Charity. All that he knew about the nun came from the scant biographical notes provided by Oliver Hunkin, head of the Religious Broadcasting Department at the BBC.

The parties involved arranged to conduct the interview at the Holy Child Convent, a religious house near Portland Place in London. Mother Teresa was late. Muggeridge was annoyed. Finally, she appeared on the set—small, frail, and badly wrinkled, even at the age of fifty-eight. "It was, for me," Muggeridge later recalled in his book *Something Beautiful for God*, "one of those special occasions when a face, hitherto unknown, seems to stand out from all other faces as uniquely separate and uniquely significant, to be thenceforth for ever recognizable."

The interview did not appear to go well. Mother Teresa seemed to be halting and nervous. Her answers were rambling and, at times, inarticulate. Muggeridge thought it was a complete bust.

Meeting Point, the half-hour series, thrived on confrontation during this era of sex, drugs, and rock and roll; of street demonstrations and anti-war protests, of conflicts between pigs and peaceniks; of Abbey Hoffman, Jerry Ruben, H. Rap Brown, Eldridge Cleaver, and Angela Davis. Who would find anything captivating about a talking—not even a singing—nun from Calcutta?

When the producers first saw the interview, they made plans to broadcast it in the dead of night, when few Brits would be sipping tea and watching the telly. "The verdict on the Mother Teresa interview," Muggeridge later wrote, "was that it was barely usable, and there were some doubt as to whether it was good enough for showing at all except late at night." But, on second thought, Oliver Hunkin fancied that it was so ordinary that it might seem unique. The BBC aired the program in May 1968.

The reaction to the program was phenomenal. Checks and money—orders for Mother Teresa's work, ranging between a few shillings to hundreds of pounds, came pouring into the studio. No one expected this reaction because Mother Teresa made no appeal for donations during the broadcast. The contributions came from every social and economic class—young and old, educated and uneducated, Catholic and non-Catholic—throughout the United Kingdom. What came across during the broadcast were her innocence and her complete lack of cynicism. These qualities were no doubt responsible for the outpouring of generosity.

Due to popular demand, the interview was aired again, with the same astonishing results. What had happened, Muggeridge later said, was inexplicable. An obscure nun of Albanian origin—neither glib nor photogenic—touched the English people "as no professional Christian apologist, bishop, or archbishop, moderator or knockabout progressive dog-collared demonstrator ever has."

In 1969, the BBC sent Muggeridge to India to make a fifty-minute documentary about Mother Teresa and her work. The crew included Peter Chafer, who served as line producer and director, and ace cameraman Ken Macmillan, who had filmed the Kenneth Clark series *Civilization.*

Arriving in Calcutta for the five-day shoot, they went immediately to the Motherhouse of the Missionaries of Charity at 54A Lower Circular Road, where Mother Teresa waited for them in the courtyard. While the crew went about setting up for the opening sequence, Mother Teresa invited Muggeridge to join her in the chapel for a time of prayer.

Entering the large meeting room, Muggeridge was surprised to find no pews or kneelers and no adornments of any kind except a statue of Mary. He was obliged to kneel on the hard floor before the common table that served as the altar, with a simple chalice placed upon it. They remained kneeling for an extended period of time. Finally, Muggeridge decided to have a go at it and say a prayer. The only prayer that came to his mind was that of St. Augustine: "Oh, God, stay with me. Let no word cross no lips that is not your word, no thought enter my mind that is not your thought, no deed ever be done or entertained by me that is not your deed."

The old curmudgeon and communist had been cleansed and sanctified. In this state of grace, he left the chapel with Mother Teresa to begin the filming. Muggeridge was no longer an objective reporter, but a devout believer. The transformation had occurred within an expanse of fifteen minutes. That was the first miracle assigned to Mother Teresa. Others were soon to follow.

Muggeridge began the interview a few minutes later. At the start of the program, Muggeridge asked Mother Teresa about her childhood in Serbia and her decision to enter a convent. "Did you ever have any doubts, any hesitations, about taking on this difficult life?" he asked. Mother Teresa replied with a coy smile. "At the beginning, between twelve and eighteen, I didn't want to become a nun. We were a very happy family. But when I was eighteen, I decided to leave my home and become a nun, and, since then, this forty years, I've never doubted for a second that I've done the right thing; it was the will of God." She uttered no word about the assassination of her father, the effect of this terrible crime on her family, the years of political oppression and humiliation, and the smoldering animosity between Serbs and Albanians. She made no mention of the fact that she sought to have her vows as a nun revoked and to leave the convent under an indent of secularization to become a social worker. She seemed innately to realize the first principle of mass communications: The semblance is more important than the reality.

The interview proceeded with Mother Teresa telling Muggeridge that she had a very happy life at Loreto until she heard "a call within my vocation" to go out in the streets and "serve the poorest of the poor." She said that she received this call in 1946, while traveling on a train to Darjeeling "to make my retreat." Naturally, she made no mention that she had been dismissed as headmistress of the Loreto School in Calcutta on charges of incompetence.

Muggeridge, who had visited the Loreto Convent, spoke of it as one of the most beautiful places in Calcutta, an oasis in the midst of a wasteland. He said, "It must have been hard to walk out of that beautiful garden, out of that quiet, peaceful place unto these terrible noisy streets." Mother Teresa bowed her head and said, "It was a sacrifice."

The topic changed to that of Kalighat. Mother Teresa described how she took a woman "half eaten by rats and ants" to a hospital that refused to admit poor people about to expire. She went on to relate how this experience led to a creation of a Home for the Dying at the temple of Kali. "I was very happy to have that place for many reasons, and especially knowing that it was a center of worship and devotion of the Hindus. Within twenty-four hours we had our patients there and we started the work of the home for the sick and the dying who are destitute. Since then we have picked up over twenty-three thousand people from the streets of Calcutta, of which about fifty percent have died."

Of course, Mother Teresa made no mention of the lack of medical care for the patients, nor did she admit that neither anesthetics nor pain killers (not even a glass of *bangla*) were administered to those in agony. She also left out the fact that most of the bodies were carted off by the sisters for burning at the pagan temple of the goddess of death and destruction.

Bangla is a liquor that is made in the garbage dumps of Calcutta. All kinds of refuse—along with animal innards and cane juice—are fermented for a month in a vat at the bottom of a fetid pool. The concoction is then poured into cast-off bottles and containers for sale in the bustees. Bangla kills more people in Bengali than malaria. Nevertheless, it has two distinct advantages. First, it is extremely powerful and immediately dulls the senses. Second, it is quite cheap. Evading tax levies, a quart of bangla costs six rupees, five times less than a quart of the cheapest government rum.

Muggeridge then turned to the subject of Shishu Brawan and the work of the Missionaries of Charity with children. "Some people say that there are too many children in India, and yet you're saving children many of who might otherwise die." "Yes," Mother Teresa replied, "many would die, especially among those children that are unwanted. Quite possibly they would have been thrown away or killed. But that way is not for us; our way is to preserve life, the life of Christ in the life of the child." Muggeridge timidly queried, "So you wouldn't agree with people who say there are too many children in India?" The question provoked this blissful response from his subject: "I do not agree because God always provides. He provides for the flowers and the birds, for everything in the world He has created. And those little children are His life. There can never be enough." Muggeridge, the old cynic, offered neither comment nor criticism. To the amazement of the BBC crew, the man who ripped apart show business and political personalities with razor-sharp wit was now wagging his tail like a lapdog before the small and unassuming nun.

Muggeridge moved on with more ingratiating questions to the subject of Titagarh. "Then about the lepers?" Malcolm asked. "How did your work for them begin, Mother?" He appeared to glow in her presence. Mother Teresa answered, "Among the lepers there are many well-educated people, many rich and capable people. But owing to the disease, they have been thrown out of society, out of their homes, by their relatives, and very often even their own children do not want to see them any more. They get isolated from their families and have no alternative but to turn to begging. Very often you see people coming up to Bengal from the south and the Bengal people going to the furthest north just to be far away from the people and from the places where they have been known and served and loved. We have among the lepers here in Calcutta very capable people who have had very high positions in life. But owing to the disease, they are now living in the slums, unknown, unloved, and uncared for. Thank God our sisters are there to love them and to be their friends and to bring the rich closer to them." No word about the sisters spreading the contagion by encouraging leprous couples to have children and to refrain from all forms of artificial birth control.

By the end of the program, the interviewer all but genuflected before his revered subject while proclaiming her sanctity to millions of viewers. Muggeridge said, "But one thing that would strike, I think, anybody from looking on is the magnitude of what you're tackling and, apart from your own extraordinary faith and the marvelous faith of your Sisters, the smallness of your resources. Don't you ever feel discouraged? Some people believe that these things should be done by great state organizations, they feel that a few loving souls trying to tackle such a thing is absurd. What do you think about all that?" The Mother gave him a pious smile and said: "If the work is looked at just by our own eyes and only from our own way, naturally, we ourselves we can do nothing. But in Christ we can do all things. That's why this work has become possible, because we are convinced it is He, He who is working with us and through us in the poor and for the poor."

The shooting of the documentary proceeded without a hitch. There were no breakdowns, no crises, and no complaints—not even among the technicians in the sweltering heat. Muggeridge later commented, "All this, as anyone with experience of filming expeditions will know, amounted to a kind of miracle."

But neither the conversion of Muggeridge nor the smoothness of the shoot prepared them for the real miracle that was about to occur when the British crew entered the Home of the Dying. That miracle, more than anything else, propelled Mother Teresa past the status of celebrity into the ranks of sainthood.

Chapter 13

The Miracle

The miracle took place within Kalighat. Muggeridge was uncomfortable about filming within the Home for the Dying because of the inadequate lighting. "The Home for the Dying," he wrote, "is dimly lit by small windows high up in the wall and Ken [Macmillan] was adamant that filming there was quite impossible."

Muggeridge's description of Kalighat is far from accurate. The three sections of arched windows are approximately six feet from the floor and measure three feet, six inches high by three feet across. The ceilings are less than ten feet high. What's more, Ken Macmillan, according to his own testimony, never said that filming within the home would be impossible. He rather saw it as a challenge to experiment with film newly developed by Kodak.

Macmillan, however, did agree that it would be wise to shoot scenes in an outside courtyard where patients were sitting in the sun, in case the scenes within Kalighat were murky and useless. After shooting several scenes of religious sisters caring for patients in the daylight, Macmillan turned his camera to the dark interior of the Home of the Dying.

When the film was processed, the scenes in the courtyard that were shot in the sunlight were dim and confused. However, the scenes within Kalighat were bathed in a soft, beautiful light—the light of heaven. Muggeridge maintained that there was no explanation for the illumination because it appears to come from a supernatural source. He said, "I myself am absolutely convinced that the technically unaccountable light is, in fact, the kindly light (John Cardinal) Newman refers to in his well-known exquisite hymn ('Lead, Kindly Light')."

Attempting to elucidate the ineffable, the former agnostic wrote, "Mother Teresa's Home for the Dying is overflowing with love, as one senses, upon entering it. This love is luminous, like the haloes artists have seen or made visible round the heads of the saints. I find it not at all surprising that the luminosity should register on a photographic film." Not only was the Home illuminated by heaven, according to Muggeridge, but it was also filled with perfect peace and serenity. He went on to say:

One thing everyone who has seen the film seems to be agreed about is that the light in the Home for the Dying is quite exceedingly lovely. This is, from every point of view, highly appropriate. Dying derelicts from the streets might normally be supposed to be somewhat repellent, giving off stenches, emitting strange groans. Actually, if the Home for the Dying were piled high with flowers and resounding with musical chants—as it may well have been in its Kali days—it could not be more restful and serene. So, the light conveys perfectly what the place is really like; and outward and visible luminosity manifesting God's inward and invisible omnipresent love. This is precisely what miracles are for—to reveal the inner reality of God's outward creation.

Muggeridge saw the light and, as a result, converted to Catholicism. He became one of the most ardent defenders of the faith until the time of his death in 1990. He opposed abortion and euthanasia while supporting the rights of the mentally and physically handicapped. His opposition to birth control resulted in his controversial resignation as Rector of Edinburgh University. Muggeridge never tired of giving testimony to "the first authentic photographic miracle." He said, "It so delighted me that I fear I talked and wrote about it to the point of tedium, and sometimes of irritation. Miracles are unpopular today—to the scientifically minded because they seem to conflict with so-called scientific miracles, like bumping television programs across the world by satellite, or going to the moon; to the ostensibly religiously minded because they remind them of miraculous claims made in the past and now discredited, which they wish to forget."

Word of the "miracle" immediately spread throughout the United Kingdom. The day after Ken Macmillan previewed the processed film, reporters called for his reaction to the "kindly light from heaven" that emanated from the Home for the Dying. The documentary had yet to be shown, let alone edited, and it was already creating a national sensation.

While the final cut of the film was being made, Mother Teresa wrote to Muggeridge, "I can't tell you how big a sacrifice it was to accept the making of a film—but I am glad now that I did so because it has brought us closer to God. In your own way try to make the world conscious that it is never too late to do something beautiful for God."

That catch phrase, "Something Beautiful for God," became the title of the documentary that was first shown in December 1969. It quickly became one of the most popular broadcasts in the history of the BBC.

Following the interview, Mother Teresa appeared on the cover of magazines and periodicals throughout the world. The rich and the famous sought to meet her. In the wake of the civil war in Pakistan, Senator Edward Kennedy traveled to Calcutta as chairman of the Committee on Refugees of the United States Senate. Mother Teresa was the recipient of numerous awards and honorary degrees, including a Doctorate of Human Letters in Washington. She appeared on leading talk shows—sometimes with Muggeridge as a double act. On the *Today* show, Barbara Walters introduced Mother Teresa to millions of viewers as a "great humanitarian."

The story of the miracle of the light emanating from the Home of the Dying remained central to her success and her status as a "living saint" who was above criticism and reproach. It was now assumed that God was directing the life and work of Mother Teresa, and to question anything she did or said was to question divine providence. Now Mother Teresa declared that anyone who appeared to be less than enthusiastic of her efforts was "fingered by God" for some misfortune on earth or a stint of hard time in purgatory.

In 1971, millions of refugees—most of them near death from starvation and exhaustion—came pouring into Calcutta from the area soon to become known as Bangladesh. A bloody civil war broke out between East and West Pakistan in which three million people were killed. The emergency in Pakistan began in 1970 when a cyclone as forceful as ten three-megaton H bombs capable of razing New York City to the ground swept over three hundred thousand Pakistanis to the streets of Calcutta. Shortly afterward, fighting erupted with reports of mass murders. The uprooted made their way to Bengal, where they considered themselves lucky to find shelter in a sewer pipe.

Two years after the program, Muggeridge published a book called *Something Beautiful for God* that contained a transcript of the program and a series of black-and-white photographs of the Sisters at work and prayer. It also contained a long and pious introduction and closing comments by Muggeridge himself. It quickly went through twenty reprints, was translated into thirteen languages, and sold close to four hundred thousand copies.

But what of the miracle? Was it real? Was the Home of the Dying radiated with divine light? Ken Macmillan, the celebrated cameraman, later said that the "first authentic photographic miracle" was no miracle at all, but rather the result of newly developed super-speed film from Kodak. He provided this testimony:

During "Something Beautiful for God," there was an episode where we were taken to a building that Mother Teresa called the House of the Dying. Peter Chafer, the director, said, "Ah well, it's very dark in here. Do you think we can get something?" And we had just taken delivery at the BBC of some new film made by Kodak, which we hadn't had time to test before we left, so I said to Peter, "Well, we may as well have a go." So we shot it. And when we got back several weeks later, a month or two later, we were sitting in the rushes theater at Ealing Studios and eventually up came the shots of the House of the Dying. And it was surprising. You could see every detail. And I said, "That's amazing. That's extraordinary." And I was going to go on and say, you know, three cheers for Kodak. I didn't get a chance to say that, though. Because Malcolm, sitting in the front row, spun around and said: "It's divine light! It's Mother Teresa. You'll find that it's divine light, old boy." And three or four days later I found I was being phoned by journalists from London newspapers who were saying things like, "We hear you've just come back from India with Malcolm Muggeridge and you were the witness of a miracle."

Peter Chafer, the director, remains uncertain about the validity of the miracle. He acknowledges that Macmillan was a brilliant cinematographer who experimented with a new film with a new emulsion that he exposed for longer than required, to attain maximum exposure. But he adds that Macmillan tried to achieve the same effect with the same film in a Cairo nightclub, with disappointing results. Chafer says, "All I know is, I was extremely grateful to have my film. But it was not my film that put Mother Teresa on the map. No, it was her. If she had not had her own charisma, it would not have worked. She definitely has something going on right."

Chafer was to meet Mother Teresa again when she came to England a few months after the airing of the film to open a Motherhouse in Southgate. She invited various dignitaries to a small service to commemorate the opening, including Muggeridge, Chafer, and Cardinal Heenan. The Cardinal replied that he was too busy to accept the invitation but would send along a deputy in his place. Mother Teresa wrote back and said, "It is such a pity you cannot come as Jesus Christ will be there." The Cardinal immediately relented and changed his plans. Mother Teresa could now summon a prince of the Church to do her bidding.

By January 1972, just when *Something Beautiful for God* was appearing in bookstores, the situation in Bangladesh went from atrocious to nightmarish. Millions of innocent civilians were rounded up and put to death, and more than two hundred thousand women were raped by Pakistani troops. The barbarous situation was described by Joyce Goldman in *Ms.* magazine. Goldman wrote about women being kept in barracks and used as "cigarette machines." One soldier told her, "We used the girls until they died." Goldman also described the case of an eight-year-old girl who was found to be too small and tight to meet the needs of the soldiers. The child was slit open to the navel and raped by the soldiers until she died.

Mother Teresa announced that she was going to the newly created nation along with ten Sisters on "a project of assistance for the very many women who underwent violation from the Pakistani troops and are now in an advanced state of pregnancy."

Mother Teresa and company traveled to Khulna, Pabna, Rajshahi, and Dacca. They were disappointed with the turnout— not many of the violated women showed up for medical assistance and counseling. Mother Teresa attributed this to her hard-line position on abortion. "But one thing I told them was that we would take all the babies and find homes for them. Killing, I said, is killing even if the child is not yet born."

A local bishop gave the Missionaries of Charity a one hundred-year-old convent to serve as a home for the women. Not all of the raped women conceived, and many of those who did tried to abort themselves. Those who delivered abandoned their "offspring of hate" in streets and alleys. Some were left on the doorstep of the convent. Overnight, the shelter for violated women became another Shishu Bhawan, a home for unwanted babies.

The situation at Dacca gave rise to one of the first and fiercest critics of Mother Teresa, the radical feminist Germaine Greer, author of *The Female Eunuch*. Greer wrote, "When she [Mother Teresa] went to Dacca two days after its liberation from the Pakistanis in 1972, three thousand naked women were found in the army bunkers. Their saris had been taken away so that they would not hang themselves. ... Secular workers told me at the time that women with complications of late pregnancy, caused by physical abuse and malnutrition, as well as women miscarrying, were turning up at the clinics claiming to have been accused of attempted abortion and turned away by Mother Teresa's nuns ...."

At the end of the year, Mother Teresa traveled to England to receive the first Templeton Award for Progress in religion for her work at Dacca and elsewhere. Prince Philip (Queen Elizabeth's husband) presented this award in London's Guildhall in the presence of his wife, who, as Christopher Hitchens points out in his vitriolic book, *The Missionary Position: Mother Teresa in Theory and Practice*, "holds the title of 'Defender of the Faith' against all the works of Rome." The Lord Mayor of London, Lord Mais, who served as chairman of the ceremony, said that the prestigious award with a cash prize of thirty-four thousand pounds was unique because it transcended all religious barriers. The next morning, London's *Daily Express* published a feature article on "the nun who offers hope for the world." By an odd coincidence, an ad for Virginia Slims cigarettes appeared on the facing page with the slogan: "You've come a long way, baby." And, indeed, she had.

Mother Teresa and Robert Morgan, on behalf of Youth Corps, release a dove as a symbol for peace in front of twenty thousand people at Varsity Stadium.

(© Bettmann/CORBIS)

Chapter 14

The Power and the Prize

Even after elevating Mother Teresa to international celebrity status with *Something Beautiful for God*, Malcolm Muggeridge still believed that the saintly nun had not received her full measure of honor, awe, and admiration. For this reason, he began a tireless campaign for Mother Teresa to receive the ultimate statement of recognition: the Nobel Peace Prize.

In 1972, Lester B. Pearson, the former Canadian Prime Minister and recipient of the 1957 Peace Prize, submitted Mother Teresa's name to the Nobel Committee at Muggeridge's urging. The committee, in turn, asked Pearson for elucidation of Mother Teresa's work to advance the cause of peace. They asked several pointed questions. Had she stopped a war? Had she negotiated a peace treaty? Had she organized a peace movement? Had she helped to abate the problem of overpopulation throughout the world?

Muggeridge labored to produce the necessary documentation for Pearson. Concerning these efforts, Muggeridge said, "I tried to explain how, by dedicating her life wholly to Christ, by seeing in every suffering soul her savior and treating them accordingly, by being, along with her Missionaries of Charity, a sort of powerhouse of love in the world, she was a counterforce to the power mania, cupidity, and egoistic pursuits out of which violence, individual and collective, in all its forms, comes."

The labor was in vain. Despite his persistent communication with the Norwegian committee, Mother Teresa did not win that year. In fact, no peace prize was granted to anyone that year. In 1973, the award was presented to Henry Kissinger and Le Duc Tho for the creation of the peace settlement in Vietnam.

But Muggeridge was undeterred. He was bound and determined to snag the prize for his saint. At Muggeridge's urgings, the name of Mother Teresa was again submitted to the Nobel committee in 1975, this time by the Right Honorable Shirley Williams, a member of British Parliament. The nomination was endorsed by Robert McNamara, former secretary of state and president of the World Bank; Maurice Strong, head of the United Nations Environmental Program; and four United States senators—Edward Kennedy, Mark Hatfield, Hubert Humphrey, and Peter Domenici. Numerous organizations submitted strong letters of support, including the National Council of Catholic Women and the United States National Council of Christian Churches. But the Herculean effort came to naught. In 1975, the award went to Russian scientist and human rights advocate Andrei Sakharov.

Overlooking Mother Teresa again seemed to be an intolerable slight to Muggeridge. He queried the committee, seeking reasons why they again dismissed his subject. The committee informed him that the award was not granted to those who engage in humanitarian endeavors, such as feeding the poor and providing shelter to the homeless, but rather to those who advance the cause of world peace. This caused Muggeridge and other supporters of Mother Teresa to scratch their heads. What had Mother Teresa really done for world peace? They couldn't come up with much.

Finally, Muggeridge pointed out that Mother Teresa had spoken out for peace on several occasions. On October 18, 1971, he argued, she appeared with Jean Vanier, founder of the ARC (Association of Retarded Citizens) communities for people with handicaps, to speak on the "Secret of Peace" in Toronto. On that occasion, she had said that peace begins with "loving word and a smile." Surely such words made her deserving of the Nobel Prize! The committee didn't buy the argument, and Malcolm went back to the planning board.

In 1977, Muggeridge geared up for another go for the gold. This time, Lady B. Ward, the author and environmentalist, placed Mother Teresa's name in nomination. A host of dignitaries were solicited to voice their support, but the award went to Amnesty International that year.

When she was passed over for the third time, Mother Teresa told the press: "I had a good laugh over the Nobel Prize. It will come only when Jesus thinks it is time. We have all calculated to build two hundred homes for the lepers if it comes, so our people will have to do a lot of praying."

Meanwhile, Mother Teresa was continuing to obtain awards and honors from organizations throughout the world. In August 1975, the Food and Agriculture Organization of the United Nations issued its Ceres Medal to Mother Teresa on behalf of her attempts to feed the hungry of the world. The specially designed medal bore an image of Mother Teresa depicted as the Roman goddess of agriculture. The nun had come a long way from Albania indeed. She was now identified with Mother Earth.

One month later, in September 1975, Mother Teresa was awarded the Voice of America's International Women's Year Pin for her work in India. In October, she received the Albert Schweitzer International Prize at the University of North Carolina. The next day, she addressed the Spiritual Summit Conference in New York. Despite her lack of theological training, she was selected to speak for Christianity as one of the five spiritual leaders of the five leading world religions. Two days later, she was honored at the National Shrine of the Immaculate Conception in Washington, D.C., where Cardinal O'Boyle presented her with a plaque and a monetary gift on behalf of the thousands of visitors to the shrine.

The next month, Mother Teresa was granted an honorary Doctor of Laws degree at St. Francis Xavier University in Antigonish, Nova Scotia. "I don't know why universities and colleges are conferring titles on me," she said. "I never know whether to accept or not; it means nothing to me. But it gives me a chance to speak of Christ to the people who otherwise may not have heard of Him."

In December, Mother Teresa became the subject of a *Time* magazine cover story. For the cover, she posed for hours while photographers snapped shots of her in prayer. For every snapped photo, Mother Teresa said she asked God "to free one suffering soul in purgatory." By the end of the session, several hundred souls gained their freedom. The cover story, titled "Saints Among Us," proclaimed, "Mother Teresa's own luminosity prompts many to bestow on her a title she would normally reject. She is, they say, a 'living saint.'"

On March 3, 1976, Indira Gandhi, in her capacity as chancellor of the Viswa Bharati University, bestowed upon Mother Teresa the institution's highest honor, the *Deshiko Hama* (Doctor of Literature) scarf in recognition of her humanitarianism. It was a strange honor to bestow upon an individual who was not known as a lover of literature. "She is tiny to look at," Mrs. Gandhi said of the recipient, who had been flown in by helicopter for the ceremony, "but there is nothing small about her."

In June 1977, Mother Teresa received an honorary Doctorate of Divinity from the University of Cambridge. The educated crowd was surprised to hear the distinguished guest speak without any prepared notes. "Her remarks," Professor Don Hoffman later said, were "rambling, repetitious, and often ungrammatical." In later years, her unprepared discourses often taxed the limit of the most patient listener. Often a short acceptance speech would turn into a long oration on her favorite subjects: abortion or birth control.

The honors and awards kept coming until Mother Teresa became the most decorated woman in the history of civilization. And along with distinction came privilege. She was granted visa privileges and customs exemptions that were reserved for top governmental officials. She received free travel on airlines and railways, free accommodations at five star hotels, and free medical care at leading medical institutions. By the mere raising of a finger, everyone halted their activities and hurried to serve her.

Finally, on October 16, 1979, the Nobel committee pronounced Mother Teresa as the year's recipient of the Peace Prize. Hundreds of reporters and photographers stormed the Motherhouse in Calcutta to catch her reaction. "I am unworthy," Mother Teresa told them, "but thank God for this blessed gift for the poor." Then turning full-face to the U.S. television cameras, she said, "And now I am going someplace to hide." The next morning, she confided to the Sisters, "Last night it was like vultures had descended." Then she caught herself and added, "But vultures can be beautiful."

Alfred Nobel was born in 1833 in Stockholm, Sweden, to a family of engineers. He invented dynamite in 1866 and later established companies and laboratories in more than twenty countries. When he died in 1895, he left his vast fortune to the Nobel Foundation for the awarding of the Nobel Prizes. In addition to Mother Teresa, other recipients of the Nobel Peace Prize in the latter half of the twentieth century include Yasser Arafat, Shimon Peres, Yitzhak Rabin, Nelson Mandela, Fredrik Willem De Klerk, Mikhail Gorbachev, the Dalai Lama, Desmond Tutu, Lech Walesa, Mohamed Anwar Sadat, Menachem Begin, Martin Luther King Jr., General George Catlett Marshall, and Albert Schweitzer.

On December 8, 1979, Mother Teresa landed in Oslo with her two traveling companions, Sister Agnes and Sister Gertrude. It was ten degrees below zero. Mother Teresa and the Sisters descended to the tarmac dressed only in their white saris without coats and sandals without woolen socks. In its own way, their dress seemed outrageously ostentatious. The usual banquet was cancelled at Mother Teresa's request. She said that the money should be spent on those who really needed a good meal, not international dignitaries who did not. The nun was bound and determined to teach the prestigious committee a lesson in charity.

On December 10, 1979, in the presence of King Olaf V, Crown Prince Harald, and Crown Princess Sonja, Mother Teresa accepted the gold medal and the money "unworthily but gratefully in the name of the poor, the hungry, the sick and the lonely."

At the Great Hall at the University of Oslo, the chairman of the Nobel Committee, Professor John Sannes, introduced Mother Teresa to the eight hundred guests. He said, "There would be no better way of describing the intentions that have motivated the decision of the Norwegian Nobel Committee than the comment of the President of the World Bank, Robert S. McNamara, when he declared, 'Mother Teresa deserves the Nobel Peace Prize because she promotes peace in the most fundamental manner by her confirmation of the inviolability of human dignity.'"

When she came to the podium, Mother Teresa made the sign of the cross and then bowed her head in silent prayer. She then called upon the audience to join her in the prayer of St. Francis that had been placed on every seat: "Lord, make me an instrument of thy peace that where there is hatred I may bring love." Many in attendance looked at the other guests with befuddlement. They didn't expect to participate in a Catholic prayer service.

Dressed in her sari and sandals, Mother Teresa reminded the crowd that God had become man to proclaim the good news, and the good news was peace to men of good will. This sounded comforting. The audience sat back in contentment. Then she broke into her tirade:

> I was amazed when I learned that in the West so many young people are on drugs. I tried to understand the reason for this. Why? The answer is because in the family there is nobody who cares about them. Fathers and mothers are so busy they have not time. Young parents work, and the child lives in the street and goes his own way. We speak of peace. These are the things that threaten peace. I think that today peace is threatened by abortion, too, which is a true war, the direct killing of a child by its own mother. In the Bible we read that God clearly said: "Even though a mother did forget her infant, I will not forget him."
>
> Today, abortion is the worst evil and the greatest enemy of peace. We who are here today were wanted by our parents. We would not be here if our parents had not wanted us.
>
> We want children, and we love them. But what about the other millions? Many are concerned about the children, like those in Africa, who die in great numbers either from hunger or for other reasons. But millions of children die intentionally, by the will of their mothers. Because if a mother can kill her own child, what will prevent us from killing ourselves, or one another? Nothing.

This, of course, is not what the audience expected. When the speech was over, many appeared to be victims of shellshock with their jaws dropped to their chests. Others politely applauded. One dignitary quipped, "Hell hath no fury like an old nun's scorn."

However, the overall reaction to the scolding was positive. One Norwegian journalist wrote in the newspaper *Aftenposten*, "How good it is to experience the world press for once spellbound by a real star, with a real glitter, a star without a wig, without a painted face, without false eyelashes, without a mink and without diamonds, without theatrical gestures and airs. Her only thought is how to use the Nobel Prize in the best possible way, for the world's poorest of the poor."

Mother Teresa accepting the Nobel Peace Prize from Chairman of the Norwegian Nobel Institute, John Sanness, in 1979.

(© Bettmann/CORBIS)

Chapter 15

Nun to the Rescue

The banner headline on the front page of *The Calcutta Statesman* when Mother Teresa received the Nobel Prize read, "Joy Sweeps Calcutta." Jyoti Basu, the communist Chief Minister of West Bengal, held a reception in her honor. He said, "You have been the Mother of Bengal, now you are the Mother of the World."

Indeed, Mother Teresa had become the Mother of the World. Everything about her life underwent an immediate change. She was surrounded by hordes of reporters, photographers, admirers, and gawkers wherever she went. There was scarcely a moment when she was off-camera.

In February 1980, Mother Teresa became one of only three Indians ever to be honored by a reception within the ramparts of Delhi's historic Red Fort, a complex of buildings enclosed by a high, red sandstone wall that once served as the imperial palace of India's Mughal emperors. The only other recipients of such honor had been Nehru and Indira Gandhi. In attendance were all the dignitaries of the capital—the prime minister, cabinet officials, diplomats, and prominent business leaders. When Mother Teresa took the podium, she spoke to the crowd of a ragged beggar who rang the bell of the Motherhouse in Calcutta the previous night:

> It was a leper shivering with cold. I asked him whether he
> needed anything from me. I wanted to offer him food and
> a blanket to protect himself from the bitter night in
> Calcutta. He replied in the negative. He showed me his

*begging bowl. He told me in Bengali: "Mother, people
were talking that you had received some prize. This morning I decided that whatever I got through begging today, I
would hand over to you this evening. That is why I am
here." I found in the begging bowl 75 paise (2 cents).
The gift was small. I keep it even today on my table
because this tiny gift reveals to me the largeness of a
human heart. It is beautiful.*

Everyone applauded warmly. They were touched by the tender
story that displayed not only the largeness of the leper's heart but
also the greatness of the esteemed Mother's heart. After she
returned to her seat, Mother Teresa let out a shriek of alarm. The
Nobel Prize medal was missing. A frantic search ensued. Finally,
the medal was found among the coats in the entrance hall.
Someone obviously was planning to steal it. So much for largeness
of the human heart!

She was next transported to Rashtrapati Bhawan, the presidential palace in Delhi, where the president presented her with the
nation's highest civilian award, the Bharat Raatna or "the Jewel of
India." The government grants this award for national service in
such areas as art, literature and science. While there was no formal
provision that recipients should be Indian citizens, this remained
the general assumption since the awards were established in 1888.
Mother Teresa became the first naturalized Indian citizen to
receive this honor. The only non-Indian to receive the award was
Nelson Mandela in 1990.

With the flood of publicity came a flood of new recruits to the
Missionaries of Charity. Before the awarding of the Nobel Prize,
there were 158 Missionaries of Charities houses for religious
women. The following year, in 1980, fourteen more opened in
Bangladesh, two in Belgium, two in Rome, Papua New Guinea,
Nepal, Ethiopia, France, Yugoslavia, Spain, Argentina, Chile, and
Miami, Florida. In 1981, eighteen more homes were created, along
with twelve in 1982 and fourteen in 1983. Within the next seven
years, more than one hundred seventy additional Motherhouses
were opened in the United States alone, in such sites as Harlem
and Greenwich Village in New York; San Francisco; Baton Rouge;

Little Rock; Dallas; Memphis; Los Angeles; Brooklyn; Phoenix; Denver; Boston; Norristown, Pennsylvania; Plainfield, New Jersey; Chichiltah and Gallup, New Mexico; Lafayette, Louisiana; and Jenkins, Kentucky.

By the end of 1980, one short year after Mother Teresa received the Nobel Prize, the Missionaries of Charity boasted one hundred forty slum schools, a daily feeding program for fifty thousand at three hundred four centers, seventy orphanages housing more than four thousand children; eighty-one homes for the dying that provided care to thirteen thousand patients; a host of vocational training sites where more than twelve thousand poor women learned to earn their living, and six hundred mobile health clinics that treated more than six million sick people. The Missionaries of Charity was the only religious order within the Roman Catholic Church to demonstrate growth—and it was growing by leaps and bounds.

Thousands of visitors descended upon the Motherhouse at 54A Lower Circular Road in search of Mother Teresa. If present, she consented to see them. Rarely did she make herself unavailable. Many who came were industrialists or politicians who wanted to present her with a check. Others simply sought a blessing or an autograph.

An amazing aspect of Mother Teresa's life is that her capacity for work seemed to increase with advancing age. Her schedule, by any standard, was exhausting. She managed to function on three to four hours sleep. She rose every morning at 4 A.M. and attended Mass at 6. From 8 until 11 A.M., she visited her homes, shelters, and work sites in a station wagon. She returned to the Motherhouse at noon for lunch, prayers, paperwork, and the reception of visitors. After the 6 P.M. Mass, she made another round of visits to the workplaces and then had dinner. While the other Sisters slept, she caught up with her correspondence on an old typewriter. Rarely did she delegate duties. Her energy was incredible.

Her room was simple and unadorned, furnished with a small cot and a dresser. It contained no comforts, not even a fan, let alone a telephone or a television set.

In 1982, Mother Teresa was called into the crisis in West Beirut when war broke out between Israel and Syria. In a dramatic rescue, she and her sisters traveled in a Red Cross van, while mortar shells exploded all around them, to save thirty-six mentally ill children who were trapped in a bombed-out asylum without food or water. A Red Cross official said at the time, "What stunned everybody was her energy and efficiency. She saw the problem, fell to her knees, prayed for a few seconds, then she was rattling off a list of the supplies she needed—nappies, plastic pants, chamber pots. The problem is that in wartime most of the attention is focused on the casualties. But the blind, the deaf, the insane, and the spastics tend to be forgotten just when they need help the most. Mother Teresa understood that right away."

At the end of 1984, another emergency brought Mother Teresa's help. Twenty-five hundred people were killed by a poisonous gas leak from a pesticide plant owned by Union Carbide in Bhopal. Thousands more were left permanently ill with severe respiratory ailments. State officials initiated no plan to evacuate the city as attempts were made to contain the leakage of the methyl isocyanate gas in the underground tanks.

As the gas continued to seep into the air, Mother Teresa arrived to offer her assistance. She was greeted at the airport by thousands of gas victims who turned to her for a solution to the problem. She joined her hands together in a gesture of prayer and said, "Forgive, forgive." The words were of little comfort to the victims who were seeking to escape the poisoned city. Visiting the hospitals, where patients were coughing up black bile, she said, "I am here to give love and care to those who need it most in terrible tragedy." Before she was whisked away like visiting royalty, Mother Teresa again told the crowd, "I say, forgive." The Missionaries of Charity offered no aid or assistance to the people of Bhopal. The appearance of Mother Teresa was deemed sufficient for public solace. Five years later, Union Carbide agreed to pay $470 million in compensation to the Indian government; the Indian government, in turn, agreed to drop criminal charges against the company and its former chairman, and, by so doing, showed its capacity to "forgive."

The AIDS crisis next absorbed her attention. Calling AIDS "the new leprosy of the West," she opened a hospice for victims of the disease in Greenwich Village. Manned by four Sisters, the facility was called "Gift of Love." Her new enterprise soon made headlines after she managed to obtain the release of three young men—Antonio Rivera, Jimmy Matos, and Darryl Monsett—who had been sentenced to Sing-Sing for violent crimes. All three men had AIDS. Repeated attempts to free them by humanitarian and gay activist groups had failed. When the situation was brought to Mother Teresa's attention, she simply telephoned New York Governor Mario Cuomo and said, "In God's name, please let these men die in peace." Within twenty-four hours, the three were transferred to the Greenwich Village Home for the Dying.

The Daily News hailed the release as "a miracle in Manhattan." Mother Teresa said, "We are hoping these poor unfortunate men will now be able to live and die in peace. We plan to give them tender loving care because each one is Jesus in a distressing disguise. We are not here to sit in judgment on these people, to decide blame or guilt. Our mission is to help them to make their dying days more tolerable and we have Sisters who are dedicated to do that."

Later she spoke of an AIDS victim to whom she had ministered in the Gift of Love. One day, the young man had asked to speak to her in confidence about the lessons he had learned from her hours of counseling. "What did he say after twenty-five years of being away from God? 'When I get the terrible pain in my head, I share it with Jesus and suffer as He did when He was crowned with thorns. When I get the terrible pain in my back, I share it with Him when He was scourged at the pillar. And when I get the pain in my hands and feet, I share it with Him when He was nailed to the cross.'" Mother Teresa responded to this pious utterance by asking permission to take the young man "home." When he gave his consent, she took him to the chapel where he "talked to Jesus" as she had never seen anyone talk before: "so tenderly and full of love." Three days later, she said, the young man died in peace.

> The Roman Catholic Church condemns homosexual acts as particularly heinous sins. The "Declaration on Certain Problems of Sexual Ethics," promulgated by the Vatican in 1975, advises priests to be "considerate and kind" in their care of homosexuals in their congregations by instilling within them the hope of one day overcoming their difficulties. "However," the Vatican document continues, "it is not permissible to employ any pastoral method or theory to provide moral justification for their actions, on the grounds that they are in keeping with their condition. Sexual relations between persons of the same sex are necessarily and essentially disordered according to the objective moral order. Sacred scripture condemns them as gravely depraved and even portrays them as the tragic consequence of rejecting God."

Within the next few years, Mother Teresa established Gifts of Love in Washington, D.C.; San Francisco; Denver; Los Angeles; and Ethiopia. By 1990, 661 patients had been treated at the 6 shelters.

The Gifts of Love hospices were governed by strict rules. The walls were decorated with colored pictures of the saints and the Pope. Visitors were permitted only between 4 to 5:30 P.M. The patients were allowed to listen to radio but not to watch television. These rules were widely criticized. Elgy Gillespie, part-time editor of *The San Francisco Review of Books*, voiced this complaint about the time she spent at the San Francisco home:

> Sent to cook in her [Mother Teresa's] hostel, tactfully
> named "The Gift of Love," I found a dozen or so very sick
> men; but those who weren't very sick were exceptionally
> depressed, because they were not allowed to watch TV or
> smoke or drink or have friends over. Even when they are
> dying, close friends are not allowed. They are never allowed
> to drink, even at the funerals of their friends and room-
> mates, and some have been thrown out for coming home in
> drag! When I mentioned the Olympics to them, they looked
> even more depressed. "We are not watching the Olympics,"
> said a sister from Bombay, "because we are making our
> Lenten sacrifice." When they're very sick and very

*religious, this doesn't matter, but with brighter men or older
men it seems intolerable.*

*A Guatemalan writer that I befriended there was desper-
ate to get out, so a friend of mine who also cooks there—an
African American who is a practicing Catholic—adopted
him for as long as she could. He became much sicker and
when she begged him to go back because she couldn't mind
him, he begged her to keep him because he knew they didn't
medicate enough, or properly, and was afraid he would
have to die without morphine ....*

Until 1995, Mother Teresa, for some strange reason, saw no
need to set up a Gift of Love in Calcutta. For years, the Indian government sponsored an AIDS Awareness Program that promoted
monogamy and heterosexual sex by the use of erotic drawings and
a man and woman engaging in various positions of sexual inter-
course from the *Kama Sutra*. But the program was not a success. An
article in the medical journal *Nature Medicine* said: "The serious-
ness does not seem to have sunk in yet as ignorance, apathy, corruption, and lack of commitment at all levels are still the most
powerful allies of the galloping AIDS virus." By 1995, India had
more than three million HIV-infested inhabitants—more than any
other country in the world. Shiv Lal, project director of India's
National Aids Control Organization, said, "We are in trouble.
From high-risk groups the virus has gone to the general public."

As the epidemic spread, Mother Teresa opposed any governmental program that involved the distribution of condoms, not
even to wives whose husbands tested positive to HIV. She maintained this position even when informed that the disease can be
transmitted from mother to baby and may endure a long period of
gestation during infancy and early childhood before the first symptoms appear.

Finally, on Christmas Day 1995, the first Gift of Love opened in
India. When asked what she could do to help prevent the spread
of AIDS in light of her opposition to condoms, Mother Teresa said:
"Nothing. It is God's will. They must die in peace with God."

Commenting on Mother Teresa's position on AIDS, Anne Sebba, in *Mother Teresa: Beyond the Image* wrote …

> Mother Teresa's response … is, like so much else of hers, paradoxical; far from taking the line that this was a self-inflicted gay plague that she would have nothing to do with, she has been in the forefront of those trying to help AIDS sufferers die with peace, love and dignity. The homes may be Spartan, without televisions and other luxuries, or without the best medical care. But they represent a response to a crisis for which she has won praise. On the other hand, the crisis will continue and deteriorate dramatically unless the causes are addressed. In the case of AIDS this means educating the people about sex in general and teaching them to wear condoms in particular. It is unprotected sex which has caused the virus to spread so fast, and if anybody has the power to do good anywhere, surely it is better to prevent someone becoming ill than to help them die once they are ill.

Chapter 16

The Movie Deal

After receiving the Nobel Peace Prize in 1979, a noticeable change took place in Mother Teresa's demeanor, speech, and appearance. By glancing at photographs of her through the years, you can see this remarkable transformation. In early photos—even during her sessions with Malcolm Muggeridge during the filming of *Something Beautiful for God*—she appears animated and physically relaxed with her arms comfortably by her side and an easy smile on her face. She does not emanate poise or a sense of extreme self-consciousness. Her body language is open and inviting. In later photos, those taken during the last twenty-eight years of her life, her appearance is radically altered. She appears stiff and imposing. Her hands are always carefully folded in prayer, often wrapped with rosaries. Even when she is among children, her mannerisms never alter. She bows before a child in a crib in one photo in the same way she bows before a statue of the Blessed Virgin Mary. It seems so studied, so poised, so artificial.

In early photos, she faces the camera with her bright, dark eyes. In later shots, she turns her head—at all times—to the floor in a gesture of humility. Watching her walk to her Black Maria (her private touring car), she appears to be heading toward the confessional.

Her vocal expression was similarly studied. In later years, she never said anything that expressed the slightest emotion, not even physical distress. From dawn to dusk, she uttered pieties to

everyone around her. Every sentence seemed to be carefully calculated to convey her saintliness. She rarely spoke a sentence without a reference to God or a member of the Holy Family. She also
developed a habit of interrupting her pontifications by pointing up
to heaven with her crooked index finger, while saying such things
as, "I do it all for him."

Mother Teresa insisted that she detested media exposure.
Referring to the press coverage of the Nobel Peace Prize, she said,
"For that publicity alone, I should go straight to heaven." When
the Indian Prime Minister Narasimba Rao presented her with
another national award in 1993, she said, "This publicity, these
lights, I accept this, as I did the Nobel Prize, only as a recognition
of the poor." And yet she never banished cameras and always
informed the press of the next place she would make an appearance.

Mother Teresa never appeared out of character and, despite her
claims of humility, took herself and her image very seriously. With
her approval, signs were posted in her homes for children that read,
"Of all the nice things in the world, the nicest must be Mother."
She also insisted that the signs of her ambulances, buses, cars, and
mobile vans be changed from "Missionaries of Charity" to "Mother
Teresa's Missionaries of Charity." She also consented to have her
face appear on religious medals and postage stamps.

The question of Mother Teresa's ego came to the fore when
moviemakers appeared at the door of her Motherhouse with plans
to make a major motion picture of her life and work. In December
1982, she signed an agreement with celebrated author Dominique
Lapierre (*Is Paris Burning?*, *Freedom at Midnight*, and *City of Joy*),
granting him exclusive rights to her story. For this exclusivity, she
received a substantial cash payment, the amount of which has
never been revealed.

Difficulties immediately surfaced with the script. As written by
Lapierre, Mother Teresa speaks as a human being. She expresses
frustration, sheds tears, displays anger, and even has a few moments
of uncertainty and doubt. Such a depiction, of course, was not
permissible, and Mother Teresa demanded a drastic alteration in
the presentation of her character.

Then came the question of who would star as Mother Teresa in this multimillion-dollar production. The filmmakers decided on Academy Award–winning actress Glenda Jackson, who had played everything from Hamlet to Hedda Gabler. She was an accomplished actress with an international reputation. It seemed permissible for her to assume the title role until Mother Teresa discovered that Glenda Jackson had appeared in some steamy sex scenes in such films as *Women in Love*, *The Music Lovers*, and *A Touch of Class*. An actress who appeared nude in film after film was certainly not right for the part of a pious nun. What's more, Jackson's personal life was riddled with scandal and her political views placed her somewhere left of Lenin.

Mother Teresa ordered Lapierre to find someone more suitable. Knowing that no one could come up to Mother Teresa's standards since Ann Blyth (the favorite Catholic film actress of the 1950s) had retired, he wisely decided to cast an unknown in the lead.

Then came the problem with the title. It couldn't be called something snappy, like *Calcutta's Saint* or *Teresa's Tears*. No, the only title acceptable to Mother Teresa was her own: *In the Name of God's Poor*. It didn't sound like a blockbuster.

After Mother Teresa continually demanded rewrite after rewrite of the script and personal control of the project, Lapierre, who had spent a small fortune in preproduction, balked at her demands. Mother Teresa responded by withdrawing permission for the filming, despite the fact that Lapierre already possessed a signed agreement.

By now, six years had flown by and Lapierre was still in Calcutta attempting to please Mother Teresa. At the request of Father Celeste, Mother Teresa's old Jesuit mentor, he agreed to send a final version of the script to Father Gaston Roberge, a fellow Jesuit, for approval. If Father Roberge found no objection, the filming could get underway.

In August 1990, Father Roberge said that he found no faults in the script and that changes had been made to comply with Mother Teresa's wishes. All seemed ready to go—until Mother Teresa again cried out in protest. The script still made her character too human and unbecoming. Moreover, certain scenes had been fabricated for the sake of a story. She wrote to Lapierre, "The permission I had given you was given upon my own misunderstanding of your intentions. I mistakenly believed that anything that would be written would be a factual account of our work and our life as Missionaries of Charity, for the honor and glory of God, and that it would serve the poorest of the poor."

She later intimated that her reservations about the movie project were underlined by the publicity arising from Dominique Lapierre's new book, *Beyond Love*, that drew unwelcome and inaccurate attention to the work of the Sisters in the Gifts of Love for AIDS patients.

Lapierre had had enough. He had spent eight years on the project, had submitted to Mother Teresa's every demand, and had spent millions with nothing to show except the signed contract. He appealed to the Vatican. Pope John Paul II, upon reading the script, expressed his full support of the project, believing the film would be of immense service to the cause of Catholic charities.

But Mother Teresa refused to abide by the Pope's wishes. She had an image to maintain and she would permit no one to tarnish it.

Eventually, a settlement was reached and the project ended up as a movie for cable television's Family Channel in 1997. Produced by Hallmark Entertainment, *In the Name of God's Poor* was filmed by director Kevin Connor in Sri Lanka. The TV movie starred Geraldine Chaplin as Mother Teresa, Keene Curtis as Father Celeste, David Byrd as Archbishop Perier, and William Katt as a fictitious character called Harry Harper.

The film depicts scenes of Mother Teresa hearing heavenly sounds on her train ride to Darjeeling; Mother Teresa drawing in the dirt with a stick to teach Bengali children the alphabet; Mother Teresa carrying a dying women through the streets of Calcutta; and Mother Teresa embracing a group of lepers. It ends with Mother Teresa receiving the Nobel Prize to thunderous applause.

One reviewer wrote, "The movie itself is a dull account of Mother Teresa's life as a missionary to the poor of Calcutta. It chooses to present the facts as if it were reporting them to a disinterested group of her peers. The moviemakers treat her condescendingly; she's relegated to the status of a well-loved grandmother whom the family locks in her room when company is expected because she might embarrass them."

The moviemakers received no complaints from Mother Teresa—not even about the casting of Geraldine Chaplin and William Katt. Perhaps, Mother Teresa was unaware that Ms. Chaplin, daughter of Charles Chaplin, appeared nude in several movies, including *Remember My Name*, and that William Katt exposed his bare buttocks in a film called *First Love*.

Chapter 17

The Odd Couple

They had little in common. He was scholarly, sophisticated, and highly educated, and he lived in a palace. She was earthy, unsophisticated, without college training, and she lived in a convent. He enjoyed reading works of philosophy. She enjoyed delousing street children. He was tall and blond. She was short and swarthy. But they were both eastern European and they made a perfect match.

Their relationship ripened after she received the Nobel Peace Prize in 1979. The next year, he invited her to address the World Council of Bishops in Rome. The theme of the synod was the breakdown of Christian families in the modern world. He spoke to her about his views on contraception, abortion, and the duty of the Church to reaffirm the commandment "Thou shalt not kill," even if this meant engaging in demonstrations of pro-life movements. She listened to his word rapturously. They were of one mind. She spoke to the synod about supporting his position in the midst of a sex-crazed and godless era. She further reminded the bishops that they should follow his example by manifesting greater holiness in their work.

Their mutual admiration blossomed during his visit to India in 1986. When he arrived at Kalighat straight from the Dum Dum airport in his Popemobile, she stepped into his vehicle to kiss his feet. He blessed her with a kiss on the forehead. It was their first public display of affection.

She introduced him to the head *sevayat* at the Temple of Kali—the smiling figure was standing behind her and all but wagging his tail—and then escorted him to the podium erected in his honor so that he could address the large crowd. Before he spoke, she placed a garland of flowers on his head and blushed. He smiled coyly, removed the garland, and placed it around her neck. She beamed with joy.

He spent more than an hour with her in Nirmal Hriday, feeding some of the patients and blessing others. He paid rich tribute to her work among the poor. "For the destitute and the dying," he said, "Nirmal Hriday is a place of hope. This place represents the profound dignity of every human person." She, too, was full of praise for him. She told the reporters, "He touched the very life of everybody here. He blessed and touched everybody. We are happy to have the Holy Father touch our poor."

In the evening, the Catholic and civic authorities held a reception in his honor at St. Xavier College. The reception included a Mass and a prayer service.

When the reception was over, she walked along the specially laid red carpet with military and police escorts. He already had left to return to Rome. Still, he had traveled thousands of miles just to see her. She was ecstatic. "This is the happiest day of my life," she said. The remark was telling. The happiest day in her life was not the day she entered the convent, not the day she became a Bride of Christ, and not the day she experienced her "call within a call." It was the day that he graced her with his presence at her mission.

In 1988, they again met, this time in Rome. He had issued orders for the creation of a special home for her within Vatican City. The orders were astonishing, to say the least. Vatican City was already overcrowded and small; every square inch was of incredible value. As a matter of fact, real estate in this principality is of greater worth than any place on earth. Still, he demanded a building and commissioned the talents of one of Italy's leading architects, Angelo Malfalto, for its design. The home was built adjacent to the Audience Hall. It was called *Casa Dono di Mario* ("Home of the Gift of Mary"). It contained two dining halls, each capable of seating sixty people, and a dormitory for sixty-four homeless women.

He presented her with the keys to the domicile as a token of his appreciation of her work. "All tramps and vagabonds are welcome," he said, "regardless of their religion. We do not want people sleeping under the arches of the Tiber bridges or at railway stations. People of all faiths—and those of none—will be welcomed in." She was ecstatic. It was the greatest gift she had ever received. "Now our poor have a place right in the Vatican. Our people are the only ones who can walk right into the Vatican without buying a ticket."

Some complained about the extravagance and the need of this gift. He already had given her three other large houses in Rome for her mission, and the Vatican was not a place for derelicts and drug addicts—it was parochial Disneyland, the greatest tourist attraction in the world for Catholics. But she wanted—no, insisted—on a home in the shadow of St. Peter's Cathedral. And he would do anything in his power to please her.

Her relationship with him was closer than her relationship with any other pope, even Paul VI. On several occasions, Paul VI mistakenly called her "Mother Teresa of Delhi." She later said that she refused to correct him because of her yearning for "anonymity." But that could not excuse the incident on July 15, 1965. She was honored with a private audience. But when she came before his papal throne, Paul VI just stared at her with a blank expression on his face and said nothing. This continued for several minutes. Finally, he asked her for her prayers and dismissed her. The Holy Father had forgotten her name.

But this never happened with John Paul II. To him, she was the number one nun, the perfect example of a Catholic woman. He called upon her to espouse the Church's position on such issues as birth control and abortion on each and every occasion. She was happy to oblige for three reasons:

- She liked and admired him.
- She agreed with his ideology.
- She knew that he had the power to make her a saint.

The relationship was symbiotic. He was important to her because he endorsed and supported her missions, and she was important to him because she endorsed and supported his teachings.

When John Paul II ascended to the throne of St. Peter, many of the religious women in the Church were in a state of open rebellion against the Roman hierarchy. Strange to say, much of this rebellion was prompted by Mother Teresa herself. Like her, they sought to leave the convents for the streets. Like her, they refused to wear traditional habits and developed their own manner of dress. Like her, they deserted the contemplative life of the Canonical Hours for the active life of social workers. No woman is more responsible for the unrest within the women's religious orders than Mother Teresa. This is ironic because she came to represent the teachings of tradition.

> By the 1950s, the first cracks began to appear in the organization of convent life within the Roman Catholic Church. Under the demands of medical practices and the shortages of trained nurses, sisters in the nursing profession were permitted to adjust their keeping of the Canonical Hours (also called "horarium") to fulfill their professional duties. The sisters who served beyond the convent bedtime were permitted to sleep beyond the five o'clock summons to prayer and were relieved of some of their daily chores. Other fissures occurred. In 1953, Sister Mary Emil Penet organized the Sister Formation Conference of the National Catholic Education association and by forceful argument obtained ecclesiastical permission for sisters engaged in the teaching profession (many of whom did not possess even a high school diploma) to depart from the routine revolving around the Divine Office to attend colleges and universities to raise the standards of Catholic education. By 1965, when Vatican II came to a close, the hours of religious sisters, by and large, were kept to their own discretion.

By 1979, when Mother Teresa received the Nobel Prize, nuns and religious sisters throughout the world had cast off their veils and wimples and appeared in blouses and blue jeans to join in boycotts, marches, and sit-ins for a variety of secular causes. As Mother Teresa left the Loreto Order to form her own religious community, others left their orders to form new religious communities that came to include married couples, Protestants, and even agnostics. Others became involved in fringe factions of the Women's Liberation Movement and shunned any semblance of adherence to the rule of Episcopal cloister. This position was exemplified by Sister Margaret Traxler, founder of the National Coalition of American Nuns, who said, "We hope to end domination by priests, no matter what their hierarchical status."

The situation went from bad to worse. In 1984, Sister Barbara Ferraro and Sister Patricia Hussey of the Sisters of Notre Dame di Namur (along with hundreds of other Sisters, including Sister Margaret Traxler) signed an advertisement in support of abortion on demand. When Pope John Paul II attempted to pressure the order into expelling the Sisters, the order responded by threatening a strike against the Church.

Catholic women throughout Western Christendom were demanding the right to perform as acolytes, to serve as deaconesses, and to receive ordination as priests.

In the Roman Catholic Church women (young girls, married, religious) are prohibited from serving the priest at the altar. The Vatican II document On the Liturgy (Liturgiae Instaurationes, 7) prohibits women from distributing Holy Communion even in women's chapels, convents, religious schools, and institutes. Women may participate in the liturgy only in the following manner:

> By proclaiming the scriptural reading, with the exception of the Gospel
>
> By offering the intentions of the Prayer of the Faithful
>
> By leading the congregational singing
>
> By providing explanatory comments to help people understand the service
>
> By serving as greeters and ushers

Women may distribute Holy Communion only when called upon to be extraordinary eucharistic ministers—that is, in circumstances when priests or deacons are not available.

Mother Teresa proved to be of extreme importance to John Paul II throughout his pontificate. She was a religious woman who was respected and revered throughout the world and who held a position of authority over hundreds of missions, hospices, shelters, and homes for children. "She is one of the very few women in the top echelons of the Church who is very orthodox," Marco Politi, Vatican expert at *La Repubblica*, said of her in 1995.

To soften the traditional teachings of the Church on women, John Paul II often attempted to speak of their special role and the so-called "feminine genius" that enables them to "give birth, raise children, and care for others." This may not seem progressive to most modern women, but it's a far cry from Pope Pius XII, who insisted that women wear doilies on their head. "Mother Teresa," Politi wrote, "embodies for John Paul II at an international level both the feminine genius of all women and the special care of the Third World, which is increasingly important as the West and the industrial world is slipping toward materialism and industrialism."

In 1990, Mother Teresa was recruited by the pope to deliver a pro-life speech at a Synod on Religious Life and was encouraged by him by speak against abortion at every opportunity. She heeded this instruction. In February 1995, as the guest speaker at the Presidential Prayer Breakfast in Washington, D.C., she delivered a forty-five-minute tirade against contraception and abortion to a ballroom of distinguished senators, congressmen, and cabinet members. President Clinton and his wife, Hillary, both in favor of a woman's right to choose, sat stony-faced before the shriveled old nun.

Surely, no one did more to champion the papacy of John Paul II than Mother Teresa. As Anne Sebba points out: "A major part of this Pope's vision has been to eradicate what he calls the culture of death and declare unequivocally the supremacy of the culture of life. In fighting this battle, Mother Teresa, as a prophetical woman sharing exactly the same values as him, has been of inestimable value. Her testimony of charity has been completely in sympathy with that of the Pope and they have been valuable collaborators of each other."

Karen Armstrong, a former nun who wrote the book *A History of God*, spoke on several occasions of the importance of Mother Teresa to John Paul II. "The Church," she said, "has often found its saints too radical and today some Roman Catholics choose to see Mother Teresa as a comforting reminder of older values. Her success, they argue, shows that the reform of the Church is unnecessary."

Armstrong also referred to the fact that Mother Teresa's act of leaving the Loreto Order in 1948 was a radical one that the conservative Pius XII, and even his liberal successor John XXIII, looked upon with suspicion. "Similarly, in the last twenty years," Armstrong said, "about a quarter of the active Roman Catholic priests throughout the world have left the conventional ministry: unlike her, they have been disowned by the Vatican. Some sixty percent of them now live and work among the destitute and are regarded by some as heralds of a new Catholicism."

Mother Teresa was so important to the pontificate of John Paul II that he discouraged her from stepping down as the Superior General of the Missionaries of Charity in 1990, even when she became gravely ill. The constitution of the order stipulates that a Superior General is elected for six years and may serve a second but not a third term. But the Vatican waived this condition—as it did for no one else—so that Mother Teresa could remain in office for eight terms—from 1950 to 1996.

By not allowing her to resign in 1990, the Pope did her a disservice. Had she disappeared from the public spotlight into the dark shadows of Kalighat or one of her missions, the controversies that plagued her during the last years of her life probably would not have surfaced and her sanctity would not have been tarnished.

What's more, during the last troublesome years, she rarely heard from her old friend John Paul II and received no special invitations to the Vatican. A year before she died, a leading journalist from a Catholic newspaper said: "As a media figure, she's almost had her day as far as the Vatican is concerned. They're looking for dynamic, young women who embrace all the tenets and are outward-looking, possibly professional women or nuns, such as Mary Ann Glandon, with a North American Order, who is part of the Vatican's team on Women's Issues." An official text *Women in the Church Today*, published in Rome in 1996, failed to even mention Mother Teresa's name.

Chapter 18

Beauty and the Beads

Mother Teresa's first encounter with the Royal Family was in 1973, when Prince Philip presented her with the first Templeton Award for Progress in Religion. John Templeton, the United States businessman who instituted the award, was concerned that religion no longer provided guidance to mankind because society had "become so topsy-turvy and when changes in direction were taken without much reflection by most of mankind." He wanted the award to go to a "creative pacesetter in religion for pioneering a breakthrough in religious thought and understanding." In his introductory remarks, Prince Philip made an attempt at humor by saying, "The Reverend Mother, whom we are delighted to see among us, would reply, if you inquired about her career, that it was of no importance."

Four years later, in 1977, the same straight and stammering Prince Philip, acting as chancellor of Cambridge University, awarded Mother Teresa an honorary Doctorate in Divinity. To some observers, this seemed odd because Cambridge was a bastion of the Reformation after the Church of England split from Rome after King Henry VIII was denied the right to divorce his wife. In her acceptance speech, she spoke to the dons about the meaning of the Eucharist.

In 1980, Prince Charles spent time with Mother Teresa watching the Sisters prepare food for more than seven thousand poor people. He also joined her on a tour of Shishu Bhawan, her home for children in Calcutta, where he stiffly shook hands with several of the urchins. Before he departed, Mother Teresa said to him, "I will pray for you so that the love and compassion you have for the poor and the needy grows and you are able to serve them better." Prince Charles responded with a smile. The Prince didn't seem to realize that a Catholic nun had just treated him with condescension. Her next encounter with the royal family took place in 1983, when Queen Elizabeth II presented her with the insignia of the Honorary Order of Merit at the Presidential Palace in Delhi. Upon receiving the gift, Mother Teresa draped it around the neck of a statue of the Virgin Mary, saying that the award really belonged to her.

Despite her friendship with the royal family, the history of the Missionaries of Charity in Great Britain was never unproblematic. The first home was opened in England in 1971 to provide shelter for impoverished women. It burned to the ground in 1980 and nine women died in the fire. Later, fire inspectors discovered that the facility lacked a fire escape. In 1983, there was a problem with the Missionaries of Charity hostel in Liverpool. The city officials said there was no need for the facility since the homeless women were provided care by existing social agencies. After talks between the city officials and representatives of the Roman Catholic Church, the sisters agreed not to use the facility as an overnight shelter but to use it strictly for daytime counseling services.

In April 1988, Mother Teresa traveled to England to meet with Prime Minister Margaret Thatcher. The prime minister, she said, was bound to see things from her point of view because she was a mother. The meeting was not very amicable. Mother Teresa informed the prime minister that she had visited London in 1970 to open a Motherhouse and had seen homeless people sleeping under the tarpaulins that draped the scaffolding of St. Martin-in-the-Fields and creating makeshift shelters under the railway arches of Charring Cross. She also said that she had spent the previous evening visiting London's Cardboard City in Waterloo. She went on to say that the poverty in London was even worse than the poverty in Calcutta. "There is much more suffering I believe here," she said, "more loneliness, more painful loneliness of people rejected by society who have no one to care for them. It hurt me so much to see our people in the terrible cold with just a bit of cardboard covering them. They were inside the cardboard box made like a little coffin. I did not know what to say. My eyes were filled with tears."

The prime minister, quite naturally, was far from pleased that the capital of England was being compared to the "city of dreadful night."

Mother Teresa was not finished with her speech. She informed the prime minister of the sufferings of a woman whom the Sisters had found frozen stiff beneath railway arches in the heart of London. She said that it was very ironic that "people here send me things when a woman in London is living like this. The prime minister informed her that such incidents were rare and that the citizens of the United Kingdom are extremely well cared for by the government. "Here you have the Welfare State," Mother replied, "the poverty of the spirit, of loneliness, and of being unwanted."

Over tea, the prime minister tried to change the subject to the plight of the poor in Africa and India. Mother Teresa held her teacup, nibbled on a cucumber sandwich, and told Mrs. Thatcher about repeated attempts of the Sisters to visit the resident of one of a row of council houses that were occupied by patients who had been discharged from mental institutions. The Sisters, Mother Teresa said, one day noticed a particularly unpleasant smell emanating from one of the row houses. They knocked at the door, but the resident refused to answer. Finally, the Sisters pried open the door to find a woman living in the house that was packed from floor to ceiling with excrement. The toilet had been blocked for months and the elderly woman was fearful of calling for help. The Sisters, Mother Teresa said, borrowed shovels and removed more than five sacks of feces. Mrs. Thatcher balked at the account, insisting that the government surely can't be blamed for such a situation.

After tea, as the afternoon droned on, Mother Teresa spoke again about the plight of the occupants of London's "Cardboard City." She insisted that the prime minister provide a property so that the Sisters could care for those sleeping in "little cardboard coffins." The prime minister told her guest that many social agencies were already in place to address that problem. Then

Mother Teresa said that if she were not given a suitable property for her new mission in London, she would bring all the drifters into the Great Hall of Westminster to sleep. Saying this, the nun chuckled, but the prime minister was not amused.

Over the next few years, Mother Teresa bitterly complained that Britain's poor had been neglected by those in power and insisted that the rejection experienced by the Missionaries of Charity in Thatcher's England was more painful to her than her worst encounters in third-world countries. As late as 1990, she expressed her frustration about finding a proper shelter for the inhabitants of Cardboard City, "I talked to the highest people, but nothing has happened. A number of people promised to do something, but we still have no home."

Shortly after her disastrous meeting with Margaret Thatcher, Mother Teresa fell into the clutches of Robert Maxwell, the notorious owner and publisher of the tabloid *Daily Mirror*. Maxwell said that he would assist the Missionaries of Charity in finding a shelter for the poor of Cardboard City. She accepted his help. Maxwell ran a series of articles in his newspaper, appealing for his "wonderful readers" to contribute as much as possible to this noble cause. The campaign seemed to serve them both. Maxwell got his photo plastered through the pages with the "living saint," and Mother Teresa got pledges of contributions for her much-desired shelter.

In all, Maxwell raised more than three hundred thousand pounds—enough to purchase two homes for Mother Teresa—that he placed in high-interest accounts. By the time of Maxwell's death, nothing had been turned over to the Missionaries of Charity. Finally, five years after Maxwell's death, a thirty-five-room hostel was eventually opened in London, and Mother Teresa attended the grand opening to thank the *Mirror* readers for their generosity. But the bulk of the money raised by Maxwell, in all likelihood, went into his own pocket.

Although Margaret Thatcher might not have been captivated by Mother Teresa and Maxwell might have used her for his own meretricious purpose, Princess Diana became an ardent admirer and, strange to say, a close friend.

On February 16, 1992, Princess Diana attempted to visit Mother Teresa at the Motherhouse of the Missionaries of Charity in London. But Mother Teresa was not in residence. She had been hospitalized in Rome. Sister Frederick welcomed the distinguished guest. She led Diana to the courtyard, where a group of novices sang, danced, and showered the princess with flower petals in traditional Indian style. In the chapel, Diana took off her shoes, knelt on the floor, and joined the sisters in prayer. Following prayer, they sang a hymn of love for the poor in Bengali.

Sister Frederick then accompanied the Princess to Kalighat. By all accounts, Diana was not afraid to touch the sick and the dying, who gave her toothless smiles, not knowing that they were in the presence of royalty.

Before Diana departed from the Home for the Dying, Sister Frederick gave her a handwritten message from Mother Teresa. The note said, "Would you please tell Princess Diana that I do not think I shall be in Calcutta when she is due to see me there, but she is welcome to come and visit me here." Within the week, Diana flew to Rome to visit the ailing nun. Mother Teresa was immediately attracted to her, perhaps more so than any other public figure. By this time, the Princess had already established her own concern for the poor, the needy, and the dying, particularly AIDS patients.

By the following June, the marriage problems between Diana and Charles were making headlines in tabloids throughout the world. When asked to comment about Diana's difficulties, Mother Teresa said, "I am praying so much for her happiness." On September 9, 1992, Mother Teresa met with Princess Diana at the Missionaries of Charity home in the Kilburn section of London. The meeting was held "in secret" so that the two would not be plagued by reporters. Such a private meeting with a dignitary was rare for Mother Teresa, and that she agreed to it shows that the young woman had captured the nun's sympathy.

In June 1993, the two again met when Mother Teresa opened a place in Southwark "for the people sleeping in the streets to have somewhere to have dinner and lay their heads at night." At this time, Diana's mother, Mrs. Shand-Kydd, was in the process of converting to Roman Catholicism and there was much speculation that Diana would follow her lead.

One of the last full-length interviews Mother Teresa granted the press concerned the subject of her relationship with Princess Diana and Diana's plans to divorce Prince Charles. Mother Teresa told Daphne Barak of *Ladies Home Journal* that the princess "is like a daughter to me." Asked about the break-up of the royal marriage, she said: "I think it is a sad story. Diana is such a sad soul. She gives so much love but she needs to get it back. You know what? It is good that it is over. Nobody was happy anyhow."

> *The Roman Catholic Church remains opposed to divorce. The Vatican II document* Gaudium et Spes *says, "Married love is uniquely expressed and perfected by the acts proper to marriage by which intimate and chaste union of the spouses takes place are noble and honorable; the truly human performance of these acts fosters the self-giving they signify and enriches the spouses in joy and gratitude. Endorsed by mutual fidelity and, above all, consecrated by Christ's sacrament, this love abides faithfully in mind and body in prosperity and adversity and hence excludes both adultery and divorce."*

It was a most unfortunate remark and seemed to undermine the Church's teaching on divorce. "Mother Teresa Sanctifies Split!" a tabloid said. The old nun was then forced by the Vatican to issue a lengthy "clarification" of her statement emphasizing that "the teachings of Jesus Christ on the indissolubility of marriage ... have been the basis of my lifelong opposition to divorce. My love and fervent prayers are with the Royal family at this difficult time .... The family that prays together stays together."

It seemed that the nun who could do no wrong now, in her final days, could do no right. Everything she said and did came under scrutiny. Like all saints, she had to endure persecution before her ascent into glory.

In early September of 1997, when Mother Teresa was informed of Princess Diana's untimely death in a car crash in Paris, she appeared before the press and spoke of Diana's love for the poor and promised to pray for her. This promise, as it turned out, proved to be Mother Teresa's last public statement.

Mother Teresa with Princess Diana.

Chapter 19

Angels of Death

Mother Teresa never sought to make the Missionaries of Charity medical establishments, but rather she wanted them to remain charitable shelters. Small wonder, then, that physicians and medical clinicians, when they began to inspect her missions, were shocked at what they found. In 1974, the British medical journal, *The Lancet*, published the first damaging report about Kalighat. After spending a day at the facility, the editor, Dr. Robert Fox, found that the medical care provided by the Sisters was substandard, at best, and barbaric, at worst. The Sisters didn't now the basics of proper care, he wrote. In fact, they didn't even know how to distinguish curable from incurable diseases by use of simple algorithms (means of finding the most likely cause of illness). He described the problems this way:

> *Algorithms can help even those without a medical training to reach a reasonable accurate diagnosis and decide what drugs can be used. This is the way primary health care is going in India, and it means that even those without a high degree of training can be taught how to diagnose common complaints and offer simple but effective treatment. However, such systematic approaches are alien to the ethos of the home. Mother Teresa prefers providence to planning; her rules are designed to prevent any drift toward materialism.*

In the article, Dr. Fox wrote of a young Bengali beggar who was treated with tetracycline and paracetamol because the nuns thought he suffered from meningitis when, in fact, he really suffered from cerebral malaria and should have been treated with chloroquine. "Could not someone have looked at a blood film?" he queried. "What happens depends on chance; it could be a Dutch or Japanese nurse or even one of the volunteers who do much of the initial assessment, and they might not immediately think of cerebral malaria."

Despite the millions in contributions that poured into the coffers of the Missionaries of Charity, Dr. Fox found that the patients of Kalighat were denied all comforts. The Sisters, he observed, did not even own an electric blender by which they could process food that patients with cancers of the throat and mouth could swallow. These types of cancer were, and remain, very common in Calcutta, where tobacco abuse by chewing and smoking runs rampant among the poor.

Finally, Dr. Fox discovered that the Sisters, many of whom were well-intentioned, were completely incompetent in managing pain. "Along with neglect of diagnosis," he wrote, "the lack of good analgesia marks Mother Teresa's approach as clearly separate from the hospice movement. I know which I prefer."

Some medical specialists stationed in India came to Mother Teresa's defense after the appearance of the article in *Lancet*. One such defender was Gilly Brown, the director of Cancer Relief India. Brown said that Indian hospitals, let alone homes for the dying, have difficulty acquiring strong analgesia (painkillers). She argued, "Even in 1994, most cancer patients whom I saw did not have access to any analgesia, because of lack of suitable drugs, of knowledge about the use of the drugs by the doctors as well as, in some instances, no understanding about pain management, and compounded by a lack of resources. Mother Teresa is to be commended for at least providing loving kindness."

Brown had never met Mother Teresa nor visited her Home for the Dying in Calcutta. Several years later, she decided that it was high time she made a visit. The defender of Mother Teresa was horrified at what she found and wrote in her Cancer Relief India report:

> I managed to speak to one of the nuns who was working
> at the center. She was unable to tell me exactly how many
> people were cared for at any one time, but it looked to me
> like there were probably about 100 men and women in
> the center, all of whom had had their heads shaved, the
> reason being that their hair may contain head lice. Some
> of the patients were clearly ill mentally, and the nun in
> charge told me quite categorically that there were no can-
> cer patients present. A doctor visits two or three times a
> week. If there are any patients with pain, they are treated
> with paracetamol or ibuprofen. When I visited there were
> two volunteers who were delivering care to the patients,
> who sleep on small, stretcher-like beds.

Brown found that she had to retract her kind works about Mother Teresa and her criticism of Dr. Fox. In the report, she wrote, "Having seen the center, I feel I am able to echo some of the sentiments written by Dr. Fox in the *Lancet*. Many of those in Kalighat will be released and have to go home without any hair; to an Indian woman, this is one of her most important assets."

Students who volunteered to work with the Sisters at Kalighat were not prepared for what awaited them. The facility was ripe with the stench of rotten flesh, urine, feces, and disinfectant. Many became physically ill upon entering and refused to return. Others were given the task of dressing sores, cleaning ears, cutting nails, shaving heads, brushing teeth, emptying bedpans, and feeding those too weak to feed themselves.

All of the patients—at Mother Teresa's insistence—were forced to receive a daily bath, even the comatose and the dying. They were placed on a tile floor and hosed down with cold water.

One of the most serious complaints about medical care at Kalighat and other facilities operated by the Missionaries of Charity was the way disposable needles and syringes were reused hundreds of times on different patients. One Missionary of Charity worker boosted to the Sisters that she had managed to inject more than five hundred children with polio vaccines with only three needles.

The conditions at hospitals in Calcutta are far from ideal. The grounds of the City Hospital are extremely well maintained, with well-manicured lawns, flowing fountains, quiet pools, and bougainvillea-lined walks. But once inside the emergency room, you encounter a chaotic nightmare: bloodstained dressings piled in hallways, broken beds serving as trash cans, and ripped mattresses crawling with cockroaches. Severely ill patients suffering from encephalitis, coronary thrombosis, tetanus, typhoid, and cholera are lying all around, including on the bare floor. In the wards, boys travel from bed to bed with water skins, charging fifty paisas (five cents) to anyone in need of a drink. In the maternity wings, it is customary to find three mothers with babies sharing the same mattress, a situation that sometimes causes asphyxia among newborns. In almost every hospital in the city, you will find expensive equipment—electrocardiograph machines and defibrillators—out of use because of lack of repair and cardiac resuscitation units closed because of lack of air-conditioning. One newspaper, reporting on conditions in the hospitals, said, "The only piece of equipment that seems to function properly, but then again, only when there are no power cuts, is the apparatus for electric shock treatment in Gobra Mental Hospital. In operating rooms, the containers of forceps, scalpels, clips, and catgut are usually empty due to theft by staff members. The pilfering of food is so widespread that meals have to be transported in padlocked carts. Large quantities of food and milk are regularly diverted to the innumerable teashops that have been set up in the vicinity of the hospitals. Newspapers reveal that the theft is so unchecked that treatments have to be given by candlelight since most of the electric light bulbs have been removed."

Mary Loudon, a volunteer worker for the Missionaries of Charity, offered this testimony about her experience at Kalighat:

My initial impression was of all the photographs and footage I've ever seen of Belsen and places like that, because all the patients had shaved heads. No chairs anywhere, there were just these stretcher beds. They're like First World War stretcher beds. There's no garden, no yard even. No nothing. And I thought, what is this? This is two rooms with fifty to sixty men in one, fifty to sixty women in another. They're dying. They're not being

given a great deal of medical care. They're not being given
painkillers really beyond aspirin and maybe, if you're
lucky, some Brufen or something, for that sort of pain
that goes with terminal cancer and the things they were
dying of.

They didn't have enough drips. The needles they used
and reused over and over and you would see some of the
nuns rinsing needles under the cold tap water. And I
asked one of them why she was doing it and she said:
"Well, to clean it." And I said, "Yes, but why are you
not sterilizing it; why are you not boiling water and sterilizing your needles?" She said, "There's no point."

The first day I was there when I'd finished working in
the women's ward I went and waited on the edge of the
men's ward for my boyfriend, who was looking after a boy
of fifteen who was dying, and an American doctor told
me that she had been trying to treat this boy and that he
had a really relatively simple kidney complaint that had
simply got worse and worse and worse because he hadn't
had antibiotics. And he actually needed an operation. I
don't recall what the problem was but she did tell me. And
she was so angry, but also very resigned which so many
people become in that situation. And she said, "Well, they
won't take him to hospital." And I said, "Why? All you
have to do is get a cab. Take him to the nearest hospital,
demand he has treatment. Get him an operation." She
said: "They don't do it. They won't do it. If they do it for
one, they do it for everybody." And I thought—but this
kid is fifteen.

Christopher Hitchens, in his ferocious attack on Mother Teresa
entitled *The Missionary Position: Mother Teresa in Theory and
Practice*, maintained that the global income of the Missionaries of
Charity would permit the Sisters to operate first-class clinics with
top-notch medical professionals but instead they choose to operate
a "haphazard and cranky institution" that promotes a "cult of
death."

Mother Teresa herself gave credence to this claim by maintaining that the purpose of Kalighat was not to cure the sick, but to offer the poor people of Calcutta, who had been stripped of all human dignity, the chance to "die beautifully." In 1973, she told Malcolm Muggeridge, "What they need ... is what we offer them. In these twenty years of work amongst the people, I have come more and more to realize that it is being unwanted that is the worst disease that any human being can ever experience. Nowadays we have found medicine for leprosy and lepers can be cured. There's medicine for TB and consumptives can be cured. For all kinds of diseases there are medicines and cures. But for being unwanted, except there are willing hands to serve and there's a loving heart to love, I don't think this terrible disease can ever be cured."

Illustrating the type of care patients received at the Home for the Dying, Mother Teresa spoke of a Bengali beggar who was in the last agonies of cancer and suffering unbearable pain. "You are suffering like Christ on the Cross. So Jesus must be kissing you." Then, with a smile, she told of the patient's reply, "Then please tell him to stop kissing me."

One of Mother Teresa's staunchest defenders remains Dr. Nicholas Cohen, a British-born physician who served as a volunteer at Kalighat. He said that the poor people of Calcutta have no alternative to the care, support, and love that is offered by the Missionaries of Charity. "There is no alternative; they can't have hospice care, so what she has done has affected the whole world. It has meant other people have started things up, too, and that is what is important, not what medicines are given or not given. Millions of mistakes are made in modern medicine anyway." What is most essential to Mother Teresa's home, according to Dr. Cohen, is "the happiness and love amongst all the people who work there, which is extremely rare in the world anywhere and gives you a sense of peace and a feeling that you can do something without any personal reward for it. It's a powerful feeling. Once you're there you're part of a brotherhood, you do your best but you are not judged. I like the idea of just caring for people but there's no judgment."

But the kind of care offered by the Missionaries of Charity appears to pose a threat to world health. At Kalighat, Nabo Jeevan, and the other homes for the dying, there is no separation between tubercular and nontubercular patients. This means that many of those treated at these facilities became infected by this highly contagious disease and return to the streets to infect others. Dr. Jack Praeger, speaking of his experience at Kalighat, said, "The tubercular patients were not simply walking among the others, they were eating together and using the same utensils. I begged Mother for a separate ward so that they would not transmit the disease, but it never happened."

Dr. Praeger has reason to be concerned about the problem of tuberculosis at Mother Teresa's homes for the poor. In recent years, the World Health Organization (WHO) warned of a drug-resistant form of tuberculosis that is poised and ready to spread throughout the globe. This new strain of tuberculosis is airborne and extremely contagious. One WHO official described it as "an AIDS epidemic with wings." Dr. Joel Almeida, medical officer for the WHO Global Tuberculosis Program, recently said: "If the multi-drug-resistant strain becomes predominant, we will be back in the pre-antibiotic days. All we will be able to do is pray and send people off to sanatoria like we did in the last century." For this reason, places like Mother Teresa's Home for the Dying that have no concern for correct medical procedure and practice might become the breeding grounds for a world-wide plague.

Chapter 20

The Mission and the Money

Mother Teresa always refused to keep records about her organization for the purposes of audit, let alone public scrutiny. This practice produced a series of problems for the Missionaries of Charity.

In 1977, for instance, investigators uncovered the fact that babies from Bangladesh were being sold to an international kidnapping ring. The ring supplied the babies for prostitution, pornography, and even more nefarious purposes. The probe revealed that at least two babies Mother Teresa had sent for adoption in Germany went to adoptive families that did not exist.

In 1987, Mother Teresa became the target of a massive swindle. A network of well-organized thieves intercepted mail for the Missionaries of Charity and cashed checks for contributions at banks in Singapore and Hong Kong. Mother Teresa and her Sisters became aware of this scheme only after a donor from the United States asked for a receipt of a donation. No one knows how much money was lost in this way, but some estimate that the amount may have exceeded two million dollars.

When questioned by the press, Mother Teresa was always open about her refusal to keep books and ledgers. She turned down all funds from private and public sources that came with a "balloon"— that is, an audit of expenditures. Navin Chawla, Mother Teresa's official biographer, explained it this way: "Keeping records would mean that in the four hundred and sixty-eight houses of the Missionaries of Charity around the world, at least one sister would be distracted from her true work of comforting and helping the lonely, the afflicted, and the despairing. It would also mean an army of accountants. Anyone who has seen the tiny office in Motherhouse, where three Sisters hammer away on antiquated typewriters to keep in touch with the work in over one hundred countries, would know that Mother Teresa would grudge every rupee spent away from the 'real work.'"

Because of her close association with Jyoti Basu, Chief Minister of West Bengal and a lifetime communist, Mother Teresa was able to obtain huge grants of land and property to care for the poor. Throughout the years, they appeared together at public functions and press gatherings concerning conditions in Calcutta. Mother Teresa served as a comforting presence for Basu and the Communist Party because she never asked any questions of them. A former Sister who left the order because of Mother Teresa's collusion with communists said, "Mother Teresa makes good friends with all the leaders, but it's not doing anything except giving them credence. The Sisters are with the people at grass roots, but if you're not taught how to grapple with the issues, how can you fight them?"

Not only did she establish ties to the Communist Party, but Mother Teresa also managed to win the support of leading capitalists in Calcutta, including Naresh Kumar. Kumar was an international tennis pro who represented India at Wimbledon for twenty-one years before becoming a successful business executive and a leader of the Bengal Chamber of Commerce. "Whenever Mother Teresa seeks my help, I consider it a privilege," Kumar told Anne Sebba. "It's so easy to work for her; you just ring people up and convey her wishes. Everybody does it for free."

Kumar mentioned one case in point. For political reasons, Jyoti Basu wanted Mother Teresa to open a house for destitute women in Tangra, a slum area in the north of Calcutta. The house was to shelter women who had recently been released from prison, ex-junkies, former prostitutes, and the mentally retarded. Kumar approached S. A. Birla, one of the richest citizens of Bengal. Birla had provided funding for a university, a hospital, a Hindu temple, a museum, an educational trust, and a planetarium. "Would the Birla family like to purchase a new home for Mother Teresa?" Kumar asked him casually at a country club. "Within five minutes," Kumar later reported, "Mr. Birla had written a check on the spot for five hundred thousand rupees."

Kumar also said that there was no reason for Mother Teresa to retain records of her income and expenditure. "You can be 110 percent sure that—with Mother—any money does not go to her or her Sisters. In any case, to whom should she account and why? I've been in business long enough to know what business accounts can be. Accounts mean very little. She has got above these things. Her mission is to look after the poor, that's her entire story."

Not everyone shares this view of Mother Teresa's record keeping. How much money has been received by the Missionaries of Charity over the past half century? Without an audit, it is impossible to tell. In addition to the millions upon millions from people around the world and the incredible support from public and parochial funding sources, the Missionaries of Charity have received a percentage of the profits from such companies as Jet Airways and Tata Tea.

In 1976, India enacted the Foreign Contributions Regulation Act that requires all charities to be registered with the government. This measure was passed to prevent funding flowing into the country to support political and terrorist activities. Once an organization is properly registered, it must undergo a complete audit every year. But Mother Teresa, through her contacts with the prime minister and top Indian officials, managed to skirt the taxing problem of yearly audits. Moreover, she arranged to channel all contributions to the Missionaries of Charity through a bank in London and the *Instituto per le Opere di Religione*, a.k.a. the Vatican Bank.

Only glimpses of the incredible wealth of Mother Teresa's worldwide missions can be obtained. One glimpse comes from Monimoy Dasgupta, a reporter for the *Calcutta Telegraph* who has kept a close watch on her operations in Calcutta. He estimates that her holdings in Bengal fall somewhere between thirty million and forty million dollars.

A second glimpse comes from the sights of the Sisters conveying traveling to Rome and London to deposit large sums of money. One former Mother Superior spoke to a reporter of her many trips abroad with stashes of checks. "I think she is a very wealthy Congregation," she said. "Apart from money, they get given so many things."

A third and final glimpse comes from this account by Susan Shields, who worked for many years as a member of the Missionaries of Charity in New York and San Francisco:

> The flood of donations was considered to be a sign of God's approval of Mother Teresa's congregation. We were told that we received more gifts than other religious congregations because God was pleased with Mother, and because the Missionaries of charity were the sisters who were faithful to the true spirit of religious life. Our bank account was already the size of a great fortune and increased with every postal service delivery. Around $50 million had collected in one checking account in the Bronx. ... Those of us who worked in the office regularly understood that we were not to speak about our work. The donations rolled in the bank, but they had no effect on our ascetic lives or on the lives of the poor we were trying to help.

The quest for private and governmental funding support of her missions brought Mother Teresa into the arena of politics and controversy. In August 1980, Mother Teresa attempted a conference on family planning in Guatemala, where she asked about liberation theology, a radical movement in the Roman Catholic Church that champions the overthrow of all forms of tyranny and oppression (including capitalism and U.S. "imperialism") in Latin America. She provided an answer that caused most in attendance to scratch their heads. "You cannot serve two masters," she wrote. "Someone once asked me whether it is better to give fish or fishing rods to people who are hungry. But the people who come to me are sick and dying: They are so weak that they cannot even hold a rod. They must be given the fish first and maybe the rod will come later."

After leaving Guatemala, she visited Haiti, one of the poorest countries in the world that had been ruled for more than three decades by the corrupt, brutal, and decadent Duvalier family. At the time of her visit, the fat and arrogant Jean-Claude Duvalier, son of the butcher Jean François "Papa Doc" Duvalier, had been named president of the island for life. His first lady, Michele Bennett Duvalier, was a sleek and elegant Creole divorcee who had squandered millions to maintain a luxurious lifestyle while the people lived in unspeakable misery.

After traveling through the island with the Duvaliers in a Rolls Royce, Mother Teresa thanked the couple for a wonderful and heart-warming visit. She then gushed to the press about the profligate Michele, "I have never seen the poor people being so familiar with their heads of state as they were with her. It was a beautiful lesson for me. I have learned something from you." She went on to say, "Madame President is someone who feels, who knows, who wishes to demonstrate her love not only with words but also with concrete and tangible actions." For the next few weeks, night after night, Mother Teresa's words of praise about the ruling couple were aired on state-sponsored television so that the unfortunate inhabitants would know the goodness and benevolence of the dictator and his wife.

In February 1994, the public outrage against the Duvalier duo boiled over into open rebellion with the people—most of whom earned less than one hundred fifty dollars a year—driving the hated couple from the island. By that time, Mother Teresa already had secured several homes from the government, along with the Haitian *Legion d'Honneur.*

Another controversy occurred when she visited her ancestral homeland, Albania, to pay a visit with the communist ruler Ramiz Alia. During the visit, Alia took her on a sightseeing tour of the countryside. She spent time with the wife of the former dictator Enver Hoxha, who had exiled her brother and caused her mother and sister to live in abject terror until their deaths in 1972. Indeed, she even visited a cemetery to lay a wreath on the grave of the

Albanian strongman, who had outlawed Christianity and pro-claimed his country to be the "world's first atheist state." The *Yearbook on International Communist Affairs 1990* noted "The world-renowned Catholic nun did not utter a word of criticism against the regime for its brutal suppression of religion."

> *In 1944, at the age of thirty-three, Enver Hoxha, as Secretary of the Communist Party's Central Committee and Political Commissar of the Army of National Liberation, gained complete control over the government of Albania. He retained this control until his death in 1985. Hoxha ruled with an iron fist. His government imprisoned, executed, and exiled hundreds of thousands of landowners, political opponents, Christian and Moslem clergy members, and peasants who resisted collectivization. Private property was confiscated, all churches and mosques were closed, and all cultural and educational institutions were put to the service of the state. In 1948, Hoxha severed relations with Yugoslavia and formed an alliance with the Soviet Union. After the death of Joseph Stalin, Hoxha's relationship with the USSR began to deteriorate because of his bitter dis-like of Nikita Khrushchev. In 1961, he severed all ties with the Soviet Union and formed an alliance with Mao Tse-tung and the People's Republic of China. In 1978, he abandoned relations with China after the death of Mao and rapprochement with the West. From that time to the end of his rule, he spurned alliances with all other countries, declaring that Albania would become a model socialist republic on its own. In 1981, he ordered the execution of leading party and government officials to ensure the succession of his close comrade, Ramiz Alia.*

Before she departed from Albania, Mother Teresa grasped the hands of Ramiz Alia and said that she was "overjoyed at all the transformations achieved in our country during the forty-five years of people's power." When she made this incredulous statement, Albania was the poorest country in Europe, with a shortage of elec-tricity and water. Most of the people lived in shacks without toilet facilities. Raw sewage was spilled in the open streets. The hospitals were infested with rats and cockroaches and there was a severe shortage of medical supplies, including morphine for cancer patients.

In return for her visit and words of praise, Mother Teresa received a gift of two Motherhouses from the government. Before she arrived in Albania, the communist officials described her in the press as merely a "well-known benefactress of Albanian origin." After she left, she became a national hero, praised for her humanitarian work. Overnight her face appeared on postage stamps and in history books. Albanian officials suddenly became to compare her to Skanderberg, the country's only other heroic figure.

Those who balked at Mother Teresa paying tribute to the persecutor of Christians and the creator of the "world's first atheist state" received this rebuke from the *Albanian Catholic Bulletin:*

> *Those who criticize Mother Teresa for showing respect are ignorant of her philosophy. She is above all a Christian following in the footsteps of Jesus Christ. The heart of the Christian message is forgiveness and, in Mother's own words, "without forgiveness there can be no real love." To view her as a pawn in the government's game is to vastly underestimate this saintly woman, who is above politics, and her lack of bitterness sets an example to us all. Yes, the government used her for public relations but thereby opened the door to forces they were ill prepared to face.*

Reading this rejoinder, Dr. Jack Pregar remarked, "The fact of the matter is that Mother Teresa is prepared to shake hands with any type of murderer who happens to be in political power. For example, when there was a diplomatic reception some two weeks after the coup in Bangladesh, she was lining up with the rest of the diplomatic corps and shaking hands with the new people in power—the very same people who had just murdered fifty of their opponents and will no doubt go on killing future opponents."

Next in her never-ending pursuit of support for her mission, Mother Teresa became a close friend of Charles Keating, the U.S. multimillionaire and financial wheeler-dealer who was sentenced to ten years in prison for his part in a savings and loan scheme that would cost U.S. taxpayers more than five hundred billion dollars in interest.

Christopher Hitchens wrote, "At the height of his success as a thief, Keating made donations (not out of his pocket, of course) to Mother Teresa in the sum of one and a quarter million dollars. He also granted her the use of his private jet. In return, Mother Teresa allowed Keating to make use of her prestige on several important occasions and gave him a personalized crucifix which he took everywhere with him."

When Keating was standing trial in federal court, Mother Teresa wrote to Judge Lance Ito, begging clemency for Keating because of his kindness and generosity to the poor. The letter, dated October 2, 1992, reads:

> *Dear Honorable Lance Ito,*
>
> *We do not mix up in Business or Politicts [sic] or courts. Our work, as Missionaries of Charity, is to give whole-hearted and free service to the poor.*
>
> *I do not know anything about Mr. Charles Keating's work or his business or the matters you are dealing with.*
>
> *I only know that he has always [sic] been kind and generous to God's poor, and always ready to help whenever there was a need. It is for this reason that I do not want to forget him now while he and his family are suffering. Jesus has told us, 'Whatever you do to the least of my brethren. ... YOU DID IT TO ME.' Mr. Keating has done much to help the poor, which is why I am writing to you on his behalf.*
>
> *Whenever someone asks me to speak to a judge, I always tell them the same thing. I ask them to pray, to look in their [sic] heart, and to do what Jesus would do in that circumstance. And this is what I am asking of you, your Honor.*
>
> *My gratitude to you is my prayer for you, and your work, your family and the people with whom you are working.*
>
> *God bless you*
>
> *M. Teresa*

Deputy District Attorney Paul Turley, who was serving as a prosecutor in the Keating case, read the letter and believed that Mother Teresa must have been unaware of the source of the money she had received from Keating. For this reason, he sought to provide the saintly nun with the unambiguous details of Keating's fraud so that she would do the right thing and return the one hundred twenty-five thousand dollars and other gifts. He wrote the following letter:

Dear Mother Teresa:

I am a Deputy District Attorney in Los Angeles County and one of the persons who worked on the prosecution of your benefactor, Charles H. Keating, Jr. I read your letter to Judge Ito, written on behalf of Mr. Keating, which includes your admission that you know nothing about Mr. Keating's business or the criminal charges presented to Judge Ito. I am writing to you to provide a brief explanation of the crimes which Mr. Keating has been convicted, to give you an understanding of the source of the money that Mr. Keating gave to you, and to suggest that you perform the moral and ethical act of returning the money to its rightful owners.

Mr. Keating was convicted of defrauding 17 individuals of more than $900,000. These 17 persons were representative of 17,000 individuals from whom Mr. Keating stole $252,000,000. Mr. Keating's specific acts of fraud were that he was the source of a series of fraudulent representations made to persons who bought bonds from his company and he also was the repository of crucial information which he chose to withhold from bond purchasers, thereby luring his victims into believing they were making a safe, low-risk investment. In truth and in fact, their money was being used to fund Mr. Keating's exorbitant and extravagant lifestyle.

The victims of Mr. Keating's fraud come from a wide spectrum of society. Some were wealthy and well educated. Most were people of modest means and unfamiliar with high finance. One was, indeed, a poor carpenter who did not speak English and had his life savings stolen by Mr. Keating's fraud.

The biblical slogan of your organization is "As long as you did it to one of these My least brethren, You did it to Me." The "least" of the brethren are among those whom Mr. Keating fleeced with flinching. As you well know, divine forgiveness is available to all, but forgiveness must be preceded by admission of sin. Not only has Mr. Keating failed to admit his sins and his crimes, he persists in self-righteously blaming others for his own misdeeds. Your experience is, admirably, with the poor. My experience has been with the "con" man and the perpetrator of the fraud. It is not uncommon for "con" men to be generous with family, friends, and charities. Perhaps they believe that their generosity will purchase love, respect, or forgiveness. However, the time when the purchase of "indulgences" was an acceptable method of seeking forgiveness died with the Reformation. No church, no charity, no organization should allow itself to be used as salve for the conscience of a criminal. We all are grateful that forgiveness is available but we all, also, must perform our duty. That includes the Judge and the Jury. I remind myself of the biblical admonition of the Prophet Micah: "O man, what is good and what does the Lord require of you. To do justice, love mercy and walk humbly."

We are urged to love mercy but we must do justice.

You urge Judge Ito to look into his heart—as he sentences Charles Keating—and do what Jesus would do. I submit the same challenge to you. Ask yourself what Jesus would do if He were given the fruits of a crime; what would Jesus do if He were in possession of money that had been stolen; what Jesus would do if He were being exploited by a thief to ease his conscience?

I submit that Jesus would promptly and unhesitatingly return the stolen money to its rightful owners. You should do the same. You have been given money by Mr. Keating that he has been convicted of stealing by fraud. Do not permit him the "indulgence" he desires. Do not keep the money. Return it to those who worked for it and earned it!

If you contact me I will put you in direct contact with the rightful owners of the property now in your possession.

Sincerely,
Paul W. Turley

Mother Teresa apparently failed to see Jesus in the poor carpenter who did not speak English and had his life savings stolen by Mr. Keating's fraud. The letter from Mr. Turley remained unanswered by Mother Teresa or any member of the Missionaries of Charity. And the money has never been returned.

Chapter 21

The Whirling Dervish

Mother Teresa knew the importance of press attention and traveled every place a major disaster struck, from Ethiopia to Chernobyl. Her photos always appeared among victims of war, hunger, pestilence, and natural disaster. Small wonder that she became seen as an angel of mercy. Her travel, she insisted was part of her mission. "If there are poor on the moon," she said, "we will go there."

As soon as she returned to the Motherhouse in Calcutta from a long journey, she wanted to head out for another. "I have the itch to go," she said. Nothing—not even serious illness—seemed to be able to hold her to one place. Mother Teresa especially experienced the "itch" when the heat and humidity in Calcutta became unbearable. From 1978 until the time of her death, she spent every summer and every monsoon season—barring 1994—in Europe and the United States. Her pattern was to leave Calcutta in early June and return in early October when the torrential downpours finally gave way to mellow weather.

In 1981, she was diagnosed with spondylitis, an acute affection of the vertebrae that caused her to stoop and rounded her shoulders. While being treated for this disease, she suffered her first heart attack. Most people would have been infirm for months, but she was not like most people: She was up and about in days. A look at her agenda for the year she recuperated from heart failure shows her incredible energy and drive. She traveled to Tokyo, Rome, the German Democratic Republic, Glasgow, Venezuela, Rome (again), Venezuela, Dublin, St. Louis, Mexico, and Washington, D.C., where she first met President Ronald Reagan and his wife, Nancy. She also found time to travel to Brazil to address the 72nd Rotary International Convention; to Corrymeela, Northern Ireland, to address a peace conference; and to London for the launching of the International Prayer for Peace. The Prayer, attributed to her, appeared in newspapers throughout the globe:

> Lead me from death to life,
> From falsehood to truth;
> Lead me from despair to hope,
> From fear to trust;
> Lead me from hate to love,
> From war to peace;
> Let peace fill our hearts, our world, our universe.

Later it was discovered that Hindu poet Satish Kumar had composed the lines as a prayer mantra.

Mother Teresa was so involved in global travel and affairs that she neglected to come to the bedside of her brother, Lazar, who died—after repeatedly asking for her—in a hospital in Palermo on July 3, 1981.

The next year, she had the same hectic schedule, with trips to Bangladesh, Japan, Glasgow, London, Mexico, Rome (for a private Mass in the Chapel of Castle Gandolfo with Pope John Paul II), Lebanon (where she performed a heroic rescue in Beirut), Assisi (for the eight hundredth anniversary of the saint), St. Louis for a Right to Life Convention, Dublin for a news conference organized by the Society of the Protection of the Unborn Child, and Caracas, Venezuela. In between, she managed to travel the length and breadth of India several times.

She started 1983 at the same feverish pace with trips to London, the United States, and Rome, where she suffered another heart attack and was confined to the Salvator Mundi Hospital under the care of Dr. Vincenzio Bilotti, a renowned heart specialist. He kept her in his care for several weeks and gave her instructions never to lift another child. Upon her release, she traveled to Poland and next to New York, where she received a gift of a property in the Bronx from Cardinal Cook. Then she headed back to Rome before heading off to East Germany, where she opened a second house, this one in Karl Marx Stadt.

In 1984, she traveled to Rome, where she suffered another weak spell and was confined again to a hospital bed. Then doctors told Mother Teresa that she must avoid climbing stairs. Nevertheless, she managed to tour Poland and Eastern Europe, attend the funeral of Indira Gandhi, travel to her homes throughout India, and visit Bhopal in Madhya Pradish in the wake of the industrial disaster that instantly killed two thousand five hundred people.

At the start of 1985, Mother Teresa visited her missions in Ethiopia, including the famine-stricken province of Wollo. On this trip, she met the pop singer Bob Geldorf of The Boomtown Rats, who was raising money for the starving children of Africa under a project called "Band-Aid." Geldorf, who can barely utter a sentence without a slew of profanities and who has lived a lifestyle decadent even by MTV standards, struck up a friendship with the old nun. Later, Geldorf said that he was astonished by her appearance and her uncanny ability to manipulate the media with a "frail old lady shtick." He said, "She is astonishingly tiny. When I went to greet her I found that I towered more than two feet above her. She was a battered, wizened woman. The thing that struck me most forcefully was her feet. Her habit was clean and well cared for, but her sandals were beaten up pieces of leather from which her feet protruded, gnarled and misshapen as old tree roots." Geldorf said that he bent to kiss her because it seemed the proper protocol. "She bowed her head so swiftly," he recalled, "that I was obliged to kiss the top of her wimple. It disturbed me. I found out later that she only lets lepers kiss her."

From Africa, she went to Washington, D.C., to attend a conference on AIDS, made a stop at the "Gift of Love" in the Bronx, and headed off to Cuba to meet Fidel Castro. In 1986, she opened a home in Cuba at Castro's request, visited the Sudan where a bloody civil war was raging, and made a stop at Tanzania, where she became part of a particularly gruesome accident. After visiting the Sisters, who were working in the Mathari Valley, one of the poorest sections of Nairobi, Mother Teresa boarded a light aircraft to head off to Kenya. The aircraft, gathering speed for take-off, veered off the runaway and into the crowd of people who were waving good-bye. Five victims—including three small children— were cut to pieces by the plane's propellers. The press reported Mother Teresa as saying, "My coming is behind the accident." She went on to Rome, Assisi, and Cuba (again) with yet another visit with her new friend Fidel.

While planning a trip to Japan in 1987, Mother Teresa suffered another heart attack and was forced to cancel her plans. She dispatched this letter:

> Dear Japanese people,
>
> I have been looking forward to come to you all. As you know, I am suffering from heart [sic] and found that I will not be able to make the journey and do the work there during these days. That's why I had at the last moment to cancel my going to Tokyo. I would have loved to be with you all but I think physically I will not be able to do it. But my message to you all is that God has a special love for the people of Japan.
>
> And the message is to love one another as God loves each one and this love begins at home. The family that prays together stays together and if you stay together you will love one another as God loves each one of you.
>
> This is my prayer for you that through this love for one another, you grow in the love of God.
>
> God bless you and keep you in his heart.
>
> Mother Teresa

Despite this setback, Mother Teresa managed to make trips to San Francisco, New York, Austria, Poland, Africa, London (for her encounter with Margaret Thatcher), and the Soviet Union, where she met with survivors of the Chernobyl disaster and received the Gold Medal of the Soviet Peace Committee. Soviet officials gave her permission to open a home of the Missionaries of Charity in Moscow.

The globe-trotting continued the following year with trips to Africa; to the India-Nepal border, to visit victims of a massive earthquake that left eight hundred dead; to Armenia, the site of another major earthquake; and finally to Moscow, where she received permission from Soviet officials to establish a home of the Missionaries of Charity in Moscow. This gesture was significant because all religious organizations had been banished from the USSR since the time of the Revolution.

In 1989, Mother Teresa set off for Budapest, Peru, Switzerland, and Albania. When she returned to Calcutta in September, she suffered a near-fatal heart attack, underwent heart surgery, and was fitted with a pacemaker.

The frantic, almost frenetic, travel was essential to promulgate Mother Teresa's image as a "living saint." The visits always resulted in photo sessions and opportunities to make pious pronouncements about the "poorest of the poor" to foreign dignitaries and members of the press. With ubiquity came her aura of transcendence over every race and nationality, over every political ideology and system of government. Wherever she went, Mother Teresa was greeted as a figure of reverence. When she spoke about her work, few questioned the veracity of her statements—not even the most outlandish claim or the most self-contradictory pronouncement. It was assumed by everybody that such a holy and devout nun would ever mouth a mendacity.

But many of her statements were blatantly untrue, if not self-serving fabrications. Raising funds in London in 1977, Mother Teresa said: "We spend 20,000 rupees a week just on food at the fifty-nine centers we have in Calcutta." Fifty-one centers in one city would represent the most massive social and religious undertaking in human history. But no one questioned the veracity of this statement—not even the most hard-nosed reporter from London's daily tabloids. Nor was the statement about the fifty-one centers a simple slip of the tongue. She went on in the same speech to say, "They (the Sisters) go all over the city—in Calcutta alone, we have fifty-one centers, the home of the dying is only one of them. The Sisters travel everywhere with a rosary in their hand." But the Missionaries of Charity, in truth, operated and continue to operate less than seven centers, including the residences for the Sisters, in the city of joy. The fact that no one—not even the public officials of Calcutta—took her to task for this claim is cause of wonder. In 1979, she upbraided the Indian Prime Minister Morarji Desai for refusing to outlaw abortion in India. In a letter that appeared in newspapers throughout the country, Mother Teresa wrote: "In Calcutta alone we have one hundred and two centers where families are taught self control out of love." No one asked the location of these centers, what services the centers provided, or how these centers obtained financial support. Thirteen years later, Father Edward Le Joly, a spokesperson for the Missionaries of Charity and another figure whom Mother Teresa called her "second self," gave the global total of the Missionaries of Charity family planning centers as sixty-nine. Father Le Joly further admitted that none existed in Calcutta.

Never taken to task for misstatements, Mother Teresa had the temerity to provide false figures not only to the international press but also to the distinguished members of the Nobel Prize Committee. Accepting her award in 1979, Mother Teresa said that members of her religious order "picked up" over thirty-five thousand dying men, women and children for care at Nirmal Hriday. Strange to say, no one took the time and effort to verify this claim. A mere visit to the Home of the Dying by any public official or member of the press would have revealed that the facility only possessed the capability to care for ninety-five patients and that only four to five hundred new patients are admitted each year.

Similarly, even a casual observer visiting Calcutta would realize that the Missionaries of Charity actually "picked up" few, if any, people from the streets, since the fleet of ambulances that were donated to the religious order had been stripped of all provisions to carry stretchers and to administer emergency medical care. Although the ambulances retained sirens and flashing red beacons, they were used solely to transport the religious sisters from one section of the city to another. Indeed, if anyone called the Missionaries of Charity to pick up a dying beggar, the caller would have been told to contact a city ambulance by dialing 102.

Yet throughout her life, Mother Teresa would perpetuate the myth of sisters combing the wretched slums of Calcutta day and night in search of poor souls in need of a place to die with dignity. In December 1989, she told *Time* magazine that her order had "picked up" more than fifty-four thousand for care at Nirmal Hriday and that "23,000 something" had died in peace. Volunteers who journey to Calcutta to assist in the work of the Missionaries of Charity are inevitably disappointed that they can't act as part of an angelic team to scrape up the dying dregs of the poorest of the poor from the gutters of the city.

Despite the fact that the ambulances of the Missionaries of Charity merely served as taxis for the sisters, one ambulance remained parked at the entrance of Nirmal Hriday day and night. But the vehicle served as window dressing. Once a day, the ambulance left the parking spot. At precisely 3:45 P.M., it departed from the Home of the Dying to transport ten or twelve sisters, who had completed their work for the day, to the Motherhouse for religious devotions.

Regarding the work of the sisters at the Home of the Dying, Mother Teresa said, "The sisters go out at night to work, to pick up people from the street." But this was not the case in Calcutta. Until 1995, Nirmal Hriday did not have any sisters staying overnight to provide comfort and solace to the sick and dying. The patients were left to the mercy of two or three janitors.

There were other facts and figures that Mother Teresa twisted in order to enhance her image. In 1983, she told Kathryn Spink, her friend and biographer, "In Calcutta alone, we cook for 7,000 people every day and if one day we do not cook they do not eat. Several years later, she told Jose Luis Gonzalez-Bolodo, another friend and biographer, "You must know that just in Calcutta we feed 9,000 daily. But the kitchens of the Missionaries of Charity in Calcutta, according to a member of the religious order, never prepared meals for more than five hundred on any given day, and that figure including not only those in need but Mother Teresa's vast army of sisters, novices, brothers and volunteers. Realizing the problem with Mother Teresa's figures, Gonzalez-Bolodo attempted to explain her exaggerated claims by writing, "Mother Teresa is among those who least worry about statistics. She has recently expressed that what matters is not how much work is accomplished but how much love is put into the work."

Similarly, she told the press—including Malcolm Muggeridge in the interview that skyrocketed her to international fame—that the Missionaries of Charity received no financial support from government agencies or the Roman Catholic Church. "We depend solely on providence," she said. "We don't accept Church donations." The statement was untrue. Over ninety-five percent of the buildings and land received by Mother Teresa for her work among "the poorest of the poor" came as grants or loans from the state or the Church. Nirmal Hriday had been obtained free and clear from the Calcutta Corporation and, for many years, this public organization subsidized the on-going operation of the Home of the Dying by payments for every patient.

Above the entrance of the Home of the Dying was a sign that read, "Corporation of Calcutta, Nirmal Hriday." Mother Teresa received Dum Dum, her shelter for homeless boys, from the West Bengal state government, along with the vast tracts of land for her leprosaria. The Motherhouse at 54A Lower Circular Road had been purchased by the Archbishop of Calcutta with church funds. Mother Teresa's order also received from the church two other properties in Calcutta, one by the Sealdah railway station and the other on expensive Park Avenue in the "white" section of the city.

The one property that she did not receive from public or parochial sources was a hone in the Tangra section of Calcutta. Mother Teresa would claim that her order was obliged to rent this property. But later it was discovered that the land was leased by the Missionaries of Charity from the government at the rate of one rupee (one and a half cents) a year. Mother Teresa confided to Father Le Joly, "It is good that the ownership of the land remains with them (the government) because if the roads need repairs, they will have to do it, as it is their property."

The fanciful stories about the tireless and Herculean acts of charity by Mother Teresa were also perpetuated by friends and admirers who penned flowery and reverential books that were based solely upon her fractured facts and bloated figures. Some of these accounts are so bizarre and naïve that even the most accepting and uncritical readers must shake their heads with disbelief.

In "For the Love of God: Mother Teresa of Calcutta," father Georges Goree, yet another "second self," tells of the vigilant search by Mother Teresa and her sisters for fetuses in the streets of Calcutta. He writes: "… in the dustbins, the drains, under the bus seats, there were living fetuses given to the dogs to eat." Anyone who has attempted to board a bus in Calcutta knows that the vehicles are so crowded that a fly could scarcely find room, let alone a pack of stray dogs. In "Meditations by Mother Teresa," Sean Patrick Lovett writes of a leprosy hospital operated by the Missionaries of Charity within the confines of Calcutta. He even manages to describe an inscription above the entrance. But no such hospital exists in Calcutta or anywhere else.

To the end of her life, Mother Teresa would twist the truth in many of her public pronouncements. On June 18, 1996, she traveled to Swansea to open her first center in Wales. She told the press and the local dignitaries that the center would provide care and counseling to victims of AIDS and other incurable diseases. But the telephone number for the center remained unlisted and the sisters who lived in the center remained in cloistered seclusion. A priest at nearby St. Joseph's Cathedral said, "The nuns don't do any counseling; their only charitable work is visiting the elderly at home."

Why did she make such fantastic claims and such outrageous pronouncements? It appears that her intent was to inflate the magnitude of her work and her status as a Christian saint. The amazing thing is that Mother Teresa remained beyond reproach until 1994 with the airing of a program called "Hell's Angel" in Great Britain. Until that time, no one attempted to question the veracity of the old, wrinkled and kindly nun who was hailed as the "holiest person in the world."

President and Mrs. Reagan say good-bye to Mother Teresa after
a lunch in the White House.

Chapter 22

Nun's Last Run

By 1990, Mother Teresa could barely walk without assistance. She visited her homes throughout Calcutta in her Black Maria. Inside the specially equipped vehicle was an easy chair and several attendants to provide medical care and administer oxygen, when necessary. Sister Gertrude, a trained physician, became Mother Teresa's constant companion in all of her excursions outside the Motherhouse.

She now informed the pope that she wished to resign as Superior General, but the Sisters, when they gathered for an election, became deadlocked in the choice of a successor. One Sister argued that a younger and more active leader was needed because there existed a danger that "the good work of Mother Teresa will be negated by her ill health." The words fell on deaf ears. One Sister working at Mother Teresa's home in the Vatican later said that if Mother Teresa had resigned, she would have been able to attend to the internal affairs of her order and, thereby, to avoid much of the misery and criticism that lay ahead.

In terms of the opening of new homes for the Missionaries of Charity in Communist countries, 1990 was particularly fruitful. By the spring, she had opened five houses—two in Moscow, two in Albania, and one in Georgia—and had received permission from Fidel Castro to increase the number of houses in Cuba from four to seven. She established the first soup kitchen in Budapest and a children's home in Bucharest.

The following year, she set off for Washington, D.C.; Cambodia; Rome; and, finally, Albania, where the government gave her several properties to serve as homes and shelters. In Tirana, she attended the reopening Mass of the Cathedral Church of the Sacred Heart that had served as a movie theater since the ban on churches had been imposed in 1945. After the Mass, she informed President Ramiz Alia that his government should reopen a few mosques for the Moslems.

From Albania, she visited Romania to visit her newly established houses for handicapped and retarded children and then set off to establish more homes for the homeless in the United States.

In 1992, after a stay in Los Angeles where the Sisters were suffering from a particularly virulent form of the flu, Mother Teresa flew to Tijuana to open a new house. At Tijuana, she became ill and was diagnosed as suffering from bacterial pneumonia. The hospital at Tijuana was no place for such a celebrated figure. She was transported to the Scripps Clinic and Foundation, one of the most prestigious and expensive medical facilities in the world, where doctors performed a balloon angioplasty to force open a blocked blood vessel.

Later that year, Mother Teresa traveled to Iraq on behalf of the United Nations to visit with Saddam Hussein. In Baghdad, she made plans to open a mission to care for the thousands who had been left wounded or homeless by Operation Desert Storm. Before the national press, with Hussein by her side, Mother Teresa said, "The fruit of war is so terrible, one cannot understand how any human being can do that to another—and for what?" She also met with Minister of Health Mohammed Sai to make arrangements for the shipment of food and medical supplies to offset the effects of the boycott. No one in the United States or the United Nations accused her of aiding and abetting the enemy.

The following year, she traveled to Belgium to celebrate the eightieth birthday of her old friend Jacqueline De Decker and to dissolve the International Association of Co-Workers.

From there, the wandering nun went to Ireland to speak to a Pro-Life Convention. She said, "Let us make one strong resolution that in this beautiful country of Ireland no child may be unwanted. Let us promise Our Lady who loves Ireland so that we will never have in this country one single abortion. Let us promise that there will be no more divorce." Two days later, she received the Freedom of the City of Dublin Award and headed off to Edinburgh and London.

Next came a series of severe setbacks. From London, she returned to Rome, where she fell and broke several ribs. In July, she collapsed from exhaustion in Calcutta and was placed in a Bombay hospital. One month later, when she was in New Delhi to receive yet another award, she suffered an attack of malaria and was treated at the All-India Institute of Medical Science. On September 17, Mother Teresa was once more struggling for her life as doctors opened another blocked heart vessel and told the press that she had "a close call." She was no longer traveling from country to country, but from hospital bed to hospital bed. Pope John Paul II sent her a note that said, "The whole world needs you."

While in the hospital, Mother Teresa received word of the death of her old friend and mentor, Father Celeste Van Exem, who had drafted the constitution for her religious order and guided her through difficult times with the Church hierarchy. "He had gone straight to God," she said. "He was a very holy man."

On September 15, four days before his death, Father Celeste sent this letter to Mother Teresa:

Dear Mother,

Tomorrow morning I shall say Holy Mass for the following intercessions:

1. That you may have no operation.

2. That you may be in China by the 7 October 1993.

3. That the Lord may take me and not you if that is His will. His will, not mine.

I am with you and the Sisters, all of them. There is a Calvary for every Christian. For you the way to Calvary is long. But Mary has met you in the road. You did not go up the hill, this is for later.

I adore the Blessed Sacrament which, I am sure, you have in your room.

*Pray for me and all my companions, especially the
companions of Jesus Christ.
Very sincerely in O.L.
C. Van Exem, SJ*

At the end of October 1993, Mother Teresa arrived in China to open the "final door" of her spiritual journey. Here she wanted to establish yet another home so that her Missionaries of Charity would be in every major city of every country in God's creation. For once, her efforts ended in failure. The Chinese officials said there was no need for Mother Teresa to establish a mission in China because the government takes care of the poor and needy. She was devastated. Never before had she been denied a request by any world leader. And this was to be her final miracle, the last tangible proof of her incredible charisma. As a final insult she met with Chinese leader Deng Xiaoping's paraplegic son, Deng Pufang, an atheist, who rebuked her offer of prayers by saying that God cares neither for the handicapped nor old nuns.

Yet heaven continued to smile upon Mother Teresa. She may not have been everywhere when disaster struck, but she was credited with being everywhere and providing help no one else on earth would offer. On September 30, 1993, an earthquake devastated Latur in the western Indian state of Maharashtra. It was one of the country's greatest natural disasters. Five million people lost their homes and possessions, and over eight thousand were killed. But the Missionaries of Charity, along with Mother Teresa, failed to appear at the scene. Similarly, Mother Teresa's order offered no assistance to the victims of other disasters in India, including an earthquake in Uttarkashi at the foothills of the Himalayas that killed over fifteen hundred in October 20, 1991, and a flood in West Bengal on October 11, 1995, that left over three million homeless.

Nevertheless, Mother Teresa managed to gain good press from these calamities. Indian officials were criticized for being slow in spending the $246 million loan that the government of India had received from The World Bank for victims of the Latur earthquake. To gain a modicum of good publicity, the officials sought out Mother Teresa, who had stopped in Bombay on her way to

Rome. They asked her to present deeds for newly constructed houses to the earthquake victims. Mother Teresa complied. Photographs appeared in newspapers throughout the world of the old nun passing out deeds to smiling villagers. One photo carried the caption, "All in a day's work for Mother Teresa." Nearly everyone assumed that the gifts of these properties were being provided by the goodness of the saintly old nun and not the inept government.

Instead of coming to the aid of the people of Latur, Mother Teresa traveled to the United States to come to the aid of Alexander Loce, who had been arrested for trespassing in an abortion clinic in an effort to prevent his former girlfriend from having an abortion. She filed an *amicus curiae* even though she was not an American citizen. She told the court, "Like that unborn child, I can be considered an outsider. I am not an American citizen. In so many senses, I know what it is like to be without a country. I also know what it is like to be an adopted citizen of many lands."

But Mother Teresa's season in the sun was coming to an abrupt end. In 1994, all hell broke loose. *Hell's Angel*, a scathing documentary on Mother Teresa, was aired on Channel IV in Great Britain. During the program, commentator and journalist Christopher Hitchens showed news footage of Mother Teresa with "Baby Doc" Duvalier, Robert Maxwell, Charles Keating, Hillary Clinton, and Washington, D.C., Mayor Marion Barry, and then accused the "leathery old saint" of "simpering to world leaders and wealthy businesspeople rather than serving those most-in-need."

Hitchens said, "For someone whose kingdom is not of this earth, Mother Teresa has an easy way with thrones, dominions, and powers." He accused her of spending millions on convents rather than hospitals and of serving as "a roving ambassador of a highly publicized papacy." He concluded the program by saying:

> In a godless and cynical age it may be inevitable that people will seek to praise the self-effacing, the altruistic, and the pure at heart. But only a complete collapse of our critical faculties can explain the illusion that such a person is manifested in the shape of a demagogue, an obscurantist, and a servant of earthly powers.

Calls flooded the station calling the program insulting, blasphemous, sacrilegious, obnoxious, disgusting, sick, satanic, and ungodly. But everyone did not denounce the broadcast. Hugh Hubert, a reviewer for *The Guardian*, wrote:

> Hitchens is right to question the Teresa cult. Idolatry is bad for us, canonization of the living worse. But despite the air of smug self-congratulation that is habitual to the professional iconoclast, he unwittingly reminds us that, as conscience salvers go, our credit card charity is cheap at the price. So Hitchens, the gadfly reporter of Vanity Fair, becomes another of Mother Teresa's accomplices.

Appearing on the popular Indian talk show *Ananda Bazar Patrika*, Mother Teresa, looking old and haggard, said, "It is for you to decide how you want to live. As far as I am concerned, I know that I have to keep doing my work." She went on to say that she forgave the program producer, Tariq Ali, and Hitchens not on behalf of God, but on behalf of herself. Hitchens responded by saying, "This was odd, since we had not sought forgiveness from her or from anyone else. Odder still if you have any inclination to ask by what right she assumes the power to forgive. There are even some conscientious Christians who would say that forgiveness, like the astringent of revenge, is reserved to a higher power."

In the same year, she attended a "National Prayer Breakfast" in Washington, where she gave a very long speech before President Bill Clinton and First Lady Hilary Clinton about the sanctity of human life and the evil of abortion. At the end of her address, no one at the front table where President and Mrs. Clinton were sitting applauded. To compound her misery, Mother Teresa visited one of her homes in Delhi and was bitten by a dog. She was forced to receive several stitches and a course of antirabies injections.

But things went from bad to worse. The year 1995 began with the publication of *The Missionary Position: Mother Teresa in Theory and Practice*, by Christopher Hitchens. It became an international best-seller. The Sisters at the Motherhouse in Calcutta told the press that their leader was going through the same trials and tribulations as Jesus Christ.

The book opened a floodgate of harsh criticism that seemed to have been pent up against Mother Teresa for decades. Some came from Co-Workers and Sisters who had left the order. One particularly damning story appeared in the *Calcutta Telegraph*. It concerned Shahida Kapoor, a fifteen-year-old pavement dweller who was married with a child. While cooking a meal in her *chula*, her sari caught on fire and Shahida became engulfed in flames. Dr. Amitabha Das, a doctor from the charitable organization HEAL, found her some days later lying outside the Calcutta Corporation building with third-degree burns and severe cuts to one arm. She had been begging the Corporation for help. After examining her, Dr. Das said, "Though the immunity of pave dwellers is high, bacteraemia and other infections could set in at any time and she will die. She needs skin grafting. Otherwise, she will develop contracture, that is, her calves will get stuck to her lower legs." He managed to have the young woman admitted to an overcrowded government hospital. But without money, Shahida was unable to pay for medication. One month later, she was back in the gutter. The wound had become infected. It had turned green and the young girl was unable to stop the bleeding and to keep flies from covering every inch of her body. She sought out the help of Meher Murshed, a reporter at *The Calcutta Telegraph*. "The pain is so great," she said, "and even when I try to sit up, blood trickles down my legs." Murshed contacted the Missionaries of Charity.

An ambulance was dispatched and Shahida was taken, with Murshed, to Mother Teresa's homes: Kalighat, Shishu Bhawan, and Prem Dan.

At Kalighat, Shahida was turned away because she was not dying. At Shishu Bhawan, she was denied entrance because she was not an orphan. At Prem Dan, she was turned away because she was neither insane nor suffering from tuberculosis. In the end, she landed back in the streets without any place to turn for assistance. She was found dead a few weeks later.

While this was happening, Mother Teresa was meeting in Washington with Senator Bob Dole. She gave the Senator a "miraculous medal" and a card that read:

The fruit of silence is prayer.
The fruit of prayer is faith.
The fruit of faith is love.
The fruit of love is service
The fruit of service is peace.

Meher Murshed had written the first negative story about Mother Teresa to appear in India. Others would follow in the pages of the Indian newspapers.

One such story that appeared on August 30, 1996, concerned Noor Jehan, a poor young woman, and her children who had been ousted from Shishu Bhawan, Mother Teresa's orphanage in Calcutta. Driven from her shack near the Hoogly River by her violent husband, Noor Jehan and her two small girls, one aged two months, the other two years, had no food and no place to live. They were directed to Shishu Bhawan, where they were admitted by the night porter and permitted to sleep in the courtyard.

At 5 A.M., the poor family was awakened by the sisters and tossed out in the streets. Noor Jehan begged and pleaded to be let in, but the doors remained shut and locked. Local shopkeepers took pity on the woman and her children and gave them milk and bread. Bystanders, outraged at the behavior of the sisters, banged on the door and demanded an explanation. The sisters said that they could not provide for the family unless the mother signed over complete custody of her children to the Missionaries of Charity. Such a form, the sisters said, only required the imprint of Noor Jehan's left thumb.

But Noor Jehan refused to relinquish custody of her children. The door of Shishu Bhawan remained locked until the poor family disappeared in the mean streets of Calcutta never to be heard of again. The incident, as the story in *The Telegraph* pointed out, contradicted Mother Teresa's oft-quoted claim: "There is always room for another child in my house."

Still more bad press was to follow. On November 18, 1996, Mother Teresa attended a prayer service at the Sacred Heart Cathedral in Delhi to launch a nationwide campaign to demand Scheduled Caste status for Christian Dalits, or Untouchables.

With such status, they would be eligible for entitlement programs like their Hindu counterparts.

> The Untouchables in the Indian cast system call themselves the "Dalits," literally "the depressed ones." Until the late 1980s, they were called the Harijan, meaning the "children of God." This name was given to them by Mahatma Gandhi. According to Indian government policy, the Dalits are entitled to positive discrimination. Fifteen percent of all government jobs must be allotted to them, and fifteen percent of the students in any public school or college must come from this caste. Tension in modern India has been created by these policies. First, Moslem and Sikh Dalits demanded these entitlements, and the government acquiesced. Second, high-caste communities complained that they were victims of reverse discrimination because of this arbitrary quota system. Despite this controversial policy, most of the degrading jobs are performed by Dalits, while the Brahmans remain at the top of the hierarchy as doctors, lawyers, professors, engineers, and business executives.

The government refused to grant Christian Dalits Scheduled Caste (SC) by stating that once a person becomes a Christian, his caste becomes irrelevant. Indeed, much of the appeal of Christianity to the poor of India resided in the claim that once they became Christians, caste no longer mattered and they were no longer "untouchables." Vir Sanghi, a leading religious commentator in India, wrote, "This is the argument that is always offered to prospective converts and to thousands of children in convent school in India. How can anybody claim that there is a caste of Christians who are so low down the religious ladder that they deserve the same affirmative action as Hinduism's unfortunate Harijans? If they are Christians they can't be Dalits. If they are Dalits, then they are Hindus and Mother Teresa has nothing to do with them."

The issue over Scheduled Caste status for Christian Dalits resulted in bloody riots throughout the country, and Mother Teresa's involvement aroused the rage of Hindu nationalists. In a widely syndicated article, Sushma Swaraj tore into Mother Teresa and her involvement in the prayer service, writing, "Christianity does not recognize Chaturbvarna which creates untouchables.

Instead of fighting this evil practice, Mother Teresa has introduced it into her own religion. The very basis of Christianity is a caste-less society. We believe the demand will do no good to society, the country, or her own religion and definitely not to Harijans."

Rather than letting the matter simmer, Mother Teresa added fuel to the fire by holding a press conference to refute the charges and to insist that she had no idea what the prayer service was all about when she attended it. "I realized only later that a demonstration demanding reservations was taking place," she told the reporters.

By making this statement, Mother Teresa infuriated the Dalit Christians, the very Christians she was supposed to represent. In an effort to clarify matters, Father S. Lourduswarmy, secretary of the National Coordination Committee for Scheduled Caste Christians, issued this statement about Mother Teresa and her involvement at the prayer meeting:

A written invitation was sent to Mother on 1 November by the Most Reverend Alan de Lastic, Archbishop of Delhi. After she accepted the invitation, Bishop Vincent Consessao, Auxiliary Bishop of the Archdiocese of Delhi, met her and explained to her that the purpose of the meeting was to demand equal justice for Scheduled Caste Christians. Then Brother Jose Daniel, convener of the program, also briefed her.

What's more, the Bishop of Delhi had even sent Mother a background paper on the issue explaining why reservation was necessary even for Christian converts. After all of this, if Mother Teresa had still failed to grasp the nature of the meeting she was attending, then she was even more otherworldly than had been previously believed.

Mother Teresa had created a mess. One of her most vocal critics in this affair was the Rev. Somen Das, who said, "I feel she has been foolish to apologize and backtrack. It is as if she was suffering from severe amnesia. We should take her words with a pinch of salt and forget about it. The fact is that Mother Teresa, with her impractical views on abortion and family planning, is quite obsolete now."

Obsolete! The words couldn't have been more biting. The woman who devoted her life to serving the poorest of the poor was being denigrated as an obsolete amnesiac by her fellow Christians in her beloved country, the country that once called her "Mother."

Still, there were more awards and honors—the papal award *Pro Ecclesia et Pontifice* and the U. Thant Award for her "sleepless service to humanity." And there were more trips—to the Maharashtra region of central India to aid victims of an earthquake, to California to plead for the life of a killer on death row, to Rwanda in the wake of a bloodbath, and to Wales to open the 565th home of her religious order.

But the health problems became insurmountable. In June 1996, she fell out of bed and broke her collarbone. Three months later, she landed in the Woodlands Nursing Home after another heart attack. Her heart stopped beating every time she was taken off a respirator. Last rites were administered. By the end of September, she was pronounced well enough to return to the Motherhouse. In November, she was rushed to the B. M. Birla Heart Institute, where blockages were removed from two arteries.

Even these incidents became targets of criticism. Hitchens and others pointed out that Mother Teresa received treatment by the finest physicians in the most expensive medical facilities while the dying in Kalighat were placed on stretchers and denied simple painkillers.

In January 1997, Mother Teresa officially resigned as Superior General of the Missionaries of Charity. She was replaced by Sister Nirmala, a Hindu convert from a Brahman family. Sister Nirmala's first trip outside India as the new leader of the order was to Nairobi (not China, as Mother Teresa may have wished), to open a new children's home. At the airport, she was greeted by a Jesuit priest who said, "Mother Nirmala, welcome to Nairobi and Africa." She corrected him by saying, "Father, please call me Sister Nirmala because we have only one mother, Mother Teresa."

On April 9, 1997, Sister Agnes, the first Sister to join the Missionaries of Charity, died of cancer. But, as usual, Mother Teresa displayed no outward sign of affection at the loss of a loved one or close companion.

In the late summer of 1997, Mother Teresa experienced heart problems and was again rushed to the B. M. Birla Heart Institute for additional treatment. At the hospital, she came into contact with Archbishop Henry D'Souza of Calcutta who was undergoing similar treatment. The doctor treating Mother Teresa reported that she was having trouble sleeping. "There was no medical reason for that," Archbishop D'Souza later told Chandra Banerjee of the Associated Press. "It struck me that there was some evil spirit which was trying to disturb her." The Archbishop visited Mother Teresa who requested an exorcism. A priest, with training in the casting out of evil spirits, was summoned to Mother Teresa's bedside and an exorcism was performed. After the ritual, Archbishop D'Souza said, Mother Teresa participated in a "prayer of protection" and "slept peacefully after that."

Attempting to downplay the significance of the exorcism, Archbishop D'Souza said that Mother Teresa's need for an exorcism was a sign of her humanity. "Mother Teresa was not possessed ... it did not hurt her sanctity," he said. "Human dimension in a saint is quite normal. It was rather a sign of closeness to God."

But Catholic experts do not accept Archbishop D'Souza's argument. The Reverend Richard McBrien, a professor of theology at Notre Dame, called the exorcism and the archbishop's explanation of it "bizarre." He said that exorcism is used only when a person is believed to be possessed by the devil. Scott Appleby, director of the Cushwa Center for the Study of American Catholicism at Notre Dame, said that exorcism is extremely rare in the Roman Catholic Church and is only employed in dire circumstances when no psychological or physical explanation can be found for dramatic personality changes.

On Friday, September 5, several days after the exorcism, the exhausted heart of Mother Teresa finally gave out. Her body was conveyed to the chapel of the Motherhouse, where only invited guests were permitted to view it.

Chapter 23

Saint Teresa

Of course, she will be a saint. In popular piety, she already has been canonized. This is evident by the titles of the books that have appeared about her: *Something Beautiful for God*, by Malcolm Muggeridge; *Mother Teresa: Helping the Poor*, by William Jay Jacobs; *Mother Teresa: The Glorious Years* and *Mother Teresa: A Woman in Love*, by Edward Le Jolly; *Mother Teresa: Protector of the Sick*, by Linda Carlson Jackson; *Mother Teresa: Servant to the World's Suffering People*, by Susan Ulstein; *Mother Teresa: Friend of the Friendless*, by Carol Greene; and *Mother Teresa: Caring for All God's Children*. Coupled with these are *Mother Teresa: The Authorized Biography*, by Navin Chawla, and *Mother Teresa: A Complete Authorized Biography*, by Kathryn Spink. If you read the titles out loud, Christopher Hitchens points out, you seem to be engaging a litany to the Blessed Virgin Mary or forming a new version of the "Hail Mary" that focuses on Holy Teresa.

Sure, there are stumbling blocks. Mother Teresa sought to renounce her vows and to become a secular social worker. She made statements that smack of unorthodoxy, including her belief in the validity of all religious expressions and her denial of the exclusivity of the Christian claim to the truth.

And there are things that must be overlooked, such as her embarrassing statements about "Baby Doc" Duvalier and Albanian dictator Enver Hoxha; the photographs of her smiling face with Fidel Castro, Saddam Hussein, and Yasser Arafat; her support of such scoundrels as Charles Keating; and her many misstatements and distortion of the truth.

Sure, there are other problems, including the exorcism and the bizarre possibility that the greatest saint of the twentieth century might have been possessed by a devil. But such things pale in comparison to her achievement. At the time of her death, the Missionaries of Charity boasted more than four thousand Sisters working in six hundred homes in one hundred thirty countries.

The process of canonization usually begins at a minimum of five years after an exemplary figure's death with the presentation of a petition to the Vatican, pleading that a "clause" (an ecclesiastical word for "case") be opened. Such petitions are rarely approved quickly. An initial examination of the merits of the petition must be conducted, simply to substantiate the person's reputation for holiness. Some cases are not opened for more than one hundred years, as is the case of Father Michael J. McGivney, the founder of the Knights of Columbus. Mother Teresa's petition, however, has received special priority and approval of her petition for sainthood has already been approved.

> In the eighteenth century, Pope Benedict IV produced the definitive book on canonization. Called The Beatification of the Servants of God and the Canonization of the Beatified, the four-volume work laid down requirements for sainthood that remain in effect to the present day. The three basic requirements are as follows:
>
>   a. Doctrinal purity
>
>   b. Heroic virtue
>
>   c. Miraculous intercession after death
>
> The process often takes hundreds of years and is quite expensive. The average cost for sainthood now exceeds two million dollars.

Once the Vatican declares that the clause can proceed, the candidate for sainthood is granted a temporary title of "Servant of God." Next comes research into the person's life by a Vatican team of censors who pour over every aspect of the candidate's life and everything the candidate has ever written—every letter, every document, and every speech. Because of the high level of scrutiny, not many subjects for sainthood have engaged in theological or philosophical speculation. This process, too, has been accelerated because of Mother Teresa's tremendous following.

Following the inspection by censors, witnesses are called before a papal tribunal. In Mother's Teresa case, the Sisters who worked with her throughout the years already have been summoned and provided testimony of her holiness.

After this testimony has been gathered, the Vatican appoints a committee to write a *positio* or "position paper" about the subject. The first section of this study consists of a detailed biography. The second provides evidence of her faith, piety, and charity. In August 2001, the *positio* on Mother Teresa was submitted to the Vatican. It numbered more than thirty-five thousand pages.

The next step in the process will be the exhumation of her body. Her remains will be studied for weeks by a team of forensic experts. They will look for special marks or signs. They also will establish proof of her virginity.

Along with this forensic evidence, the position paper will be submitted to the Vatican's Congregation for the Causes of Saints, a committee consisting of twenty-five cardinals and bishops. If the committee approves of the findings, the name of Mother Teresa will be submitted to the pope, who must provide his agreement. When this happens, Mother Teresa will receive the title "Venerable." Following this, she must be beatified.

Beatification is a papal decree that permits Catholics to venerate or to offer petitions to a person after his death. It is a preliminary step to canonization, although it does not guarantee sainthood. To be beatified, Mother Teresa must perform a miracle *after* her death, which will offer tangible proof that she is with God in heaven. Regarding the miracles that will be expected of Mother Teresa, Father Peter Gumpel, a member of the Vatican's saint-making commission, said, "We do not accept any cure as a miracle unless we are scientifically, humanly certain that the cure has been instantaneous, not expected, and complete. If God intervenes and works a miracle, He doesn't do it halfway."

If all goes well and if the dead Agnes Gonxha Bojaxhiu is alive in heaven and performs a miracle of two, she will receive the title "blessed" and her "cult" (or "following of supporters") will receive papal approval.

When all this is accomplished and more than two miracles are verified, the pope will pronounce Mother Teresa a saint. Her name will be listed among the "holy ones" who stand in the presence of God and submit petitions and pleas of residents of "this vale of tears" who call upon them for divine intercession. Her remains will become incredibly valuable—strands of her hair, swatches of her sari, beads from her Rosary, and her rare and sanctified bones will become relics to bless ordinary people, including, as she would have wanted, the "poorest of the poor."

Mother Teresa in prayer several days before her death.

Appendix A

Letter to Bush

L etter written by Mother Teresa to U.S. President George Bush and Iraqi President Saddam Hussein at the outbreak of Desert Storm.

54A, A.J.C. Bose Road,
Calcutta—16
2nd January, 1991

Dear President George Bush and President Saddam Hussein:

I come to you with tears in my eyes and God's love in my heart to plead to you for the poor and those who will become poor if the war that we all dread and fear happens. I beg you with my whole heart to work for, to labour for God's peace and to be reconciled with one another.

You both have your cases to make and your people to care for but first please listen to the One who came into the world to teach us peace. You have the power and the strength to destroy God's presence and image, His men, His women, and His children. Please listen to the will of God. God has created us to be loved by His love and not to be destroyed by our hatred.

In the short term there may be winners and losers in this war that we all dread but that never can nor never will justify the suffering, pain and loss of life which your weapons will cause. I come to you in the name of God, the God that we all love and share, to beg for the innocent ones, our poor of the world and those who will become poor because of war. They are the ones who will suffer most because they have no means of escape. I plead on bended knee for them. They will suffer and when they do we will be the ones who are guilty for not having done all in our power to protect and love them. I plead to you for those who will be left orphaned, widowed, and left alone because their parents, husbands, brothers and children have been killed. *I beg you please save them.* I plead for those who will be left with disability and disfigurement. They are God's children. I plead for those who will be left with no home, no food and no love. Please think of them as being your children. Finally I plead for those who will have the most precious thing that God can give us, Life, taken away from them. I beg you to save our brothers and sisters, yours and ours, because they are given to us by God to love and to cherish. It is not for us to destroy what God has given to us. Please, please let your mind and your will become the mind and will of God. You have the power to bring war into the world or to build peace. PLEASE CHOOSE THE WAY OF PEACE.

I, my sisters and our poor are praying for you so much. The whole world is praying that you will open your hearts in love to God. You may win the war but what will the cost be on people who are broken, disabled and lost?

I appeal to you—to your love, your love of God and your fellowmen. In the name of God and in the name of those you will make poor do not destroy life and peace. Let the love and peace triumph and let your name be remembered for the good you have done, the joy you have spread and the love you have shared.

Please pray for me and my sisters as we try to love and serve the poor because they belong to God and are loved in His eyes so we and our poor are praying for you. We pray that you will love and nourish what God has so lovingly entrusted into your care.

May God bless you now and always.

Mother Teresa

Appendix B

In Her Own Words

On the Love of God

"Thou shalt love the Lord thy God with thy whole heart, with thy whole soul and with thy whole mind." This is the commandment of the great God, and he cannot command the impossible. Love is a fruit in season at all times, and within reach of every hand. Anyone may gather it and no limit is set. Everyone can reach this love through meditation, spirit of prayer and sacrifice, by an intense inner life.

On Prayer

It is not possible to engage in the direct apostolate without being a soul of prayer. We must be aware of oneness with Christ, as he was aware of oneness with his Father. Our activity is truly apostolic only in so far as we permit him to work in us and through us, with his power, with his desire, with his love. We must become holy, not because we want to feel holy, but because Christ must be able to live his life fully in us. We are to be all love, all faith, all purity, for the sake of the poor we serve. And once we have learned to seek God and his will, our contacts with the poor will become the means of great sanctity to ourselves and to others.

Love to pray—feel often during the day the need for prayer, and take trouble to pray. Prayer enlarges the heart until it is capable of containing God's gift of himself. Ask and seek, and your heart will grow big enough to receive him and keep him as your own.

On Silence

We need to find God, and he cannot be found in noise and restlessness. God is the friend of silence. See how nature—trees, flowers, grass—grow in silence; see the stars, the moon and sun, how they move in silence. Is not our mission to give God to the poor in the slums? Not a dead God, but a living, loving God. The more we receive in silent prayer, the more we can give in our active life. We need silence to be able to touch souls. The essential thing is not what we say, but what God says to us and through us. All our words will be useless unless they come from within—words which do not give the light of Christ increase the darkness.

On Holiness

Our progress in holiness depends on God and ourselves—on God's grace and on our will to be holy. We must have a real living determination to reach holiness. "I will be a saint" means I will despoil myself of all that is not God; I will strip my heart of all created things; I will live in poverty and detachment; I will renounce my will, my inclinations, my whims and fancies, and make myself a willing slave to the will of God.

On Humility

Let there be no pride or vanity in the work. The work is God's work, the poor are God's poor. Put yourself completely under the influence of Jesus, so that he may think his thoughts in your mind, do his work through your hands, for you will be all-powerful with him who strengthens you.

On Submission

Make sure that you let God's grace work in your souls by accepting whatever he gives you, and giving him whatever he takes from you.

True holiness consists in doing God's will with a smile.

On Suffering

Without our suffering, our work would just be social work, very good and helpful, but it would not be the work of Jesus Christ, not part of the Redemption. Jesus wanted to help by sharing our life, our loneliness, our agony, our death. Only by being one with us has he redeemed us. We are allowed to do the same; all the desolation of the poor people, not only their material poverty, but their spiritual destitution, must be redeemed, and we must share it, for only by being one with them can we redeem them, that is, by bringing God into their lives and bringing them to God.

On Joy

Joy is prayer—Joy is strength—Joy is love—Joy is a net of love by which you can catch souls. God loves a cheerful giver. She gives most who gives with joy. The best way to show our gratitude to God and the people is to accept everything with joy. A joyful heart is the normal result of a heart burning with love. Never let anything so fill you with sorrow as to make you forget the joy of Christ Risen.

We all long for heaven where God is, but we have it in our power to be in heaven with him right now—to be happy with him at this very moment. But being happy with him now means:

loving as he loves,
helping as he helps,
giving as he gives,
serving as he serves,
rescuing as he rescues,
being with him twenty-four hours,
touching him in his distressing disguise.

On Kindness

Be kind and merciful. Let no one ever come to you without coming away better and happier. Be the living expression of God's kindness: kindness in your face, kindness in your eyes, kindness in your smile, kindness in your warm greeting. In the slums we are the light of God's kindness to the poor. To children, to the poor, to all who suffer and are lonely, give always a happy smile—give them not only your care, but also your heart.

On Our Lady

Let us ask our Lady to make our hearts "meek and humble" as her Son's was. It is so very easy to be proud and harsh and selfish, so easy; but we have been created for greater things. How much we can learn from our Lady! She was so humble because she was all for God. She was full of grace. Tell our Lady to tell Jesus, "They have no wine," the wine of humility and meekness, of kindness and sweetness. She is sure to tell us, "Do whatever he tells you." Accept cheerfully all the chances he sends you. We learn humility through accepting humiliations cheerfully.

On Thoughtfulness

Thoughtfulness is the beginning of great sanctity. If you learn this art of being thoughtful, you will become more and more Christ-like, for his heart was meek and he always thought of others. Our vocation, to be beautiful, must be full of thought for others. Jesus went about doing good. Our Lady did nothing else in Cana but thought of the needs of others and made their needs known to Jesus.

On Leaving Loreto

Our Lord wants me to be a free nun, covered with the poverty of the Cross. But today I learned a great lesson. The poverty of the poor must be so hard for them. When looking for a home (for a centre) I walked and walked until my legs and arms ached. I thought how much they must ache in soul and body looking for a home, food and health. Then the comfort of Loreto came to tempt me, but of my own free choice, my God, and out of love for you, I desire to remain and do whatever be your holy will in my regard. Give me courage now, this moment.

Peace

We shall make this year a year of Peace in a particular way—to be able to do this we shall try to talk more to God and with God and less with men and to men. Let us preach the peace of Christ like he did. He went about doing good; he did not stop his works of charity because the Pharisees and others hated him or tried to spoil his Father's work. He just went about doing good. Cardinal Newman wrote: "Help me to spread thy fragrance everywhere I go—let me preach thee without preaching, not by words but by my example—by the catching force; the sympathetic influence of what I do, the evident fullness of the love my heart bears to thee." Our works of love are nothing but works of peace. Let us do them with greater love and efficiency—each in her own or his own work in daily life; in your home—in your neighbour. It is always the same Christ who says:

I was hungry—not only for food, but for peace that
comes from a pure heart.

I was thirsty—not for water, but for peace that satiates
the passionate thirst of passion for war.

I was naked—not for clothes, but for that beautiful
dignity of men and women for their bodies.

I was homeless—not for a shelter made of bricks, but
for a heart that understands, that covers, that loves.

This year let us be this to Christ in our neighbour wherever the Missionaries of Charity and their Co-Workers be. Let us radiate the peace of God and so light his light and extinguish in the world and in the hearts of all men all hatred and love for power. Let the Missionaries of Charity and the Co-Workers, in every country wherever they are, meet God with a smile—everywhere they go in everyone.

Apostle of the Unwanted

The biggest disease today is not leprosy or tuberculosis, but rather the feeling of being unwanted, uncared for and deserted by everybody. The greatest evil is the lack of love and charity, the terrible indifference towards one's neighbour who lives at the roadside assaulted by exploitation, corruption, poverty and disease.

As each one of this Society is to become a Co-Worker of Christ in the slums, each ought to understand what God and the Society expect from her. Let Christ radiate and live his life in her and through her in the slums. Let the poor seeing her be drawn to Christ and invite him to enter their homes and their lives. Let the sick and suffering find in her a real angel of comfort and consolation, let the little ones of the streets cling to her because she reminds them of him, the friend of the little ones. Our life of poverty is as necessary as the work itself. Only in heaven we will see how much we owe to the poor for helping us to love God better because of them.

Holy Communion

In Holy Communion we have Christ under the appearance of bread. In our work we find him under the appearance of flesh and blood. It is the same Christ. "I was hungry, I was naked, I was sick, I was homeless."

Daily Prayer
JESUS, MY PATIENT

Dearest Lord, may I see you today and every day in the person of your sick, and, whilst nursing them, minister unto you. Though you hide yourself behind the unattractive disguise of the irritable, the exacting, the unreasonable, may I still recognize you, and say:

> *Jesus, my patient, how sweet it is to serve you. Lord, give me this seeing faith, then my work will never be monotonous. I will ever find joy in humouring the fancies and gratifying the wishes of all poor sufferers.*
>
> *O beloved sick, how doubly dear you are to me, when you personify Christ; and what a privilege is mine to be allowed to tend you.*

Sweetest Lord, make me appreciative of the dignity of my high vocation, and its many responsibilities. Never permit me to disgrace it by giving way to coldness, unkindness, or impatience.

And O God, while you are Jesus, my patient, deign also to be to me a patient, Jesus, bearing with my faults, looking only to my intention, which is to love and serve you in the person of each of your sick.

Lord, increase my faith, bless my efforts and work, now and for evermore. Amen.

Go Tell Everyone

> *God's Spirit is in my heart,*
> *He has called me and set me apart,*
> *This is what I have to do,*
> *What I have to do.*

He's sent me to give the good news to the poor,
Tell prisoners that they are prisoners no more,
Tell blind people that they can see,
And set the down-trodden free,
And go tell everyone the news that the kingdom of
God has come,
And go tell everyone the news that God's kingdom
has come.

Just as the Father sent me,
So I'm sending you out to be
My witnesses throughout the world,
The whole of the world.
Don't carry a load in your pack,
You don't need two shirts on your back,
The workman can earn his own keep,
Can earn his own keep.
Don't worry what you have to say,
Don't worry because on that day,
God's Spirit will speak in your heart,
Will speak in your heart.
When I was hungry, you gave me to eat,
When I was thirsty, you gave me to drink.

Whatsoever you do to the least of my brothers,
that you do unto me.
Now enter the house of my Father.

When I was homeless, you opened your doors,
When I was naked, you gave me your coat,
When I was weary, you helped me find rest,
When I was anxious, you calmed all my fears,
When I was little, you taught me to read,
When I was lonely, you gave me your love,
When in a prison, you came to my cell,
When on a sick bed, you cared for my needs,
In a strange country, you made me at home,
Seeking employment, you found me a job,
Hurt in a battle, you bound up my wounds,
Searching for kindness, you held out your hand,

When I was Negro, or Chinese, or White,
Mocked and insulted you carried my cross,
When I was aged, you bothered to smile,
When I was restless, you listened and cared,
You saw me covered with spittle and blood,
You knew my features, though grimy with sweat,
When I was laughed at, you stood by my side,
When I was happy, you shared in my joy.

Appendix C

Nobel Prize Lecture

As we have gathered here together to thank God for the Nobel Peace Prize, I think it will be beautiful that we pray the prayer of St. Francis of Assisi which always surprises me very much. We pray this prayer every day after Holy Communion, because it is very fitting for each one of us. And I always wonder that four hundred to five hundred years ago when St. Francis of Assisi composed this prayer, they had the same difficulties that we have today as we compose this prayer that fits very nicely for us also. I think some of you already have got it—so we will pray together:

Let us thank God for the opportunity that we all have
together today, for this gift of peace that reminds us that
we have been created to live that peace, and that Jesus
became man to bring that good news to the poor. He,
being God, became man in all things like us except in sin,
and he proclaimed very clearly that he had come to give
the good news.

The news was peace to all of good will and this is
something that we all want—the peace of heart. And God
loved the world so much that he gave his son—it was a
giving; it is as much as if to say it hurt God to give,
because he loved the world so much that he gave his son.
He gave him to the Virgin Mary, and what did she do
with him?

As soon as he came in her life, immediately she went
in haste to give that good news, and as she came into the
house of her cousin, the child—the unborn child—the
child in the womb of Elizabeth, leapt with joy. He was,
that little unborn child was, the first messenger of peace.
He recognized the Prince of Peace, he recognized that
Christ had come to bring the good news for you and for
me. And as if that was not enough—it was not enough to
become a man—he died on the cross to show that greater
love, and he died for you and for me and for that leper
and for that man dying of hunger and that naked person
lying in the street not only of Calcutta, but of Africa, and
New York, and London, and Oslo—and insisted that we
love one another as he loves each one of us. And we read
that in the Gospel very clearly: "love as I have loved you;
as I love you; as the Father has loved me, I love you."
And the harder the Father loved him, he gave him to us,
and how much we love one another, we too must give to
each other until it hurts.

It is not enough for us to say: "I love God, but I do
not love my neighbour." St John says that you are a liar if
you say you love God and you don't love your neighbour.
How can you love God whom you do not see, if you do
not love your neighbour whom you see, whom you touch,
with whom you live? And so this is very important for us
to realize that love, to be true, has to hurt.

It hurt Jesus to love us. It hurt him. And to make sure
we remember his great love, he made himself the bread of
life to satisfy our hunger for his love—our hunger for
God—because we have been created for that love. We
have been created in his image. We have been created to
love and be loved, and he has become man to make it possible for us to love as he loved us. He makes himself the
hungry one, the naked one, the homeless one, the sick
one, the one in prison, the lonely one, the unwanted one,
and he says: "You did it to me." He is hungry for our
love, and this is the hunger of our poor people. This is the

hunger that you and I must find. It may be in our own home.

I never forget an opportunity I had in visiting a home where they had all these old parents of sons and daughters who had just put them in an institution and forgotten, maybe. And I went there, and I saw in that home they had everything, beautiful things, but everybody was looking toward the door. And I did not see a single one with a smile on their face. And I turned to the sister and I asked: How is that? How is it that these people who have everything here, why are they all looking toward the door? Why are they not smiling?

I am so used to see the smiles on our people, even the dying ones smile. And she said: "This is nearly every day. They are expecting, they are hoping that a son or daughter will come to visit them. They are hurt because they are forgotten." And see—this is where love comes. That poverty comes right there in our own home, even neglect to love. Maybe in our own family we have somebody who is feeling lonely, who is feeling sick, who is feeling worried, and these are difficult days for everybody. Are we there? Are we there to receive them? Is the mother there to receive the child?

I was surprised in the West to see so many young boys and girls given into drugs. And I tried to find out why. Why is it like that? And the answer was: "Because there is no one in the family to receive them." Father and mother are so busy they have no time. Young parents are in some institution and the child goes back to the street and gets involved in something. We are talking of peace. These are things that break peace.

But I feel the greatest destroyer of peace today is abortion, because it is a direct war, a direct killing, direct murder by the mother herself. And we read in the scripture, for God says very clearly: "Even if a mother could forget her child, I will not forget you. I have carved you in the palm of my hand." We are carved in the palm of his hand; so close to him, that unborn child has been carved in the hand of God. And that is what strikes me most, the beginning of that sentence, that even if a mother could forget, something impossible—but even if she could forget—I will not forget you.

And today the greatest means, the greatest destroyer of peace is abortion. And we who are standing here—our parents wanted us. We would not be here if our parents would do that to us.

Our children, we want them, we love them. But what of the other millions? Many people are very, very concerned with the children of India, with the children of Africa where quite a number die, maybe of malnutrition, of hunger and so on, but millions are dying deliberately by the will of the mother. And this is what is the greatest destroyer of peace today. Because if a mother can kill her own child, what is left for me to kill you and you to kill me? There is nothing between.

And this I appeal in India, I appeal everywhere—"Let us bring the child back"—and this year being the child's year: What have we done for the child? At the beginning of the year I told, I spoke everywhere and I said:

Let us ensure this year that we make every single child born, and unborn, wanted. And today is the end of the year. Have we really made the children wanted?

I will tell you something terrifying. We are fighting abortion by adoption. We have saved thousands of lives. We have sent word to all the clinics, to the hospitals, police stations: "Please don't destroy the child; we will take the child." So every hour of the day and night there is always somebody—we have quite a number of unwedded mothers—tell them:

"Come, we will take care of you, we will take the child from you, and we will get a home for the child." And we have a tremendous demand for families who have no children, that is the blessing of God for us. And also, we are doing another thing which is very beautiful. We are teaching our beggars, our leprosy patients, our slum dwellers, our people of the street, natural family planning. And in Calcutta alone in six years—it is all in Calcutta—we have had 61,273 babies less from the families who would have had them because they practice this natural way of abstaining, of self-control, out of love for each other. We teach them the temperature method which is very beautiful, very simple. And our poor people understand. And you know what they have told me? "Our family is healthy, our family is united, and we can have a baby whenever we want." So clear—those people in the street, those beggars—and I think that if our people can do like that how much more you and all the others who can know the ways and means without destroying the life that God has created in us.

The poor people are very great people. They can teach us so many beautiful things. The other day one of them came to thank us and said:

"You people who have evolved chastity, you are the best people to teach us family planning because it is nothing more than self-control out of love for each other." And I think they said a beautiful sentence. And these are people who maybe have nothing to eat, maybe they have not a home where to live, but they are great people.

The poor are very wonderful people. One evening we went out and we picked up four people from the street. And one of them was in a most terrible condition. And I told the Sisters: "You take care of the other three; I will take care of this one that looks worse." So I did for her all that my love can do. I put her in bed, and there was such a beautiful smile on her face. She took hold of my hand, as she said one word only: "thank you"—and she died.

I could not help but examine my conscience before her. And I asked:

"What would I say if I was in her place?" And my answer was very simple. I would have tried to draw a little attention to myself. I would have said: "I am hungry, I am dying, I am cold, I am in pain," or something. But she gave me much more—she gave me her grateful love. And she died with a smile on her face—like that man who we picked up from the drain, half-eaten with worms, and we brought him to the home—"I have lived like an animal in the street, but I am going to die like an angel, loved and cared for." And it was so wonderful to see the greatness of that man who could speak like that, who could die like that without blaming anybody, without cursing anybody, without comparing anything. Like an angel—this is the greatness of our people.

And that is why we believe what Jesus has said: "I was hungry, I was naked, I was homeless; I was unwanted, unloved, uncared for—and you did it to me."

I believe that we are not really social workers. We may be doing social work in the eyes of the people. But we are really contemplatives in the heart of the world. For we are touching the body of Christ twenty-four hours. We have twenty-four hours in his presence, and so you and I. You, too, must try to bring that presence of God into your family, for the family that prays together stays together. And I think that we in our family, we don't need bombs and guns, to destroy or to bring peace—just get together, love one another, bring that peace, that joy, that strength of presence of each other in the home. And we will be able to overcome all the evil that is in the world. There is so much suffering, so much hatred, so much misery, and we with our prayer, with our sacrifice, are beginning at home. Love begins at home, and it is not how much we do, but how much love we put in the action that we do. It is to God almighty—how much we do does not matter because he is infinite, but how much love we put in that action. How much we do to him in the person that we are serving.

Some time ago in Calcutta we had great difficulty in getting sugar. And I don't know how the word got around to the children, and a little boy of four years old, a Hindu boy, went home and told his parents: "I will not eat sugar for three days. I will give my sugar to Mother Teresa for her children." After three days his father and mother brought him to our house. I had never met them before, and this little one could scarcely pronounce my name. But he knew exactly what he had come to do. He knew that he wanted to share his love.

And this is why I have received such a lot of love from all. From the time that I have come here I have simply been surrounded with love, and with real, real understanding love. It could feel as if everyone in India, everyone in Africa is somebody very special to you. And I felt quite at home, I was telling Sister today. I feel in the convent with the Sisters as if I am in Calcutta with my own Sisters. So completely at home here, right here.

And so here I am talking with you. I want you to find the poor here, right in your own home first. And begin love there. Be that good news to your own people. And find out about your next-door neighbour. Do you know who they are?

I had the most extraordinary experience with a Hindu family who had eight children. A gentleman came to our house and said: "Mother Teresa, there is a family with eight children; they have not eaten for so long; do something." So I took some rice and I went there immediately. And I saw the children—their eyes shining with hunger. I don't know if you have ever seen hunger. But I have seen it very often. And she took the rice, she divided the rice, and she went out. When she came back I asked her: "Where did you go, what did you do?" And she gave me a very simple answer: "They are hungry also." What struck me most was that she knew—and who are they? a Muslim family—and she knew. I didn't bring more rice that evening because I wanted them to enjoy the joy of sharing.

But there were those children, radiating joy, sharing the joy with their mother because she had the love to give.

And you see this is where love begins—at home. And I want you—and I am very grateful for what I have received. It has been a tremendous experience and I go back to India—I will be back by next week, the 15th I hope, and I will be able to bring your love.

And I know well that you have not given from your abundance, but you have given until it has hurt you. Today the little children, they gave—I was so surprised— there is so much joy for the children that are hungry. That the children like themselves will need love and get so much from their parents.

So let us thank God that we have had this opportunity to come to know each other, and that this knowledge of each other has brought us very close. And we will be able to help the children of the whole world, because as you know our Sisters are all over the world. And with this prize that I have received as a prize of peace, I am going to try to make the home for many people that have no home. Because I believe that love begins at home, and if we can create a home for the poor, I think that more and more love will spread. And we will be able through this understanding love to bring peace, be the good news to the poor. The poor in our own family first, in our country and in the world.

To be able to do this, our Sisters, our lives have to be woven with prayer. They have to be woven with Christ to be able to understand, to be able to share. Today there is so much suffering and I feel that the passion of Christ is being relived all over again. Are we there to share that passion, to share that suffering of people—around the world, not only in the poor countries. But I found the poverty of the West so much more difficult to remove.

When I pick up a person from the street, hungry, I give him a plate of rice, a piece of bread, I have satisfied. I have removed that hunger. But a person that is shut out, that feels unwanted, unloved, terrified, the person that has been thrown out from society—that poverty is so *hurtful and so much, and I find that very difficult. Our Sisters are working amongst that kind of people in the West.*

So you must pray for us that we may be able to be that good news. We cannot do that without you. You have to do that here in your country. You must come to know the poor. Maybe our people here have material things, everything, but I think that if we all look into our own homes, how difficult we find it sometimes to smile at each other, and that the smile is the beginning of love.

And so let us always meet each other with a smile, for the smile is the beginning of love, and once we begin to love each other, naturally we want to do something. So you pray for our Sisters and for me and for our Brothers, and for our Co-Workers that are around the world. Pray that we may remain faithful to the gift of God, to love him and serve him in the poor together with you. What we have done we would not have been able to do if you did not share with your prayers, with your gifts, this continual giving. But I don't want you to give me from your abundance. I want that you give me until it hurts.

The other day I received $15 from a man who has been on his back for twenty years and the only part that he can move is his right hand. And the only companion that he enjoys is smoking. And he said to me: "I do not smoke for one week, and I send you this money." It must have been a terrible sacrifice for him but see how beautiful, how he shared. And with that money I brought bread and I gave to those who are hungry with a joy on both sides. He was giving and the poor were receiving.

This is something that you and I can do—it is a gift of God to us to be able to share our love with others. And let it be able to share our love with others. And let it be as it was for Jesus. Let us love one another as he loved us. Let us love him with undivided love. And the joy of loving him and each other—let us give now that Christmas is coming so close.

Let us keep that joy of loving Jesus in our hearts, and share that joy with all that we come in touch with. That radiating joy is real, for we have no reason not to be happy because we have Christ with us. Christ in our hearts, Christ in the poor that we meet, Christ in the smile that we give and the smile that we receive. Let us make that one point—that no child will be unwanted, and also that we meet each other always with a smile, especially when it is difficult to smile.

I never forget some time ago about fourteen professors came from the United States from different universities. And they came to Calcutta to our house. Then we were talking about the fact that they had been to the home for the dying. (We have a home for the dying in Calcutta, where we have picked up more than 36,000 people only from the streets of Calcutta, and out of that big number more than 18,000 have died a beautiful death. They have just gone home to God.) And they came to our house and we talked of love, of compassion. And then one of them asked me: "Say, Mother, please tell us something that we will remember." And I said to them: "Smile at each other, make time for each other in your family. Smile at each other."

And then another one asked me: "Are you married?" And I said, "Yes, and I find it sometimes very difficult to smile at Jesus because he can be very demanding sometimes." This is really something true. And there is where love comes—when it is demanding, and yet we can give it to him with joy.

Just as I have said today, I have said that if I don't go to heaven for anything else I will be going to heaven for all the publicity because it has purified me and sacrificed me and made me really ready to go to heaven.

I think that this is something, that we must live life beautifully, we have Jesus with us and he loves us. If we could only remember that God loves us, and we have an *opportunity to love others as he loves us, not in big things, but in small things with great love, then Norway becomes a nest of love. And how beautiful it will be that from here a centre for peace from war has been given. That from here the joy of life of the unborn child comes out. If you become a burning light of peace in the world, then really the Nobel Peace Prize is a gift of the Norwegian people. God bless you!*

10 December 1979

Index

Paul L. Williams

Paul L. Williams holds a Ph.D. in historical theology from Drew University. His dissertation won the National Book Award for literary and scholastic merit. He has served as a professor of theology and philosophy at the University of Scranton and Wilkes University and as senior editor of Northeast Books, the publishing arm of The Fellowship of Catholic Scholars. He has written feature articles on religion for *National Review* and has appeared on *Firing Line*, *People Are Talking*, and *Larry King Live*. He has also penned a series of scripts for CBS and Allied Artists.

As a newspaper reporter for *The Metro*, Williams captured three first-prize Keystone Press Awards in three different categories in the same year—a feat unequaled in the history of Pennsylvania journalism. His previous books include *The Complete Idiot's Guide to the Crusades* (Alpha Books, 2002), *The Complete Idiot's Guide to the Lives of the Saints* (Alpha Books, 2002), *Everything You Always Wanted to Know About the Catholic Church but Were Afraid to Ask for Fear of Excommunication* (Doubleday, 1990), and *The Moral Philosophy of Peter Abelard* (The University Press of America, 1980).

He lives in Clarks Green, Pennsylvania, with his wife, Patricia, and daughter, Katie.